SIDE ORDERS

Small Helpings
of Southern Cookery & Culture

SIDE ORDERS
Small Helpings
of Southern Cookery & Culture

John Egerton

PEACHTREE PUBLISHERS
Atlanta, Georgia

Published by
PEACHTREE PUBLISHERS, LTD.
494 Armour Circle, NE
Atlanta, Georgia 30324

Illustrations by Jacelen Deinema Pete
Cover and book design by Jacelen Deinema Pete
Calligraphy by Cynthia Tyler

Manufactured in the United States of America

10 9 8 7 6 5 4 3 2 1

Library of Congress Cataloging in Publication Data

Egerton, John.
   Side orders : small helpings of Southern cookery & culture / John
   Egerton.
      p.   cm.
   Includes index.
   ISBN 1-56145-005-7 (hardcover) : $14.95
   1. Cookery, American—Southern style.   I. Title.
   TX715.2S68E34   1990
   641.5975—dc20
90-41766
                                                                CIP

This book is for
the next generation—
Mark and John,
Janet, Graham, David, and Mary,
Hardin, Judy, Doug, Rowland, and John,
Brooks and March—
to help them remember
how sweet it was.

CONTENTS

C U L T U R E

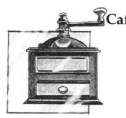

ACKNOWLEDGMENTS

All of the essays in this book were written originally for magazines and newspapers, and most were published, in somewhat modified form than they appear here, between January 1987 and February 1990. I wish to acknowledge with thanks the cooperation of those periodicals.

Southern Magazine published about a dozen of the pieces; *Atlanta Magazine, Southern Living, Food & Wine, Travel & Leisure, Country Home, The Journal of Gastronomy, The New York Times,* and *The Washington Post* published one or two each. Most of the rest appeared as weekly columns in these newspapers: *The Nashville Banner, The Atlanta Journal & Constitution, The Chattanooga Times, The Huntsville Times, The Shreveport Times, The Tampa Tribune, The Anniston Star, The Hattiesburg American,* and *The Herald* of Rock Hill, South Carolina.

INTRODUCTION

"Show me what the people eat," someone wise once said, "and I will tell you about their journey through history."

It could have been Chaucer who gave us that brilliant burst of insight, or the French food philosopher Brillat-Savarin, or a cultural anthropologist such as Peter Farb, or a food historian such as Waverley Root, or—perhaps especially—an oyster-gulping, history-loving observer and recorder of the human comedy such as A. J. Liebling.

Or, it simply could have been any one of the numberless thousands of country sages who have ministered to the insatiable appetites of Southern eaters over the past four centuries—people like Aunt Arie Carpenter of *Foxfire* fame, or Louis "Hawk" Rogers of Colonel Hawk's Restaurant in Bardstown, Kentucky, or Ma-Ma and Rebecca, the two women who gave Eugene Walter of Mobile, Alabama, his simultaneous introduction to Southern food and life.

Whoever said it first, the words bore a timeless and universal truth. Show me what the people eat, and I will tell you who they are and where they have come from and what their lives have been like.

Nowhere—except perhaps in France—is this gastronomical perspective of history more applicable than here in the southeastern corner of the United States. The boundaries are never well marked, of course—being Southern has always had less to do with geography than with a state of mind and being—but draw a line from Baltimore to El Paso by way of Louisville and Oklahoma City, and almost anywhere you go below that line is apt to be a place where food permeates history like butter in a bowl of steaming-hot grits or sauce on a shoulder of pork barbecue.

Southern food has been praised and maligned, coveted and scorned, imitated and mocked for lo these many generations; it has clung to tradition, and yet somehow adapted to endless currents of change; it has embraced and integrated elements of Indian, European, and African culture into a diverse but distinct and united family of cooking styles. Fads and trends come and go, but Southern food survives, endures, prevails.

The grits and cornbread and roasting ears—and whiskey—that are so closely identified with the South are direct by-products of Indian maize, the ancient grain that our predecessors on this continent cultivated thousands of years ago. Our meats and sweets were first the pork and puddings of Spanish and English explorers. Our peas and greens and yams came from Africa, our rice and spice and citrus from the

Orient. And from the once-exotic offerings of other lands has evolved a rich array of pilaus and gumbos and simmering blends of seasoned delight that are the heart and soul of Southern cookery.

The food of the South has outlived African slavery and Indian exile. It has survived military defeat and economic depression and racial segregation. Now, it is even withstanding—if only barely, and for the moment—the incursions of fast-food restaurants and microwave ovens and the sobering admonitions of diet- and health-conscious guardians of the commonweal.

To be sure, old-fashioned Southern cooking no longer dominates the daily diet of people in this region, as it once did. But here and there, in restaurants and private homes scattered across the landscape, remnants of the genuine old cookery remain, and in those places you will find food that offers comfort and satisfaction and even identity, food for thought and conversation as well as nourishment.

When I wrote *Southern Food: At Home, On the Road, In History* a few years ago, I came across many more fascinating tales of cookery and culture than I could possibly hope to use, and others have found their way to me since the book was published. In order to pass that material along and keep a conversation going with readers interested in the subject, I have continued to write about Southern food in magazine articles and in a series of weekly newspaper columns published by several dailies in the region. It is from those essays, most of them written between the summer of 1987 and the fall of 1989, that this collection of *Side Orders* has been gathered.

In these small servings of foodlore and folklore, I have deliberately kept the perspective as broad as possible. Thus, there are recipes and kitchen secrets from places as widely scattered as the Cajun and Creole precincts of Louisiana, the mountain redoubts of Appalachia and the Ozarks, the ethnic ports of Florida, and the landlocked country and soul food enclaves of the Southern heartland.

Part of the food heritage of the South is derived from the elaborately sumptuous hospitality of the plantation era. Part of it also comes from times of pervasive hunger and need—from the Civil War and the Great Depression. Within and between those extremes, Southern cooks have historically drawn upon the woods and waters and cultivated fields—and upon their own inventive imagination—to create the most distinctive and enduring regional cookery in America. Little wonder, then, that I or any recorder would find a virtually inexhaustible supply of subjects about which to write.

And so I have collected in these pages some of the extra helpings of *Southern Food* that somehow ended up in the kitchen and pantry and workroom where I spend my days. All the familiar comfort foods are here—country ham and barbecue, catfish and pan-fried chicken, hot breads, fresh garden vegetables, iced tea and other potables, and of course the obligatory array of cakes and pies and cobblers. Here also is some less common fare, from corn light bread and wilted lettuce salad to Minorcan pastries and Huguenot tortes. Most of this food is rich in caloric content as well as in tradition and history. Pork fat and butter figure prominently in it, as do sugar, cream, eggs, salt—all out of favor now in the trend toward lighter eating. But it's a mistake to think of Southern cooking as only an amalgam of the greasy, the sweet, and the heavy—and it would be an even bigger mistake to throw out all the classic old dishes with the dishwater.

At its best, Southern food is the antithesis of today's fast foods and highly processed, chemically-laden products. Slowly prepared from scratch with the freshest ingredients, carefully seasoned with just the right spices and flavorings, the traditional cookery is elevated by master cooks to a level of perfection seldom achieved in any cuisine. It can be rich, yes, but it can also be irresistibly appealing and delicious— and even nutritious.

The social and cultural dimensions of Southern food are as important as its appearance and taste and quality. A barbecue in the South is not just a piece of meat cooked over an open fire—it's an occasion, an event, a ritual. The same is true of a fish fry, an oyster roast, a crawfish boil. It is not just the food itself that matters; it's also the people, the setting, the precedents.

Down through our history, Southern food has given strength to the weak, solace to the troubled, hope to the discouraged. It has offered relief from discrimination and poverty and hunger. For generations on end, it has stimulated the memories and animated the conversations of Southerners far and near, no matter what their age, sex, race, religion, or occupation. It's our oldest and most persistent cultural asset—and perhaps our most important one. At the very least, it deserves praise for the pleasures it has given in good times and bad.

The organization of these pieces is simple—just Cookery and Culture, more or less arbitrarily subdivided into six smaller units for the former and three for the latter. Everything is in narrative form, including the recipes. What it all comes down to, finally, is just talk— kitchen talk, table talk. It's the lubrication of human exchange, here in the South as much as anywhere else in the world.

Now help yourself to some side orders of Southern comfort, and pass to your left. There's plenty to go around.

Nashville, Tennessee
June 1990

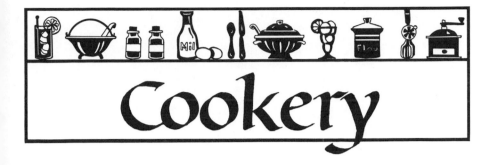

Cookery

Savories

SOUTHERN HERBS

If you asked me to name the most important herbs and spices used in seasoning Southern food, I'd mention salt and black pepper, garlic and hot pepper sauce, mint and the likes of cinnamon, nutmeg, ginger, and such— and then I'd start drawing blanks.

We might argue about what's a herb (an 'erb?) and what's a spice, and whether some seasonings are neither of the above, but even if we got past those hurdles, I'd be hard-pressed to compile a long list.

And if the question called for herbs that are not only used in Southern cooking but also grown in Southern gardens, I could probably count the ones I know on the fingers of one hand.

Could, that is, until I came across *Southern Herb Growing* , by Madalene Hill and Gwen Barclay, with Jean Hardy (Shearer Publishing, Fredericksburg, Texas). Now I'm a walking encyclopedia on herb cookery—as long as I've got their book in my hands.

Madalene and Jim Hill moved to Cleveland, Texas, in 1957 to retire and grow herbs, but what started out to be a leisurely activity soon grew into a new career and a thriving business partnership for them and their daughter, Gwen.

Their Hilltop Herb Farm near Cleveland, a southeast Texas community close enough to Louisiana to be a bonafide precinct of the South, is not only a place where herbs are grown and marketed; it's also a country restaurant featuring dishes seasoned with Hilltop's herbs and spices.

Jim Hill died in 1982 and the following year a devastating tornado virtually destroyed the farm, but Mrs. Hill and her daughter have rebounded from those losses and completely restored the business. They now keep about 25 employees busy growing, cooking with, and selling herbs and related products.

Southern Herb Growing is a welcome and long-needed book, both for gardeners and cooks interested in culinary herbs and spices. Extreme fluctuations of temperature and wet-dry conditions have made herb-growing difficult in the South, but the encouraging message here is that the problems can be overcome.

Numerous examples of outstanding herb gardens in the region are cited. For instance, at the Ozark Folk Center in Mountain View, Arkansas, there's a historical garden reflecting the state's pioneer period with dozens of flowers, herbs, vines, and perennials. Jefferson Island, Louisiana, has another stunning display of herbs. Still other impressive gardens have been developed in Birmingham and Atlanta, Greensboro and Raleigh, Dallas and Houston, as well as in Garfield, Arkansas, and Jefferson City, Tennessee.

Two more features of the Hill-Barclay book are an herb growing guide and a section on cooking with herbs. The guide includes most of the ones you can find on the grocery shelf, with tips on how to grow them at home. Sweet basil, bay leaf, caraway seeds, chamomile (an old tea-maker), chicory (essential for New Orleans-style coffee), chives, coriander, dill, garlic (called here "the backbone herb" of the Southern kitchen), horseradish, marjoram, mint (for tea and juleps), oregano, parsley, rosemary, sage (for good country sausage), tarragon, and thyme are some of the more than 130 herbs included.

As for cooking, the uses of freshly harvested herbs are virtually unlimited. Most of the recipes in *Southern Herb Growing* don't sound very Southern in any traditional sense, but they do sound delicious. They also remind me of some very old regional specialties—filé gumbo, country captain, chicken pilau, and Spanish bean soup, to name a few—that owe their distinction to their seasoning of herbs and spices.

One of the recipes in the book is for basic **herb butter,** a mixture of softened **butter** or **margarine** with finely chopped **chives** and **parsley.** There are many variations on this basic blend, the subtle differences being achieved by adding one or more of the following: **lemon juice, salt, pepper, garlic, mustard, curry powder, celery seed, paprika,** and on and on. There are plenty of renowned Southern breads that would respond admirably to spreads like these.

HERB BUTTER

Madalene Hill and her daughter have advanced Southern cooking tremendously with this book. They've showed us how to make better use of the multitude of savory fragrances and flavors that grow within easy reach— and that knowledge is bound to give new strength and diversity to the region's cookery.

GARLIC

I may be imagining this, but it seems to me that garlic is gaining favor in the kitchens of the South.

If so, it's about time. This much-maligned vegetable—or herb, if you prefer—has a lot going for it, not only as a taste enhancer but as a valuable tool in the maintenance of a healthy diet.

We owe it to our Spanish, Greek, Italian, and French forebears that garlic has ever commanded any respect at all in Southern cookery, for it was they who brought it here from the Mediterranean regions of Europe and kept it in the kitchen through many long decades of British indifference.

In the Creole and Cajun foods of south Louisiana, where French and Italian influences are strongest, and in the Hispanic foods of Florida, garlic has always been a familiar ingredient. The native Indians of southern North America also included a type of wild garlic in their diet.

But by and large, Southern cooks have tended not to incorporate the distinctive flavor of garlic in their mainstay meat and vegetable dishes. They haven't shied away from onions, be they the little green ones or big yellow and white ones; but garlic, with its notorious capacity for causing offensive breath, has turned many a good cook away.

Considering how prevalent it is in most of the warm-weather regions around the globe, garlic ought to be a natural staple in Southern food, just as it is in the cookery of southern France, Spain, Italy, and Greece.

The importance of garlic to good health has been getting a good bit of attention lately. Dr. Benjamin Lau, a specialist in medical microbiology and immunology, has written (in *Garlic for Health* , Lotus Light Publications, Wilmot, Wis. 53192) that garlic may be useful in the prevention and treatment of a multitude of disorders ranging from influenza and diarrhea to hypertension, cancer, leprosy, and AIDS.

Furthermore, he asserts, garlic has been shown to be effective in reducing low-density lipoproteins—the so-called "bad" cholesterol—and other fat molecules in the blood, such as triglycerides.

These findings are consistent with the belief of some early Greek and Roman sages that eating a clove of garlic a day was an effective way to prevent a wide range of diseases.

Hippocrates, the Greek "father" of medicine, was an appreciator of the benefits of garlic. So were such diverse others as the prophet Mohammed, Mohandas Gandhi, Charlemagne, Louis Pasteur, and Eleanor Roosevelt.

Food historian Waverley Root saw the wind shifting in favor of garlic early on. "Before I left America to live in Europe in 1927," he once wrote, "you were looked down upon if you ate garlic; when I returned in 1940, you were looked down upon if you *didn't* eat it."

Garlic has come to be appreciated as "the backbone herb" of the Southern garden. A hardy perennial, it grows well in the region, and it is easily preserved in a cool, dry place. It can even be frozen in plastic bags without losing its aroma and flavor.

And, if garlic with its dragon breath turns you off, you can grow some antidotes right next to it. Munch on a few fresh leaves of parsley or sweet basil, two more herbs that do well in the South, and you'll wipe out the offensive odor of garlic in a hurry.

So there's really no reason at all not to use garlic, and plenty of it, in your cooking—for the health of it, the taste of it, and for the universal sense of food history that comes free with those smelly little cloves.

Lest you think it doesn't fit in with the traditional cooking of the South, consider this recipe for **roast pork** from *Florida Keys Cooking* , a fine little collection of native recipes published in Key West back in 1946:

ROAST PORK

"Using **3 pounds of pork shoulder**," writes the author, Patricia Antman, "season with **salt** and **pepper** and add **1/3 cup lime or lemon juice**. Slice **1 onion** and place over roast with **1/2 teaspoon oregano**. Let stand in refrigerator about 1 hour. When ready to bake, place plugs of garlic in little slits in the meat, all over the roast. Roast in oven 35 to 40 minutes per pound."

Low temperature—about 325 degrees—is best for roasts. Once this pork shoulder has been removed from its marinade for cooking, it will make its own rich pan gravy in the oven. You may want to increase the gravy volume a bit by adding a little hot water during the roasting process. But regardless, be sure you use plenty of garlic—and eat it in good health.

Pancake Sauces

Some friends of ours go to New England fairly often, and to my great delight they almost always come home bearing gifts of genuine maple syrup straight from the north country source.

I happen to love that stuff. You can get some pretty fine cane syrup in Louisiana, and all across the rural Midsouth there are traditionalists who make excellent sorghum molasses, and I've even tasted a delicious mountain elixir called hickory bark syrup, but none of them please my taste buds quite as much as the maple's clear cup of sweetness and light.

You would think that pancakes and waffles originated in Vermont or New Hampshire, so perfectly do they blend with maple syrup to make a memorable breakfast. Actually, though, it was the Dutch and the English who brought the breads here in the seventeenth century, and before that the Indians made a cornmeal batter bread that was very much like pancakes.

New Englanders, Southerners, and most other regional groups around the nation have long since adopted pancakes and waffles as their own, making these morning specialties as American as hot dogs and apple pie. But the folks up East still hold the edge in the syrup department.

Over the years, I have gained a moderately good reputation as a breakfast cook, owing mainly to the fact that my recipe for Southern-style buttermilk pancakes generally yields a hot, puffy, tender, and tasty result.

But in all honesty, it's not so much the pancakes that win approval; it's that pure maple syrup, or some good cane or sorghum or sourwood honey—or it's one of my homemade concoctions designed to forge a more perfect union between the pancakes and their sweet coating.

I'm probably prouder of those made sauces than I am of my pancakes, which are very much in line with most standard recipes. The sauces, on the other hand, are a diverse collection from far and near, and each one has an identity of its own, a story telling how it came into my collection.

There's an intensely flavorful strawberry sauce, for example, that was supposed to be freezer jam. It just wouldn't set up for me; it simply ran free, syrup-like, so all I had to do to turn bad jam into great sauce was to warm it and pour it over the cakes.

And then there's a mock maple syrup that Marion Flexner included in her fine cookbook, *Out of Kentucky Kitchens*, forty years ago. It's a simple blend of butter, brown sugar and water, but it's surprisingly good, and I've made it many times when my Vermont supply was exhausted.

I've made sauces from all sorts of berries, from rhubarb, from lemon curd and bananas and muscadines. Sauces and syrups—and of course a little butter—are what give life and meaning to pancakes and waffles. If you don't believe it, try eating them plain.

STRAWBERRY HONEY

The simple sauces are the most satisfying. Take **strawberry honey.** I got this one from the dean of Kentucky writers, James Still, who says he got it from fellow author and Southerner Katherine Anne Porter.

All you do is pour **a cup of clear honey** into a saucepan and bring it to a simmering boil. Into it you drop **15 to 20 small strawberries,** freshly picked, washed, and capped. Leave them just long enough for the two flavors to mingle—two or three minutes should do it. Pour the mixture into a pitcher and serve it warm on hot pancakes.

◇

LAGNIAPPE SYRUP

And one more for good measure—**lagniappe,** as they say in Louisiana. You need **two cups of that genuine maple syrup, 1/2 cup of clear honey, about a cup of pecan meats** (broken into small pieces), and **1/2 teaspoon or so of cinnamon.** Combine it all in a saucepan, stir and heat to near boiling, and head for the nearest stack of hotcakes.

Now there's a sauce that combines the best of North and South. It's sure to win applause wherever pancakes and waffles are served.

PEANUTS

Consider the peanut, a well-traveled fruit of the vine: It is known to have existed in South America more than 3,500 years ago. Spaniards who explored the New World in the sixteenth century took peanuts back to Europe, where they were propagated and eventually carried on to Asia and Africa.

Africans who were brought to America as slaves in the seventeenth century had peanuts among their meager possessions, and the energy-packed edibles proved to be a basic survival food.

Peanuts are more precisely peas than nuts; in fact, they're the edible subterranean seeds of a plant that looks very much like an ordinary garden pea vine. Because the vines bear so abundantly in the South, peanuts have long been associated with the region's agricultural economy, and especially with the rural poor, black and white.

Until the late 1800s, peanuts were essentially a local crop, privately grown for home consumption. For the past century their commercial production has been extensive, and now we offer to the world at large the peanut as a snack food, an ingredient in candy and cookies, a sandwich spread, and a cooking oil. Most of this country's peanuts are grown in Georgia, Virginia, Alabama, and Florida (but India and China produce eight times as many pounds of them annually as we do). Considering how abundantly they grow, how well they keep, and how nutritious they are, it's not hard to understand why peanuts have become such a popular food around the world.

George Washington Carver, the great botanist at Alabama's Tuskegee Institute almost a century ago, was more responsible than any other person for the prevalent domestication of peanuts. His studies of the nut and its numerous uses introduced Southern farmers to an alternative crop when the boll weevil was wreaking havoc in the cotton fields.

During Dr. Carver's time, mechanical equipment was introduced for planting, cultivating, harvesting, and shelling peanuts, and a physician in St. Louis, his name now forgotten, invented peanut butter and promoted it at the 1904 World's Fair as a health food. From that time since, peanuts in many forms have been an all-American favorite, like apple pie and hot dogs.

Cholesterol-free and high in protein, peanuts still qualify as a health food. Two tablespoons of peanut butter pack about 20 percent of an adult's daily protein need. Peanuts have a higher content of pure protein than eggs, or even beef, and they're rich in other nutrients too.

Jimmy Carter, the favorite son of Plains, Georgia, single-handedly elevated the humble nut to world renown in 1976 when he became the first and only peanut farmer to be elected president.

Lillian Carter, the president's irrepressible mother, touted peanuts and other Southern delicacies in a book, *Miss Lillian and Friends*, published in 1977. Among her recipes therein was a simple formula for **salted peanuts** that I have since adopted as one of my favorites.

Start with a quantity of **raw peanuts**—say, **a quart**—removed from the shells. In a deep fat fryer or a large black skillet, heat a half-pint or more of **peanut oil**—enough to cover the nuts— to a temperature of about 400 degrees. Cook the peanuts for four or five minutes, or until the red skins turn a deeper shade of brown. Lift out and spread on a tray lined with absorbent paper; **salt to taste** and, when cool, store in a tightly covered jar.

SALTED PEANUTS

A similar method is roasting. Spread the **raw peanuts** one layer deep in a shallow pan and run them into a preheated 350-degree oven for

ROASTED
PEANUTS

15 to 20 minutes, or until they take on that deep brown hue. Then coat them with **melted butter** or **margarine, salt to taste,** and store when cool in a jar.

What is surprising about these fried or roasted peanuts is how much more intensely peanutty they taste than the processed varieties you can buy in a can or jar. With peanuts, as with practically everything in the food basket, nothing can take the place of freshness.

PECANS

Thanks in the main to the all-American popularity of pecan pie, you might be inclined to assume that pecans are known and loved all over the world. Surprisingly, though, this native American nut is hardly grown or eaten at all outside the United States.

And that's just one of the interesting little twists in the history of the second most popular member of the nut family (after peanuts) in our food supply. Among the other curiosities:

♦ The name *pecan* is found in several American Indian languages, indicating that the nut was common in the seventeenth century, but little note was made of it in the first 150 years of European settlement.

♦ The pecan is known botanically as the Illinois hickory, but the tree on which it grows thrives almost exclusively in a band of the Deep South stretching from coastal Georgia to Texas.

♦ Thomas Jefferson introduced pecan trees to the East Coast from the South. Food historian Waverley Root noted in 1980 that three trees given to George Washington by Jefferson in 1775 were still growing at Mount Vernon.

♦ Texans reportedly consume more pecans than anyone, but Georgia produces the most, and Louisiana may have been first to use them in its cookery, perhaps starting with the venerable and delicious praline.

♦ There are numerous and conflicting claims regarding the origin of pecan pie, but the most surprising note may be that practically no one baked it until the mid-1930s.

The earliest recipe I can find for pecan pie is in a 1938 collection by Eleanore Ott called *Plantation Cookery of Old Louisiana*. She contended that the confection "is now an integral part of the Southern culinary scene," but acknowledged that some purists might consider it "too modern to include in a treatise on traditional cookery."

The basic ingredients in pecan pie filling—eggs, butter, brown or white sugar, corn or cane syrup—were used earlier in this century as the basis for confections called molasses pie and transparent pie. Somehow, though, the addition of pecans seems not to have occurred to many people for decades.

Once it finally did, the pie quickly became popular wherever it was taken, and now it's about as common as apple or lemon or chocolate pie from coast to coast and border to border.

Pecan production in Georgia is about equal to that of all the other states combined, and two southwest Georgia communities—Albany and Baconton—hold annual fall festivals in celebration of the nut (so does Colfax, a little town in north Louisiana).

Georgia traces its industry to 1840, when a ship captain named Samuel Flood is said to have found pecans floating at sea and planted them at his home port of St. Marys, in the southeast corner of the state.

In candy and cookies and cakes as well as pies, and even in some meat and vegetable dishes, Southerners have long found many uses for the versatile pecan.

One of my favorite recipes featuring them was published in the *Old South Cook Book,* a 1938 volume from Hot Springs, Arkansas, and later used in the Little Rock Junior League cookbook and others around the South. It's called **Cinnamon Pecans,** and it's one of those delicious confections that most people have a hard time resisting.

They're simple to prepare. Beat **2 egg whites** stiff, slowing blending into them **1/2 cup of sugar, a pinch of salt, 1 teaspoon of cinnamon, and 1 or 2 teaspoons of vanilla extract.** When well combined, add **2 cups of pecan halves** and fold them in carefully until all the nuts are covered with the mixture. Spoon onto a lightly buttered cookie sheet and separate the individual nuts as well as possible, making a single layer covering the sheet. Bake in a very slow oven (275 to 300 degrees) for about 30 minutes. Cool on a rack and then store in an air-tight container.

CINNAMON
PECANS

These little morsels come out looking and tasting like cinnamon and pecan-flavored meringues or egg kisses. That's an irresistible combination—so fine, in fact, that it would immortalize pecans even if no one had ever invented pralines or pecan pie.

Drinks

ICED TEA

That the inventor of iced tea should have slipped through a crack in history and disappeared into the void of anonymous and forgotten heroes and heroines is one of those monumental injustices for which there is no explanation and no excuse.

I have a theory that this exceedingly popular drink of the twentieth-century South was discovered in New Orleans sometime around 1868—that being the reported place and time of the beginning of commercial ice manufacturing in the United States.

Imagine this New Orleans scene in the dreary wake of the lost War of Rebellion: The iceman, a new figure in the thin ranks of Southern public servants, has just delivered a block of ice to a house in the Garden District. Our hero, a perspiring tea sipper, while wilting through one of those oppressively steamy south Louisiana summer afternoons, idly chips off some of the frozen novelty with an ice pick and puts it in a pitcher.

The intent is to make ice water, but there is a half-filled teapot on the table, left over from lunch—and impulsively, the thirsty sipper pours the remaining two or three cups of freshly brewed tea into the frosty pitcher.

Shazam! The greatest thirst-quencher in all history explodes like a clap of thunder on the dark surface of Southern consciousness.

In the grim aftermath of the Civil War, when any simple and accessible pleasure was eagerly seized upon by the weary survivors, the discovery of iced tea must have been received with as much joy and hope as a new cholera vaccine. Word of the refreshing beverage no doubt spread quickly across New Orleans and throughout the South. By the turn of the century, tall, frosty glasses of it were already being hailed as the people's choice from Virginia to Texas. For this most useful and outstanding service, the inventor of iced tea should have been immortalized in bronze somewhere. (I could see a statue or him or her, for example, in the same New Orleans French Quarter square where Andrew Jackson now sits immobile upon his rampant steed.) But alas, history has misplaced the name of our great drink-maker, and it seems highly doubtful that the noble servant will ever be known to us.

At the World's Fair in St. Louis in 1904, an iced tea concession stand was so popular that food historians have since associated that occasion with the introduction of the drink to the public. In so doing, they have failed to take into account what must have been happening in New Orleans and elsewhere in the South during the previous thirty-five years.

Iced tea is too pure and natural a creation not to have been invented as soon as tea, ice, and hot weather crossed paths. This refreshing sippage is a monument to simplicity, an uncomplicated union of tea leaves and boiling water subsequently lowered to near-freezing by copious amounts of ice. A rich burnt-umber in color and as clear as spring water, a glass of tea is sufficient unto itself, requiring nothing supplementary to make it delicious. The usual refinements—sugar, lemon, mint—are like so much frosting on a fine cake.

Considering how much a fresh glass of iced tea adds to a good plate lunch or supper, and how welcome it is almost anytime, the wonder is not that Southerners drink so much of it, but rather that the rest of the world drinks so little. It's true that the region's tea habit is spreading north and west (more than 75 percent of all the tea now consumed in this country is iced, compared to only 50 percent twenty years ago), but in practically every other nation the iced version is viewed suspiciously, if not scorned altogether.

The reasons are inscrutable. Some say the long hot summers and the relatively low cost made iced tea a hit in the South—but they also have hot summers and cheap tea in places like India, China, Indonesia, and Sri Lanka, where most of the world's tea is grown, and yet practically no one there drinks it cold. The British and the Russians drink a lot more hot tea than we Americans, and the Russians may even have discovered the lemon-and-sugar treatment before we did, but they still don't understand about ice.

Well, it's their problem, not ours. The facts are out in the open for everyone to see: iced tea's prowess as a thirst-slaker, its total absence of calories (unless you add sugar), its low caffeine level (equal, pound for pound, with coffee, but much less per unit because tea makes three or four times as many servings per pound as coffee). So if the rest of the world wants to muddle through without the soothing lubrication of a spot of cold tea, they can't say we didn't try to tell them.

It's a paradox that neither tea nor coffee, the two most common beverages consumed in the United States, has ever been produced here in any appreciable quantity. Virtually all of the tea leaves and coffee beans we have converted to liquid since they were introduced here in the seventeenth century have been imported from faraway lands. (A South Carolina company, Charleston Tea Plantation, Inc., now holds a minuscule market share with "the only tea grown in America.")

Until about 1900, tea was a luxury that only the well-to-do could afford, but the invention of colas and other soft drinks drove the price down, and the rising popularity of iced tea can be traced to that time. With the ready availability of ice in restaurants, it was practically inevitable that the virtues of iced tea would make it the South's leading beverage.

They've been drinking tea in China and Japan for well over a thousand years and in Europe for about three hundred and fifty, but all the big marketing innovations of the twentieth century originated here—tea bags, decaffeination, soluble "instant" powders, prepackaged combination flavors. Still, the staple of the industry has hardly changed at all since the turn of the century: black tea, made from a blend of the tenderest leaves and put up in bulk packages of a quarter-pound or more.

The man who introduced that processed foodstuff to the world—and thereby made tea an accessible drink for the world's masses—was Thomas J. Lipton, a Scotsman. In 1865, when he was only 15 years old, Lipton emigrated to the United States. He worked for a time in the tobacco fields of Virginia and the rice fields of South Carolina before becoming a merchant in New York City, and by the time he was twenty-one, he was back in his native Glasgow with his own store, the first of many he was soon to own all across Scotland.

In 1890, the millionaire merchant sailed for Australia, looking for new worlds to conquer. On a stop in Ceylon, then in the midst of a severe depression, he bought several tea plantations at rock-bottom prices and set about to modernize a labor-intensive colonial industry. After many trial-and-error experiments, he and a few of his associates came up with the blend they liked best, and soon they were marketing it around the world.

The two leaves nearest the end of the branches on the tea plant are called the orange pekoe and pekoe leaves, and it is these young and tender shoots that make the best tea. Two methods of processing them result in oolong and green tea, and a third technique produces what is commonly called black tea. Thomas Lipton's orange pekoe and pekoe black tea leaves became so popular that virtually all tea merchandisers copied the process. Black tea now accounts for about 95 percent of the world market.

As simple as it is to make a good pitcher of tea, lots of people still manage to botch the job. Many restaurants have given the drink a bad name by making it too strong or too weak, keeping it too long (after a day or two, it may become sour), or serving it cloudy or bitter. All too often, they use the instant stuff—distinctly inferior in taste to freshly brewed leaves.

Iced tea is a standard year-round drink in most restaurants in the South, but the quality is uneven. Now, as always, the most reliable place to get a decent glass of iced tea is at home. This is the standard method of preparing it:

ICED TEA

Bring **3 measuring cups** full of fresh **tap water** (or bottled water) to a rolling boil in a saucepan. Put in **3 heaping teaspoons of good-quality black tea** (or 4 tea bags, each of which contains a level teaspoon); turn off the heat, cover the pan, and let the tea brew or steep for 5 to 10 minutes. Then strain it into a pitcher, add 4 cups of cold water, and you'll have enough for seven 8-ounce glasses. Fill the glasses with ice, pour in the tea, season to taste with **sugar, fresh lemon,** and **tender mint sprigs,** and sip or guzzle to your heart's content.

Since most tea lovers have finely-calibrated taste sensors to tell them if their tea is too strong or too weak, they will quite naturally want to adjust this formula up or down to suit them. In general, I find that tea packagers tend to recommend too high a measure of tea to water (they sell more that way, of course), but it all comes down to a matter of individual taste.

One curious thing about iced tea in the South that has always puzzled me is the tendency of many restaurants to serve it pre-sweetened. Some places even pour it sweet without asking, their experience apparently being that about nine of every ten drinkers prefer it that way, and if you want yours plain, you have to tell them in advance. The only explanation for this routine sweetening that I can imagine is the celebrated affinity of Southerners in general for practically anything sweet.

MINT TEA

An especially popular variation on the pre-sweetened theme is a picnic favorite commonly called **mint tea.** This is a basic recipe for it: First, gather a large handful of **fresh mint**—say, about a dozen long sprigs. Then, in a large saucepan, make a strong tea by dropping **4 tablespoons or 12 individual bags** of tea into 1 quart of boiling water and letting it steep for 5 to 10 minutes. In another saucepan, make a simple syrup by dissolving **1 cup of sugar** in **1 cup of water,** adding the mint sprigs, and simmering the mixture for 5 minutes or more. (Mash the mint with a wooden spoon during this process.) Let it cool a bit before straining into the tea. Finally, add a **6-ounce can of frozen limeade concentrate** and a **6-ounce can of lemonade** to the mixture, followed by enough water to bring the total liquid to 1 gallon. Served over crushed ice, this Southern sipper is as refreshing as any drink can be. If the balance of sweet and sour seems off a bit one way or the other, you can make your own fine-tuning adjustments with more sugar or lemon juice.

Surely, sooner or later, the rest of the world will discover the glory and the wonder of freshly brewed iced tea. It's the South's gift to a thirsty world, and it may prove to be the region's most important contribution to peace and harmony among nations.

SOUTHERN SOFT DRINKS

The magnitude of one of the South's greatest success stories grows a little larger every time someone opens a soft-drink bottle or can in this country—and that's mighty often, considering that the beverages now amount to a $25-billion-a-year business.

For over a century, most of the non-alcoholic beverages marketed in the United States have originated from Southern inventions. There were a few colored, flavored, sweetened varieties of carbonated water in existence before the Civil War, mostly in the North. But the modern craze for these refreshments—quickly dubbed "soda pop" for the sound a cork made when pulled from a bottle—really took hold in the 1880s. It all began in some unlikely places, such as Rural Retreat, Virginia, and New Bern, North Carolina.

Pharmacists were responsible for many of the inventions, which they first used as general-purpose curatives (stomach and headache remedies and such) and then as refreshments. These are the most notable examples:

♦ When Charles Alderton worked in Charles K. Pepper's drugstore in Rural Retreat, a little southwest Virginia village, in the early 1880s, he experimented with a carbonated drink that he finally perfected in Waco, Texas, in 1885. Hoping to impress his former boss, whose daughter he wanted to marry, Alderton named the beverage for him—and Dr Pepper was born.

♦ John S. Pemberton, an Atlanta druggist, created a patent medicine/soft drink in 1886. His bookkeeper, Frank M. Robinson, came up with a name for it: Coca-Cola, because the formula contained extracts of the coca leaf and the cola nut. By 1893 another pharmacist, Asa G. Candler, had bought the rights to the soda syrup, added carbonated water, and put the drink on the market as a light refresher.

♦ Druggist Caleb D. Bradham came up with a similar concoction at his shop in New Bern, one of North Carolina's oldest towns, in 1896. He called it Brad's Drink at first, but within a few years he was manufacturing and bottling it under the name it has kept ever since: Pepsi-Cola.

The post-Civil War refinement and expansion of such things as soda water, carbonation, ice-making, and bottle-making all added favorably to the rise of soft drinks. In addition, two other factors gave strong impetus to the South as the primary base for this new industry.

One was the temperance movement. Though it was a nationwide reaction to excesses in alcohol consumption, the church-centered drive to combat that abuse was especially forceful in this region—and alternatives to beer and whiskey quickly gained a market foothold.

The other Southern boost for cold soft drinks was directly tied to the weather—more precisely, to the oppressive summer heat. Simply put, what better market could there be for cool and refreshing bottled beverages than in places where the temperature and humidity virtually brought midday activity to a complete halt?

Fast on the heels of the successes enjoyed by Dr Pepper, Coca-Cola and Pepsi-Cola, numerous other soda pop companies were formed, and most of them were south of the Ohio River. Several that began back around the turn of this century are still in business:

♦ Barq's Root Beer, developed by Edward A. Barq in Biloxi, Mississippi, in 1898;

♦ Buffalo Rock Ginger Ale, created by Sidney Lee of Birmingham, Alabama, in about 1901;

♦ RC Cola, developed in Columbus, Georgia, in 1933 by successors to Claud A. Hatcher, a pharmacist whose first commercial soft drink in about 1902 was a ginger ale he called Royal Crown;

♦ Blenheim Ginger Ale, first bottled by C. R. May and A. J. Matheson of Blenheim, South Carolina, in 1903.

There are still others, including Ale 81 from Kentucky, Dr. Enuf and Double Cola from Tennessee, and Pop Rouge from Louisiana.

Perhaps the most popular soft drink to originate outside the South was 7 Up in 1929. It came from St. Louis—just a short distance up the Mississippi River from this region.

And finally, there's the newest thirst-quencher, Gatorade—not a soda pop, but a phenomenally successful commercial soft drink nonetheless. Dr. Robert Cade, a kidney specialist at the University of Florida Medical School in Gainesville, invented it in 1965 as an energy booster and a quick replacement for body fluids lost during heavy exercise.

POUR LORE

Since Columbus started the parade of Europeans to this continent almost five hundred years ago, fortified libations have never ceased to lubricate the American palate.

The explorers and colonists of the sixteenth and seventeenth centuries brought plenty to drink with them—beer, wine, brandy, rum, Scotch and Irish whiskeys—and they wasted no time in replenishing the imported supply with domestic creations. They made brandy from peaches and blackberries, rum from Caribbean sugar cane molasses, wine from dandelions, cider from apples, and beer from such exotica as persimmons, spruce bark, and pea shells.

They drove the native Indians and the black slaves to drink, too. Almost everybody drank some form of alcohol—men and women and children, rich and poor, urban and rural, from New England to the Gulf Coast.

Water and milk were often unsafe; beer, wine, and cider were much more reliable table liquids. The harder stuff had many purposes, among them ceremonial, medicinal, and anesthetic.

From early on, the Southern colonies were noted for their fighting spirit—and for their love of strong drink. From Virginia down to Florida and around the gulf crescent to present-day Texas, and in the landlocked hills of Arkansas and Tennessee and Kentucky, Southerners in every generation have found celebration and solace in brewed, fermented, and distilled sippages. Little wonder that they drank a lot, given the sultry climate, the rural isolation, and the importance they attached to entertaining company. By all accounts, from old newspapers to handwritten cookbooks to travelers' diaries, white Southerners kept up the drinking habits of their European forebears; in fact, they surpassed them, inventing new intoxicants and consuming ever greater quantities of alcohol.

In most of the cookbooks to come out of the South in the nineteenth century—including those from Baptist and Methodist church women no less than secular volumes—alcoholic drinks were commonly offered. On the diverse and wide-ranging list were eggnog and milk punch, syllabub and sangaree, and much more: wines and brandies, beer and cider, and such now-obscure concoctions as shrubs, orgeats, ratafias, bounces, slings, flips, fools, smashes, caudles, rickeys, toddies, fizzes, and cordials.

When excessive drinking and its costly consequences spawned a surge in the temperance movement in the mid-1800s, the South was characteristically torn between Puritan abstinence and libertarian indulgence. With a show of schizophrenic ambivalence that has remained a trademark of its collective personality, the region somehow managed to lead the nation in the manufacture of bourbon, the production of illegal moonshine, and the clamor for prohibition—all at the same time. Even now, there are big distilleries producing legal whisky in some dry counties of the South—and little stills making illegal moonshine in wet ones.

From such a rich and colorful history is bound to flow a parade of offbeat characters and improbable tales, some of them true to life. Here are a few notes at random from the voluminous record—some tidbits of drink trivia and pour lore:

♦ A. A. Peychaud, a druggist in New Orleans in the 1790s, regularly served to his clientele a good-for-what-ails-you tonic known as bitters. He poured the compound in a little china egg cup—a *coquetier*, the French called it—and to make the medicine more palatable, he added an ounce or two of brandy. Soon, tipplers were ordering those "cocktails" in bars and coffeehouses and apothecary shops all over town. Peychaud thus not only introduced bitters as a mixer and created the first cocktail; he also invented the jigger, in the form of a china egg cup. (The origin of the term *jigger* is elusive; it surfaced as an American slang expression in the 1880s to denote—along with *shot* and *dram*— a small serving of liquor.)

♦ It was Britain's King Charles II who first imposed a colonial tax on distilled spirits in the 1660s, and the word *moonshiner* subsequently entered the language as a term for people who smuggled liquor past the tax collectors. As time went on, whiskey smuggling became more popularly known as *bootlegging*— literally, hiding a bottle in your boot top—and moonshining came to be understood as the act of distilling whiskey illegally. In most of the states of the Southeast, and particularly in southern Appalachia and the Ozarks, the making of moonshine—also known descriptively as white lightning and splode (as in explode)—has continued for centuries. The principal difference between top-quality moonshine and legal bourbon is that the latter has been aged for two years or more in charred oak barrels.

♦ The Scottish and Irish whiskey-makers who left Pennsylvania in the 1790s when the federal government taxed their spirits migrated to Kentucky, where pure limestone water and tall corn gave them the combination that in time became known as Kentucky whiskey, or Bourbon (after the county in which much of it was first made). Scottish immigrant James C. Crow, a physician and chemist, brought quality control and the sour-mash distilling process to bourbon-making in the 1820s, and both his namesake—Old Crow—and his method have been around ever since.

♦ The mint julep was known to Kentucky tipplers back when Henry Clay was a young lawmaker in the first decade of the nineteenth century. Virginia, Louisiana, and other states have made spurious claims to the invention of the julep, but Kentuckians pay them no mind. Books have been written on the history, lore, and methodology of julep-making; politicians and editorial writers and poets have soared to oratorical heights—and plumbed the depths of doggerel—in their descriptions of the elixir. Still, it remains the soul of simplicity: a delicate union of two aromas (bourbon and mint) and three flavors (bourbon, mint, and sugar). There must be ice, of course, and a frosty container helps (silver is preferred), but the rest is just talk, just old-fashioned Southern talk.

♦ Kentucky rivals Louisiana as the homeland and heartland of Southern sipping, and people such as Irvin S. Cobb did a lot to establish the reputation. Cobb was a journalist, magazine writer, and author who rose to national fame from the Ohio River town of Paducah, Kentucky, in the early part of this century. A humorist and tippler in the W. C. Fields tradition (or was Fields in the Cobb tradition?), he wrote, among many others, a book called *Red Likker* and, in 1934, a little paperback compendium of his favorite drinks. *Irvin S. Cobb's Own Recipe Book*, coming as it did the year Prohibition ended, was a celebration of the return of legal alcohol.

♦ Stanley Clisby Arthur was to New Orleans in the 1930s what Irvin S. Cobb was to Kentucky: a chronicler of liquor lore and highball history. In a paperback booklet called *Famous New Orleans Drinks and How to Mix 'em* , Arthur described the background and nomenclature of such libations as the Sazerac cocktail, absinthe drinks, juleps (eight versions), planter's punch (four kinds), Ramos gin fizz, and café brûlot. He attributed one of his drinks, The Contradiction, to a Frenchman in New Orleans who ordered "whiskey to make it strong, water to make it weak; lemon juice to make it sour, sugar to make it sweet." Then, he added, "You say, 'Here's to you'—and you drink it yourself."

HOLIDAY PUNCH

A recollection from the Fifties:
It had been what I would call a typical Southern Episcopal wedding: an impressively formal service, followed by convivial socializing at a sumptuous reception, at which the cakes were elegant and the punch was deceptively, dangerously delicious.

We were given a corked bottle of the leftover toasting drink by the generous hosts, and I stashed it under the seat in the car. Driving home in the frosty, moonlit evening, we rehashed the affair, I and my front-seat companion and two matronly relatives in the back.

"It was simply divine," said Gertrude, one of the abstemious elders.

"Did you ever taste a more wonderful coconut cake? And that punch! It was simply irresistible! I had three cups of it."

Elizabeth, her companion and sister teetotaler, was in full agreement.

"It was the most enjoyable wedding I've been to in ages," she raved. "Such an interesting service, such a beautiful bride, so many nice people—and all that food. And the punch, yes, the punch was wonderful!"

We rode along in silence for a while, each of us lost in happy thoughts. Then I heard something pop beneath me, and the warm air inside the car soon was suffused with the unmistakable bouquet of sweet citrus and rum.

As I pondered what comment to make, I glanced back and saw Gertrude gazing contentedly at the moon. Then, in a whisper, her reverie became an expression, a little song of praise.

"Ah, the punch. I can still almost taste it, smell it. What do you suppose it was made of? We should have asked for the recipe. It would be a big hit at church the next time we have a brotherhood dinner."

◇

Etymologists say that the word *punch* originated in the Hindu language of the Far East. It supposedly came from *panch* , meaning "five," and referring to the five basic ingredients—lime, sugar, spices, water, and some form of alcoholic liquid—that made up a drink popular in that part of the world as long ago as the early 1600s.

Frankly, I'm skeptical of that explanation. The stuff is called punch, don't you think, because it packs one? In other words, the name was simply descriptive of what the historic libations did—they sneaked up on you in the disarming guise of citrus and sugar, and then punched you out with a jolt of distilled or fermented intoxicant.

And did it originate in India? I doubt it. British sailors may have created punch, enamored as they were with the fruits and sugars and spices they found in the Caribbean and the Orient—and with anything alcoholic that they could lay their hands on.

In the West Indies, which the sea-faring explorers first thought were the islands of Asia, all the ingredients for punch were present, and rum was the perfect mixer. So if you want to pinpoint the historic source of this versatile beverage—at least as it has come down to us in the present age—I suggest that Puerto Rico or Jamaica might be closer to it than the countries around the Indian ocean.

San Juan and Kingston are also much closer to the American South, of course, and punch in this culture has been a popular favorite almost since the first boatload of Europeans arrived.

They made it stout in those days, potent enough to put a whole party of embibers in a drunken stupor—and they were calling it punch, too, by about 1625. Those who mixed the beverage argued endlessly about the fine points of punch-making, but regardless of the recipe, punch became enormously popular throughout the colonies.

One of the oldest surviving Southern recipes, handwritten by Eliza Lucas Pinckney of South Carolina in 1756, is for **"The Duke of Norfolk Punch."** This is it, in her words:

"Boil **twelve Gallons of Water,** as soon as it Boils put in **twelve pounds of loaf Sugar** and **the Whites of thirty Eggs.** Let them boil a quarter of an hour, and when cold strain it very clean through a coarse cloth into a rum Cask; then put in **five quarts and an half of Orange juice,** and **three quarts and a half of Lemon juice** strained. Peel **thirty Oranges** and **thirty Lemons** very thin, steep the Peel in **a Gallon of rum** four days, strain the rum off into a Cask adding **four gallons more of rum.** It will be fit to bottle in two Months. Care must be taken not to shake the cask when drawing off. It may be weaken'd with Water as you use it to the palate."

DUKE OF
NORFOLK
PUNCH

By my calculations, that works out to about 15 gallons of water and citrus juice (fortified by sugar and egg whites) and 5 gallons of rum—not an unreasonable ratio, even by today's more moderate drinking standards. But the colonists, to use a colorful and descriptive old Southern phrase, were "bad to drink," and often they fortified their punch with more spirits than anything else.

Marion Brown, in her classic *Southern Cook Book,* first published in 1951, revealed what she said was the original recipe for **Cape Fear Punch.** The formula, she said, had been kept a secret for generations, and never before had been printed. The ratio of alcoholic to non-alcoholic liquids was about two to one. This is that North Carolina original:

Make a stock of **6 tablespoons of sugar, 1 pint of lemon juice, 1 quart of strong tea, 4 quarts of rye or bourbon whiskey, 1 quart of West Indian rum,** and **1 quart of French brandy.** Mix well, pour into 2 1-gallon jars, seal and let stand for 30 to 90 days, the longer the better.

CAPE FEAR
PUNCH

When ready to serve, pour 1/2 gallon of the stock into a large punch bowl with **1 large block of ice** and add **2 bottles of sparkling water, 2 bottles of champagne,** and **2 each oranges and lemons,** sliced.

With twice as much liquor as supporting liquids, Cape Fear Punch might better have been called Stark Terror Punch.

Then there is a whole army of British and American regimental punches that have long been popular in the South, some of them even listed in nineteenth century recipe collections of blue-blooded ladies not known for their love of strong drink.

They still serve Charleston Light Dragoon's Punch in the South Carolina low country, and Chatham Artillery Punch—multiple versions of it, in fact—can be found in the former colonies of Virginia, the Carolinas, and Georgia.

One recipe for the latter that I have seen had nothing but strawberries and pineapples to offset 6-1/2 bottles of wine and spirits.

No wonder the South lost the war.

Contemporary punches tend to be much more subtle, so much so that one of their dangers is the juicy-sweet disguise that hides the alcohol. By the same token, this can also be a virtue, since it means that the alcoholic content can be adjusted down to zero without harming the flavor.

Non-alcoholic party drinks—so-called **Sunday school punches**—abound in the South, particularly in the summer months and on holidays and other special occasions. This is a typical example:

SUNDAY SCHOOL PUNCH

Combine the juice of **12 lemons** and **6 oranges** in a container that will hold 3 or more gallons. Add **1 quart of water,** the contents of a **46-ounce can of pineapple juice,** and **4 quarts of grape juice.** Sweeten to taste with simple **syrup** (made by boiling together equal parts **sugar** and **water** until clear and smooth). Cool the punch bowl mixture with a large block of ice, and just before serving, add **3 quarts of ginger ale** or sparkling water and stir lightly. You'll have almost 2-1/2 gallons of punch, enough for about 40 servings.

There's a Southern punch for every imaginable taste, and has been for nearly four centuries. It's hard to get more traditional than that.

BOILED CUSTARD AND EGGNOG

Side by side in cut-glass cups on a Christmas buffet, boiled custard and eggnog look like identical twins: pale yellow in color, creamy smooth in texture, and almost too thick to pour. They may even be topped with the same jaunty cap—a dollop of whipped cream and a light dusting of powdered nutmeg.

But for all their similarities—including British origins lost in antiquity—these two exceedingly popular holiday sippages in the South and elsewhere are actually quite different. One is a cooked mixture of eggs, sugar, milk, and flavoring; the other also begins with eggs and sugar, but then is blended with one or more kinds of bottled spirits (and, generally speaking, milk or cream too), leaving the finished product thoroughly combined but not cooked.

They may have originated as a single cup of cheer—as custard, probably, without the nog (an old English term for ale)—but by the time they reached Virginia more than two centuries ago, their separate identities had already begun to merge. Custard was rich, flavorful, soothingly delicious, and safe for children; eggnog was equally rich and tasty, but also high-spirited, potent, and wisely consumed only with a certain judicious restraint.

Teetotalers took to boiled custard, and still do. They used vanilla extract to flavor the drink (not knowing, or simply ignoring the fact, that alcohol is commonly used as the base for vanilla extract). Eggnog makers, on the other hand, got their flavors from ale, brandy, rye, sherry, rum, and finally bourbon, the present liquor of choice (at least in the South).

And so the twain parted, still siblings but tending usually to live under separate roofs. The estrangement seems to me both unnecessary and unfortunate, for both the cooked and uncooked custards can be enjoyed with or without spirits. Winifred Green Cheney, a noted cookbook author and hostess of Mississippi, is one among many to pass on plain custard recipes while observing the nog paradox. She tells how generations of her people drank only boiled custard—but also loved to pour the rich elixir over whiskey-soaked "tipsy" cakes.

Every year around the holiday season, many Southern dairies market cartons of non-alcoholic eggnog and boiled custard, and both drinks may be served with or without being laced with spirits. But the commercial blends, tasty though they may be, are no match for the real stuff, made from scratch with fresh ingredients. There are plenty of good recipes to choose from, but both eggnog and boiled custard tend to keep close fidelity to their origins. Louisiana writer Hartnett T. Kane published a recipe in the 1950s that he claimed was George Washington's personal eggnog formula. It combined brandy, whiskey, sherry, and rum to make a quart of spirits, these to be blended slowly with egg yolks and sugar, a quart each of milk and cream, and beaten egg whites. That is still the most common and popular way to eggnog glory, in Washington's Virginia and all across the South. As for boiled custard, it is now, as always, essentially a carefully cooked union of whole eggs, milk, and sugar, with the vanilla extract as a crowning taste enhancer.

Historian Joe Gray Taylor once observed that in every age there have been some unimpressed partakers who regarded eggnog as "a tragic waste of eggs and whiskey." Nevertheless, it seems safe to assert that Southerners in the main have always had a weakness for eggnog or boiled custard—or both—and have made them a necessary part of their holiday rituals and traditions.

These two ancient and treasured recipes for the libations have long been claimed by countless thousands of experts from one end of the South to the other, and beyond the region as well. They belong to the ages, and to the masses. They also provide comforting assurance that traditional quality from the distant past can be preserved in the present and future.

◊

BOILED
CUSTARD

Beat **8 whole eggs** until they're frothy. Blend in **1 cup of sugar** and **a pinch or two of salt,** and set the mixture aside. Pour **1/2 gallon of whole milk** into a large heavy pot or double boiler and warm it to a very hot level, taking care not to boil or scald it. Slowly pour small amounts of the egg mixture and the milk back and forth between the two containers until all the liquid is blended in one pot. (This method of mixing is intended to keep the milk and eggs from curdling. If they do separate, try recombining them by beating at high speed with an electric mixer; failing that, start over.)

Return the full pot to the heat, stirring constantly, and gradually increase the heat until the thickening custard leaves a coating on your metal stirring spoon. Sensing precisely when the moment is right for removing the custard from the stove is an art that can only come with a little practice. If it cooks too long, the milk and eggs again may separate (in which case, set the pan in cold water and beat the custard vigorously); if it doesn't cook long enough, the finished product will be too thin and runny. What you're striving for is a thick but pourable drink, one that can be sipped or eaten with a spoon. Remember that it will thicken somewhat when cooled.

When the custard is thoroughly cooled, stir in **1 or 2 teaspoons of vanilla extract** to suit your taste and then store it in glass jars in the refrigerator (you'll have between 2 and 3 quarts total). The flavor will improve with a day or two of cold storage, and the custard will remain fresh and tasty for a week or more—if by some miracle it should last that long. Serve it with a **spoonful of whipped cream** and **a sprinkle of nutmeg.** A slice of holiday cake makes an excellent companion treat. In fact, boiled custard and coconut cake are often mentioned in the same breath in many parts of the South.

◊

Separate **12 large eggs** and beat the yolks vigorously, adding **1 cup of sugar** slowly. When the mixture is light and smooth, slowly blend in **4 cups of bourbon,** continuing to beat. (For best results, do these chores with an electric mixer at high speed.)

Next, blend in **1/2 cup of white rum** and **1 quart of half-and-half,** and then set the mixture aside. In a separate bowl, beat **1 quart of heavy whipping cream** until stiff and fold it into the egg mixture. Finally, beat the 12 egg whites until stiff and fold them in too. You will then have almost a full gallon of thick and creamy eggnog beyond the fairest promise of anything that ever came in a plastic or cardboard carton from the supermarket.

Eggnog should be made far enough ahead of serving time that it can stand in the refrigerator for two or three days, there to mellow and ripen to a velvety smoothness. In 4-ounce servings (topped, if you like with the traditional whipped cream and/or spice), this much eggnog will make 25 to 30 cups of holiday cheer.

Boiled custard and eggnog may not be native to the South, but they've been here long enough to belong. If they're not identical twins, they're certainly fraternal, or at least siblings—and whether they're served together or separately, they hold traditional places of honor at festive Southern tables everywhere.

Breads

STONE-GROUND CORN

When the first Spaniards reached North America in the fifteenth century, the Indians who lived here had been cultivating corn for about 2,500 years.

Now, nearly five centuries later, corn is still one of the primary staples in our diet. Midwesterners grow most of it, true—but Southerners have always excelled in the preparation of it for human consumption.

I can think of at least a dozen examples of food and drink made from corn that are native to the South, from hoecake and hushpuppies and grits to corn muffins and spoonbread and bourbon.

Most of these products go back a long way in Southern food history.

Southerners who like grits—and prefer them with butter and salt rather than cream and sugar—can trace that preference back to the Indians around the Jamestown colony, who offered steaming bowls of softened maize called *rockahominie,* seasoned with bear grease and salt, to the English settlers.

Hominy came to be the name for softened corn kernels from which the hard husks had been removed. The customary way of removing them was then—and still is—to soak the kernels in a solution of water and lye, the latter made from wood ashes.

From this methodology there evolved two ways to make grits. One, still commonly used by commercial grits manufacturers, involves drying and grinding hominy.

The other, also quite traditional, is to grind hard corn kernels with a millstone and remove the husks by a sifting process called bolting.

I'm partial to stone-ground grits. They're coarser than the kind sold in supermarkets, and more flavorful. There's something almost nut-like about the taste of them. You have to cook them longer—20 or 30 minutes instead of 5—but they're well worth the extra effort.

Grits are made from white corn, and cornmeal may be either white or yellow. Most Southern cooks prefer white meal, though exceptions can be found, particularly in some coastal areas.

Scattered about the rural Southern landscape are some great old grist mills where you can still buy grits and cornmeal made by water-turned stones. It may be labeled "stone-ground" or "water-ground," but by either name it should be the genuine article.

One such place I always enjoy stopping, especially on crisp fall mornings, is at picturesque Mabry Mill on the Blue Ridge Parkway, a mile north of Meadows of Dan, Virginia.

In the little restaurant next to the mill, the breakfast menu includes cornmeal griddle cakes and Mabry Mill grits. Here's how they cook the grits:

GRITS

Pour **l cup of grits** and **1/2 teaspoon of salt** into a saucepan containing **3-1/2 cups of boiling water.** Reduce the heat to low and cook for 25 minutes, stirring occasionally. Add **2 tablespoons of butter or margarine** and cook for 5 more minutes. Serve steaming hot.

Leftover grits, when cold, become quite firm. The Mabry Mill cooks and others of that traditional bent like to serve them sliced and fried in butter or pork drippings.

Still another popular way to serve grits is as a casserole containing cheese, garlic, and perhaps other "modern" additions. You're more likely to find that dish at a Junior League brunch than at a country restaurant, but it's certifiably delicious wherever it happens to be.

Cornbread made with stone-ground meal also tastes different—and to my mind, better—than the store-bought kind. Like the grits, the meal is coarse and faintly crunchy, with a more distinct flavor.

One of my favorite kinds of cornbread is a simple pone that's very similar to the earliest Indian breads (two of which were called *suppone* and *appone).* I've seen it variously referred to as cornpone, corn dodgers, hoecake, hot-water cornbread, and johnnycake.

When you eat foods made with stone-ground grits and cornmeal, you're about as close to the first Southern cooking as you can get. And that little slice of history is made all the more interesting when you consider how good those foods still taste.

CORNBREAD

The story is told by historian T. Harry Williams in his biography of Huey Long that the political boss they called the Kingfish stirred up a Southern hornet's nest in 1930 by asserting that "cornpone hard enough to knock down a yearling" should properly be dunked, not crumbled, in a bowl of pot likker. (The Louisiana governor extolled that broth, incidentally, as "the noblest dish the mind of man has yet conceived.")

According to Long, Williams wrote, etiquette ordained that the diner hold the cornpone in the left hand and a soup spoon in the right. First a spoonful of the liquid was to be sipped, then the cornpone was to be dunked and a bite taken, and the sequence was to be repeated until either the pone or the pot likker was consumed.

The true devotee *always* dunked, Huey insisted; it was considered crude and ill-mannered to crumble the pone into the bowl.

Long's instruction was roundly assailed in a lead editorial in the *Atlanta Constitution*. The governor of Louisiana might know how to prepare pot likker, wrote editor Julian Harris, but he certainly didn't know how to eat it; anyone who fully appreciated the dish understood instinctively that it was best to crumble the cornbread. Boldly, Harris went further, charging that Long crumbled in private.

The Kingfish fired back with a hot letter to the editor in which he accused Harris of going beyond the limits of respectable journalism. It was true that he had crumbled in the presence of a few of his closest friends, the governor acknowledged, but only to demonstrate the faults of the technique.

This tongue-in-cheek exchange of more than a half-century ago serves to underscore the reverence with which Southerners traditionally have regarded both pot likker and cornbread in its many forms. And indeed, reverence seems an especially appropriate stance, particularly in regard to cornbread. It is, after all, the ancient American manna, the Southern staff of life. When the first Europeans took up housekeeping in Virginia almost four hundred years ago, the native populations thereabout were long since accomplished at making bread and other foods from ground corn. Their basic pones have survived to the present day as the most fundamental form of cornbread in the Southern diet.

The recipe for cornpone has remained essentially unchanged since the Indians discovered it: a union of cornmeal, boiling water, salt, and grease. Cooked on a hot griddle, it is commonly called hoecake (so named, wrote pioneer historian Harriette Arnow, "from the custom of the slaves in Virginia, who, given only meal, mixed it with water and baked it on their hoes" over the open fire). The same thick batter is called ashcake when it is wrapped in a cabbage leaf or simply dropped on a stone, covered with ashes, and left to steam and cook in the fire. Practically no one does that anymore.

Two other ways of cooking cornpone are still practiced here and there in the South, and both may be referred to as dodgers—for reasons unclear. The first is to immerse small dollops of batter in hot liquid—either to fry in deep fat or to simmer in boiling water or pot likker. The second is to make round patties on a cookie sheet and bake them to a brown, crusty finish in a hot oven. *The New Dixie Cook-Book*, published in Atlanta in 1889, said the batter for corn dodgers should be "thick enough to just flatten on the bottom, leaving them quite high in the center." That description of the optimum consistency would be hard to improve upon.

As delicious as the various forms of cornpone are, I am puzzled to note how rare they have become in the Southern diet. Richer and more refined kinds of cornbread have slowly crowded pone off the table. In the modern age, it is widely disdained as a primitive form of field-hand food. It's not that we don't like it; rather, it's as if we somehow think we've risen above it. For young, upwardly mobile professionals, Southern or otherwise, pone is not the bread of choice. In my darker moments, I see a looming danger that the next generation will cast *all* cornbread into outer darkness, but I try not to dwell on such depressing thoughts.

Fortunately for all of us who love cornbread, some excellent variations have evolved in the South since the frontier receded a century or more ago. The addition of eggs, milk, butter, and rising agents (baking soda, baking powder) have brought us such delights as cornbread muffins, batter cakes, skillet cornbread, corn light bread, and the unutterably delicious cornmeal soufflé called spoonbread, and for all of these we should be eternally grateful.

Speaking for myself, I certainly appreciate them, one and all, and I generally find a way to eat cornbread in some form at least a couple of times a week. I happen to love spoonbread with unbridled passion, but I have not turned my back on corn dodgers and hoecake, nor will I. That would be a betrayal of my heritage and a denial of my roots—not to mention a punishment for my taste buds. Besides, the pones are too ingeniously simple and too compatible with basic Southern cooking to be discarded and forgotten.

Tracing the evolution of cornbread from Indian suppone to elegant spoonbread is as revealing and wondrous an exercise as exploring history through the study of fossils. The social and cultural movement of people through Southern history is right there in those recipes. A crisp and crunchy baked corn dodger displays the simple creative genius of native Americans and the enduring wisdom of cooks who for four centuries have emulated them. A properly baked dish of piping-hot spoonbread, on the other hand, stands in eloquent testimony to the progress, and perhaps even the perfectability, of humankind.

Lest there be some confusion about ingredients, one more historical point needs to be made here. For at least a century, and perhaps longer, cooks in the South have shown a strong preference for white cornmeal over yellow, and have made most of their basic cornbreads with no sugar and little if any flour. (There are exceptions, I know, but this is the larger truth.)

"I don't hold with that sweet, cake-like yellow bread that stands up high in the pan and makes a pile of crumbs when you eat it," a country kitchen artist once explained to me. Without knowing it, she was echoing the sentiments of one A. W. Chase, a Yankee convert to our cornbread ways. In *Dr. Chase's Third, Last and Complete Receipt Book*, published in Detroit in 1887, he declared that "the Southern people raise the white corn only, or, at least, almost wholly so; and some people, even in the North, think it makes the best bread."

For the benefit of those who have forgotten, the satisfaction of those who remember, and the salvation of those who never knew, here are some classic and immortal recipes for corn dodgers and spoonbread, the alpha and omega of Southern breads. I make no claim of ownership to either treasure; they are every Southerner's inheritance, and they belong to the ages.

◇

In a mixing bowl, combine **2 cups of plain white cornmeal, 1 scant teaspoon of salt,** and **about 1 tablespoon of bacon grease.** Slowly stir in enough boiling water (about 2 cups) to make a mush that is thoroughly moistened but thick enough to hold its shape— not runny, in other words, but not stiff either. Drop tablespoonfuls of the batter onto an ungreased cookie sheet, shape into rounded patties, and bake on the middle rack of a preheated 450-degree oven for 30 minutes or more, or until the dodgers are light brown, crisp, and crunchy on the outside. Serve finger-burning hot with butter, and you've got the essential other-hand companion to a forkful of turnip greens, collards, or cabbage, or a spoonful of pot likker—and that's regardless of whether you dunk or crumble. The recipe will make 10 to 12 dodgers about as big around as a pint jar lid.

CORN DODGERS

◇

SPOONBREAD

In a large saucepan, combine **1 cup of plain white cornmeal with 2 cups of hot water** and add **1 scant teaspoon of salt.** Bring the mixture to a boil, then lower the heat and simmer for 5 minutes, stirring constantly. (Though the mixture will be very stiff at first, don't add more water.) Remove from the heat and very gradually stir in **1 cup of cold sweet milk,** followed by **2 well-beaten eggs** and **2 tablespoons of melted butter.**

When the mixture is thoroughly combined, grease an oven-proof casserole, heat the dish to near smoking in a 400-degree oven, and then pour the batter into the dish and bake it for about 40 minutes, or until the spoonbread is firm in the center and lightly-browned on top. Spoon out generous servings of it quickly, while it's still hot enough to fog your glasses. It goes with practically anything. This amount will make plenty for two hungry diners; for more, double the recipe.

FRIED PONE

Right smack in the middle of the winter holiday season, when everyone tends to eat a little higher on the hog, I get an unshakable hankering for some plain old Southern food. And when I think of the plainest and the oldest and the best, my mind turns quickly to cornbread.

Social scientists claim they can tell a lot about a culture by examining the language. Eskimos, they say, have dozens of words for snow and ice, and tropical populations refer in a multitude of ways to the power of the sun, and island societies make repeated references to fishing and the sea.

In the American South, you could almost write a book—perhaps even construct an entire social history—around the evolution and meaning of cornbread. "Plumb the depths of cornbread," a wise old cook once told me, "and you will discover the secret heart and soul of the South." I'm still exploring that possibility, and though I haven't attained the higher consciousness she hinted at, I've certainly enjoyed the search.

A few years back, some writers inclined to whimsy and humor put together a book they called *One Lord, One Faith, One Cornbread.* I loved that title at first, but it didn't wear well; it was a little too "high church" for me. One lord and one faith I could understand, but one cornbread? Never.

When it comes to the wonders of cornmeal, I'm strictly an ecumenical believer, an all-souls communicant. I've never met a cornbread I didn't like. Some of that crumbly, yellow, cake-like stuff you get in Northern cafeterias has tested my faith a time or two, but I didn't leave it on my plate.

From the original pones of the Indians to the elegant spoonbread soufflés of today, Southern cooks and bakers have transformed simple cornmeal and a few other ingredients into a multitude of breads as fine as any to be had elsewhere.

Dodgers, hoecake, corncakes, griddle cakes, egg bread—you name it, and chances are some Southern kitchen genius has fried or baked it, given it some new variation in flavor and a new name, even put it in a cookbook. In a hotbed of cornbread like this, there's truly nothing new under the sun.

But there's plenty old, thank goodness, and as far as I'm concerned, it'll never go out of style or off the menu. I may not eat as much of it as I used to, but that just makes it all the more appealing when it does show up on the table.

I'll cite one example: The memory of my mother's hoecake is as vivid to me now as it was when she regularly served it to her growing family in the decades of the 1930s and '40s. Almost as simple as the pone that early Southerners cooked over an open fire on the blade of a hoe (hence the name), Mom's was a crisp, lacy-edged, skillet-fried cornbread so fine that when served with a few fresh garden vegetables it made a meal fit for royalty. It was a form of pone, but we always called it hoecake.

I have tried for years to capture the essence of it, and though mine is still no match for hers, it's close enough to recharge the memory. To make this fried pone—**Beck's hoecake,** I call it— sift together **1-1/2 cups of plain white cornmeal, 1/2 cup of plain flour,** and **1 teaspoon of salt** in a pan and add enough **boiling water** (2 cups plus) to make a batter that is thoroughly moistened but too thick to pour. Stir in **1 tablespoon of bacon drippings.**

BECK'S HOECAKE

Pour about **1/4 cup of cooking oil** into a large black skillet and set it over medium heat to get quite hot but not smoking. Spoon the pone batter into the skillet, shaping it into round disks 3 or 4 inches in diameter. Reduce the heat if necessary, but cook as hot as possible without spattering. When well browned on one side, turn and pat down to fry on the other.

The batter should make about a dozen hoe-cakes. Keep the first ones on absorbent paper in a warm oven while you cook the rest, and serve them hot, with the butter plate and vegetable dishes within easy reach.

Hoecake is not quite as simple as the fried pone of the original Americans, but it's close, and it has stood the test of centuries. Sometimes in this over-complicated world, it's the simplest things that mean the most. This unbeatable bread is a case in point.

Corn Light Bread

Pass a plate of Yankee cornbread under the noses of a table full of Southerners, and chances are you won't get many enthusiastic takers. "That's not cornbread, it's cake," someone is bound to say.

Cornbread that's cakelike—dry, crumbly, sweet, yellow—has the mark of the North upon it. Southern cooks prefer white cornmeal to yellow and bacon grease to vegetable shortening. Furthermore, they don't have much use for sugar or flour in their cornmeal batters.

Yeast is another ingredient that doesn't work well in Southern cornbread. Since meal is heavier than flour, rising agents can't lift it as easily, so bakers must have decided long ago to save the yeast for their flour breads.

But of course, there's nothing like a few exceptions to prove the rule. No less an authority than *The Progressive Farmer*, the Alabama-based parent magazine of today's popular *Southern Living*, featured in its big *Southern Cookbook* in 1961 a recipe for yeast cornbread made with yellow meal—and including both sugar and flour.

That cookbook also had a recipe for corn light bread. It called for a sponge—a fermented mixture predating commercial yeast—made from meal, boiling water, and sugar or molasses.

All of this calls to mind a corn light bread recipe that is thoroughly Southern and old-fashioned. I can trace it back as far as the early 1950s, but I'm confident it's much older than that. You don't run across it too often in cookbooks of the region—perhaps because it ignores the rules of thumb concerning flour and sugar—but it's undeniably delicious.

The name probably relates to the fact that it's baked in a loaf pan, the same as wheat bread. (Light bread used to be the common name for store-bought flour loaves.)

Corn light bread made with yeast or a sponge must have been a laborious and time-consuming product. But the recipe below is simple, straightforward, and quick:

Preheat the oven to 350 degrees. Sift together **2 cups of white cornmeal, 1/2 cup of
sugar, 1 teaspoon of salt, 1/2 cup of plain all-
purpose flour, 2 teaspoons of baking powder,** and **1 teaspoon of baking soda.** Add **4 tablespoons of melted shortening and 2 cups
of fresh buttermilk.** Stir the mixture thoroughly. In a standard-size bread loaf pan,
heat **2 tablespoons of bacon grease** by setting
it in the oven. When the grease is smoking
hot, stir a little of it into the batter and then
pour the batter into the pan. Bake for 1 hour.
It will be crusty brown on top and firm in the
center, but it won't rise up the way a yeasty
wheat flour loaf does. Turn it out on a rack to
cool a bit before slicing. (It crumbles badly
when sliced oven-hot, but you can slice it cool
and warm it again just before serving.)

**CORN LIGHT
BREAD**

Corn light bread doesn't really fly in the face of all the cardinal
rules governing Southern cornbread. On the contrary, it really proves
how venerable and versatile bread made with cornmeal truly is. Even
a little sugar and flour won't necessarily ruin it—and for all I know, it
might even work with yellow cornmeal.

But this much I do know: A slice of buttered corn light bread is an
excellent thing to hold in one hand while you spoon-sip from a hearty
bowl of soup or chili or gumbo with the other.

This is a distinctive bread; it has a texture, a body, a heft of its own.
It's substantial, yet somehow light enough to invite your consideration
of a second slice. One loaf will suffice for four to six people at supper—
unless they can't resist the temptation to go for thirds.

In the land of the hot bread lovers, this one ranks right up there
with the best—proving once again that corn in all its many-splendored
forms is still one of our most basic and indispensable of foods, as it has
been throughout our history.

SOFT WINTER WHEAT

Of all the specialties I can think of that set Southern cooking apart
from the other regional styles in the country, nothing—with the
possible exception of grits—seems more exclusively ours than hot biscuits.

Soft, light, tender biscuits that let out little billows of steam when
you pull them open to admit a slice of butter have been an essential and
indispensable presence on traditional Southern tables—and only Southern tables—for longer than anyone can say.

That's a curious fact. Why on earth would people in, say, Minneapolis or Cleveland or Bismarck, North Dakota, prefer a slice of toast or even a cold hard roll to a hot biscuit on their breakfast plates?

I used to think the answer had to do mainly with ethnic background; the German and Scandinavian and East European families living in the North and Midwest simply preferred the hard, dense, chewy, cold loaves of their heritage.

But now I have been led to another theory: Midwesterners like their bread hard and cold—and Southerners prefer theirs soft and hot—because the wheat grown by their fathers and grandfathers produced those kinds of bread.

A century ago, says the Wheat Flour Institute, the flour and cornmeal consumed by this nation's 30 million people was ground from wheat and corn in more than 22,000 mills scattered across the landscape. Milling was very much a local enterprise, and the grain, too, was grown locally.

What grew in the Midwest and the Upper Plains was mostly hard red winter wheat, from which came flour high in protein and gluten, yielding a heavy, coarse, hard-crusted bread you could sink your teeth into only by biting down very hard.

A much softer kind of wheat grew in the South, though it too was of the red winter variety (red denoting the color of the chaff, and winter indicating the growing season). The flour from it was lower in protein and gluten; it produced a softer, less elastic dough and made biscuits and cakes that were light and tender.

And so the pattern was set, not by tradition but by necessity. Home bakers in the South turned their feather-soft flour into an array of biscuits, rolls, pastries, and cakes that to this day are closely identified with the region's cookery. In the North, meanwhile, bake shops sprang up in every town and village to produce rich and delicious breads and sweets that generally were made to be served cold, and tended to be on the heavy side.

Today, a few major companies operating a relative handful of mills produce the lion's share of flour used by Americans for baking, but the North-South contrast remains. Hard red winter wheat is still grown and milled in the North and upper Midwest (along with three other varieties: durum, white, and hard red spring), and the nation's two largest flour producers, Pillsbury and Gold Medal, are headquartered there.

Soft winter wheat, on the other hand, is still the source of most flour used to make biscuits and cakes, and the two largest marketers of it are Tennessee-based companies: Martha White in Nashville and White Lily in Knoxville. They also make virtually all of the self-rising flour so popular with Southern biscuit bakers.

Self-rising flour is made from soft wheat, or from a blend of soft and hard. It was developed right after World War II to ease and quicken the process of biscuit-making by putting the rising agents—baking powder and baking soda—and a little salt into the packaged flour. This was the first "convenience" mix, soon to be followed by cake mixes and others.

To strike a happy medium between the hard flour that's best for breads and the soft flour that's best for biscuits and cakes, all the major flour producers developed the balanced blend labeled "plain all-purpose."

All the other adjectives on flour sacks (enriched, fortified, bleached, bromaded, phosphated), have to do with additives to make the flour more nutritious, whiter, and easier to rise.

The leading Southern marketers of flour and cornmeal for home use have been at it since the nineteenth century. The Martha White brand was established in 1899 by Richard Lindsey and named for his three-year-old daughter. White Lily dates to 1883. There are smaller and older milling companies here and there in the region, such as the one in Hopkinsville, Kentucky, that has been marketing a brand called Sunflower since 1874.

Flour made from soft winter wheat has been sending hot biscuits to Southern tables since antebellum days, and they've improved steadily over that time as milling has become a more exact science.

A century or two is plenty of time to get people in the habit of preferring their biscuits soft, light, fluffy, tender, brown on top, slightly moist in the middle—and hot enough to burn your fingers.

The wonder is that everybody in the world hasn't followed suit.

SOUTHERN BAKING

On a driving trip through the upper Midwest a few years ago, I made a happy discovery: Somewhere near the heart of almost every little town, regardless of its size, there was a bustling bakery filled with irresistibly sweet and yeasty aromas and flavors, an institution as basic and essential in its own way as the churches and schools and businesses around it.

Memories of earlier travels in France and Germany and Scandinavia flooded back into my consciousness. Here was a wonderful European tradition transplanted and permanently preserved for the everlasting pleasure of one and all. Now, whenever I think of going to Wisconsin and Minnesota and elsewhere in that region, I salivate in anticipation of the breads and pastries and cookies waiting for me in those main street shops.

There are bakeries in my native South, of course—those of the Cubans in Florida, the Moravians in North Carolina, the French in Louisiana come quickly and pleasantly to mind—but on the basis of ubiquitous presence and sheer volume of baked goods, ours simply can't hold a cookie to theirs.

For reasons that are not altogether clear, the South's baking traditions have orbited around home kitchens, not village shops. Moreover, we have some peculiar customs of our own, such as giving proper names to some of our cakes and pies, and showing a decided preference for hot breads over cold ones, and often for cornmeal breads over wheat ones.

"In the North, man may not be able to live by bread alone," observed cookbook author Helen Woodward of Charleston in 1930, "but in the South . . . he comes mighty near to it, provided the bread is hot." More recently, Camille Glenn declared in *The Heritage of Southern Cooking* that "Southern cooks are bakers," and although that's a sweeping generalization, I think it's basically true. In a half-century of serious eating in this region, I have never met a truly great cook who wasn't an expert bread and dessert maker. More so in times past than now—but even now, in countless rural and traditional households of the region—biscuits or cornbread straight from the stove were considered standard daily fare. In many family restaurants and even in fast-food outlets, biscuits still hold a favored place on the menu, more remarked by their occasional absence than by their presence. Whether eating in or eating out, Southerners still welcome the sight, smell, and taste of hot bread on the table. Indeed, the more fortunate among them tend to take for granted that it will be there.

And this business of naming confections is another Southern peculiarity. Our bakers have seemed to delight in personalizing their creations, sometimes honoring old warriors (Robert E. Lee Cake, Jefferson Davis Pie), or the rich and famous (Lady Baltimore Cake, Dolly Madison Cake), or renowned confectioners (Lane Cake, named for Emma Rylander Lane, a turn-of-the-century baking champion in south Alabama).

I grew up in a small-town Kentucky environment that exemplified these patterns. In my mother's kitchen—and my grandmother's, nearby—I was accustomed to seeing hot biscuits on the table virtually every morning and either biscuits, yeast rolls, or some kind of cornbread there for the other large meal of the day, be it midday dinner or evening supper. Typically, the daily bread came to the table directly from the oven, and only nimble jugglers like me could apply the butter without burning their fingertips. As for desserts, well, no dinner was complete without a little something for the sweet tooth. Baked goodies seemed always to be there, within easy reach.

If there was ever a bakery in that little hamlet, I don't remember it. And who would have bought from them anyway? All the women were at home, busily turning out loaves of fresh bread, sheets of cookies, all manner of fruit and custard pies, and four-layer cakes clasped in a delicate balance by ribbons and flourishes of filling, frosting, and artful decoration.

Times have changed, of course. Practically no one bakes at home with anything like the regularity or the output of earlier years. We have gone from scratch biscuits and cakes to mixes, ready-to-bake items, and even slice-and-serve products. Still, there are times when only the finest will do, and that means fresh, homemade breads and confections faithfully prepared from proven recipes handed down through the generations.

Almost any Southern family of long duration could give you a baker's dozen of these treasures as quickly as you could write them down. Do you like cornbread? There must be a hundred ways to make it. And wheat breads? Take your pick: hot and cold, slow (with yeast) and fast (without), loaf-size and bite-size. Or what about cookies, pastries, fruit-nut breads and such? The varieties are too numerous to count. And finally, how about the grandest of all confections, the pies and cakes? Southern home bakers boast scores of classic recipes for them.

I sometimes envy Midwesterners their good fortune in having so many fine bakeries all around them, but the South's home-baking traditions certainly have their own rewards—and the more they're shared, the richer they seem to become.

Reviewing my personal list of all-time favorites, I have selected one recipe from each of five main categories of breads and baked sweets (cornbread, biscuits, fruit-nut loaves, pies, and cakes) for inclusion here. The choices are more or less whimsical, even arbitrary; I wouldn't dream of ranking them as the best of the best—but I can say with confident assurance that they're broadly representative of the South's finest baked goods.

◇

At the Beaumont Inn in Harrodsburg, Kentucky—one of the last surviving showcases of elegant Old South cookery—the cornbread is symbolic of the culture: Up from pone and hoecake, it comes to the table as a deep bronze, pancake-sized disk with a lacy edge as crisp as crinoline. The Beaumont serves these crepe-like delicacies at breakfast, and they respond deliciously to butter and jam or syrup; they're every bit as good at dinner, too, with meat and vegetables. This recipe makes about a dozen cakes as big around as wide-mouth jar lids:

Sift together **1 cup of plain white cornmeal, 1/2 teaspoon of baking soda,** and **1/2 teaspoon of salt.** Stir in **2 well-beaten eggs** and **1-1/4 cups of buttermilk,** followed by **2 tablespoons of hot bacon grease or shortening.** When the batter is well mixed, grease a griddle or black skillet, heat to near smoking, and pour enough batter in little pools to spread into cakes about 4 inches in diameter. Cook like pancakes, turning

CORNMEAL BATTER CAKES

only once. When lacy-edged, puffy in the center, and deep brown in color, they're ready to serve.

◇

Marion Flexner called these "my own biscuits" in her great old cookbook, *Out of Kentucky Kitchens* (1949). They've been my own, too, since about 1960, and I still prefer them over anybody else's.

MORNING BISCUITS

To make a dozen or so, sift together **1 cup of plain all-purpose flour, 1 teaspoon of baking powder, 1/4 teaspoon of baking soda, 1/4 teaspoon of salt,** and **1/2 teaspoon of sugar.** Using a pastry blender, cut in **4 tablespoons of lard or vegetable shortening.** Add **1/3 cup of fresh buttermilk.** Mix well and turn out on a floured surface. Knead it lightly and quickly, adding just enough flour to keep it from sticking to the rolling pin. Roll out to about 1/2 inch thick and cut with a small biscuit cutter (2-inch diameter). Bake in a hot oven (450 degrees) for about 10 minutes, or until golden brown—or bake longer at 350 degrees. Serve steaming hot with butter and anything else you like (sausage, ham, jam, honey, etc.).

◇

Fruit-nut loaves have always been a common offering in Southern kitchens where bread-making is a practiced art. Cranberries, dates, figs, and pumpkins are among the most popular flavors, and even zucchini squash makes a fine loaf. But the all-time favorite, in my book, is this moist and mellow banana bread, made with bananas so overripe that the skin is black and the fruit is deep gold and very mushy. The recipe makes 1 9-inch loaf (or two 5-inch).

BANANA NUT BREAD

Preheat the oven to 325 degrees and grease your pans well. In a large mixing bowl, blend **1 stick of softened butter or margarine** with **1 cup of sugar,** then stir in **2 well-beaten eggs.** Mash **3 large bananas** to a pulp and stir them into the mixture. Then sift **2 cups of plain all-purpose flour** with **1 teaspoon of baking soda** and combine this with the other ingredients. Finally, prepare **1 cup of coarsely chopped pecans** and add them to the batter. When well-mixed, pour into the pan and bake for 1 hour (slightly less if using 2 smaller pans). Test the center with a toothpick or broomstraw to make sure the bread is done, and take care to avoid overbaking. The finished loaf, when cooled and sliced, should be tender and moist, not dry and crumbly.

◇

Thanks to the persistence of an inspired but unknown (to me, anyway) Southern baker, the never-ending effort to improve on perfection has resulted in this divine dessert: a dynamite pecan pie with the addition of chocolate and coffee flavors. It was first served to me by Anne Griffin of Atlanta sometime in the 1970s, and it's been one of my absolute favorites ever since. In an unbaked 9-inch pie shell, this fillingbecomes a memorably rich and delicious dessert.

Preheat the oven to 350 degrees. Combine **1/4 cup of coffee liqueur** and a **1 6-ounce package of semisweet chocolate** (broken into pieces) in a saucepan and melt over low heat, stirring until smooth. In a separate pan, melt **1 stick of butter or margarine.** Set both pans aside to cool a bit. In a large mixing bowl, combine **3 large eggs, 1/4 teaspoon of salt, 1/2 cup of dark brown sugar** (firmly packed), **2 teaspoons of vanilla extract,** and **1 cup of light corn syrup.** Then add the melted chocolate and liqueur, the butter, and **1 cup of coarsely chopped pecans.**

MOCHA
PECAN PIE

When well-blended, pour the filling into the unbaked pie shell and bake for about 45 minutes, or until the pie is barely set in the center. Set on a rack to cool. For an ideal topping, whip **1 cup of heavy cream** to soft peaks with **1 to 2 tablespoons of coffee liqueur** and enough **sugar** to suit your taste, and spoon a generous puff of it onto each slice of pie.

In some widely separated parts of the South, coconut cake and boiled custard have become traditional desserts served together as the grand climax of holiday feasts. Because both the cake and the custard are exceedingly rich, only small servings are called for—but larger ones are sometimes hard to resist. This is one of many outstanding recipes for coconut cake; it can be made in two or three layers, with two being a little easier to manage when stacking and icing.

COCONUT
CAKE

You'll need at least **2 cups of grated coconut** (fresh or packaged). First make a syrup (coconut drizzle) by combining in a sauce pan **1 cup of milk** from a fresh **coconut** (or 1 cup of water) with **1/2 cup of grated coconut** and **1/2 cup of sugar.** Bring to a boil over low heat and cook an additional 3 or 4 minutes; then set the drizzle aside.

Set out **2 sticks of butter** to soften. Preheat the oven to 325 degrees and butter 2 9-inch round cake pans. Line the bottoms with wax paper and butter the paper. Using an electric mixer, cream together the butter and **2 cups of sugar** until light and fluffy. Gradually add **3 whole eggs** and **1 egg yolk** and continue beating. In another bowl, sift together **3 cups of plain all-purpose flour, 3 teaspoons of baking powder,** and **1/4 teaspoon of salt,** then sift again twice more. In another container, combine **1 cup of whole milk** and **2 teaspoons of vanilla extract.**

Stir one-third of the dry ingredients into the butter and egg mixture, followed by one-third of the milk. Repeat these steps twice more, and the batter will be finished. Divide it evenly into the cake pans and bake for about 25 minutes, or until the tops are light golden and no batter clings to a toothpick inserted in the center. For a moist cake in the end, don't overbake.

When done, turn out on cooling racks, peel off the wax paper, and set the cakes upright.

Meantime, make a 7-minute frosting by combining in the top of a double boiler **2 egg whites, 1-1/2 cups of sugar, 1/8 teaspoon of cream of tartar,** and **1/3 cup of water.** Set over rapidly boiling water and beat with an electric hand mixer on high speed for 7 minutes. Remove from heat, but leave the pan sitting over the hot water. Stir in **2 teaspoons of vanilla extract** and continue beating until the frosting is thick and forms soft peaks (this spreadable thickness will require about 4 or 5 minutes of beating).

To assemble the cake, set the first layer on a large platter, poke holes in the top with a fork, and spoon about half of the coconut drizzle evenly over the surface, followed by about **1/2 cup of grated coconut.** Set the second layer in place (anchor it with toothpicks if necessary to keep it from sliding off), poke holes in it, and spread the remaining drizzle over the top. Then spread the frosting generously all over the top and sides and sprinkle at least **1 cup of grated coconut** heavily over the entire surface. Store the finished work of art in a cake tin with a tight-fitting lid and keep it in a cool place. If by some chance there should be any left after a couple of days, it might be a good idea to refrigerate it.

Monk's Bread

Monk Baird, our neighbor down the street, showed up at the back door with a loaf of homemade bread one afternoon a few months ago, and things haven't been the same at our house since.

She said it was called yeast starter bread, but it contained no yeast. Mary Jane Evers, whose husband Charlie is president of Sunbeam Bakery, gave her the starter back in about 1982, but it didn't come from the bakery—it came from Mary Jane's hairdresser.

Even so, knowing that the loaf had passed muster in the Evers household was good enough for me. It so happens that 1989 is Sunbeam's 100th year in the bread-making business, with four generations of Everses running the company all that time. A bread recipe from a baking family with that kind of experience is potentially as valuable as a wine suggestion from the Gallo brothers or a racing tip from the Whitneys, so I paid close attention.

We liked the bread so much that Ann was on the phone the next day, asking Monk for a cup or two of the starter. (Monk, I should explain, was born Martha Ann King in Hopkinsville, Kentucky, a while back, but everybody has called her Monk since she was a child.)

Not only did she give us enough starter to bake our own loaves; she also gave us the recipe. For all these favors (and because I like the sound of it), we now call it Monk's Bread, and we'd gladly nominate its originator for sainthood, if we only knew who started the starter.

"This is a very forgiving concoction," Monk advised us, and indeed, we have found it to be extremely flexible, as well as easy to make. As for the taste of it, all I can say is this: If you can find a loaf as light, as tender, as finely textured, and as tasty, buy as much as you can and put it in your freezer. It could be worth its weight in gold.

Some people would call this sourdough bread, I suppose, and call the starter a mother. I'm not clear on all the terminology. But I do know that if you have two cups of the starter, this is what you do:

**TO FEED
STARTER**

First, feed the starter by stirring into it **3/4 cup of sugar, 1 cup of plain all-purpose flour, 3 tablespoons of instant potato flakes, and 1 cup of warm tap water.** When well mixed (a wire whisk is great for this), cover the bowl and let it stand at room temperature for several hours—even all day is okay. The mixture will bubble and take on a yeasty smell, but it won't rise. Take out 1 cup of this to make bread; store the remainder in the refrigerator, and feed it again each time you take some from it. If you have no plans to make bread for a while, you can simply give away or throw away a cup of starter and feed the remainder.

◇

MONK'S BREAD

To prepare the bread, make a stiff dough with **6 cups of bread flour, 1/4 cup of sugar** (Monk's recipe called for 1/2 cup, but we've reduced it), **1 tablespoon of salt** (optional), **1/2 cup of vegetable oil, 1 cup of starter, and 1-1/2 cups of warm water.** When well mixed, cover the dough in a greased bowl and let it rise 8 to 10 hours or overnight at room temperature.

Next, knead it well and shape it into 2 large or 3 medium-size loaves. Place in greased pans and let rise 4 to 5 hours or more. Bake in a preheated 350-degree oven for about 35 minutes (slightly less for smaller loaves). Brush the tops with butter a minute or two before you take them out, if you like. Remove immediately from the pans, let the loaves cool on a rack, and when cold, seal in plastic bags for freshness.

The recipe says the starter must be fed every three to five days, but we've waited a couple of weeks and it still worked just fine. Monk says she once left hers for six weeks and added a package of dry yeast to the feeding, and the bread that resulted was excellent.

That's what she means by "a forgiving concoction." There are other modifications you can make, too—in the amounts of sugar and salt you use, and in the kinds of flour. For example, whole wheat flour or oat bran or some other kind of dough-making ingredient can be substituted for some of the bread flour. (The combination we've come to like best is 3 cups of bread flour and 3 cups of whole wheat flour.) You can also double the recipe, or make cloverleaf rolls or jellyroll-style sweet breads or biscuits or pancakes with it. Another variation is to substitute honey or molasses for the sugar.

Knowing that all these instructions are of limited value unless you have some starter to work with, I've been trying to learn how to make starter. The late John Howard Griffin of Fort Worth, Texas, gave me a sourdough starter recipe twenty years ago, and it's exactly like one I got recently from bread maker David Holland of Brentwood, Tennessee, who got it from *Uncle John's Original Bread Book.* I'm experimenting with it now. Here's the method:

Pour 1 cup of whole milk into a crockery bowl, cover it with a plate, and let it stand at room temperature for 24 hours or more, until it clabbers. Thoroughly blend into it 1 cup of unsifted plain flour, cover the mixture with cheesecloth, and leave it out for 3 to 5 days to catch wild yeast from the air and "work"—that is, bubble and take on a sour, yeasty odor. My first attempts to use this concoction in place of Monk Baird's starter haven't worked well, but I'm still experimenting.

MONK'S BREAD REVISITED

In our earlier discussion of Monk Baird's homemade bread recipe, I noted that she called it yeast starter bread; others have said it is a form of sourdough. I dubbed it Monk's Bread, and noted that it contained no yeast and was more sweet than sour. One question was left hanging: how to acquire the starter—the bubbly, yeasty mixture that gives the bread its essential uplift and its taste. Either someone must give you a portion of it, or you must learn to make your own.

As I reported, Monk gave us two cups of starter with instructions to feed it, or add to it, as follows: Empty the mixture into a crockery bowl and, using a wire whisk or other utensil, combine with it the following: 3/4 cup of sugar, 3 tablespoons of instant potato flakes, 1 cup of plain all-purpose flour, and 1 cup of warm tap water. When well blended, cover the bowl with a plate and let it stand at room temperature for 8 to 12 hours or more. The mixture will bubble and take on a yeasty odor, but won't rise.

You will then have three or four cups of starter. When it is working well (that is, bubbly and smelling good and strong), take out a cupful to make bread and refrigerate the rest, to be fed again in a week or so.

On the matter of how to make your own starter, I said in the earlier essay that I was experimenting with methods, and invited suggestions. As it turned out, my experiments were only moderately successful; I did finally get one batch to work, but the bread wasn't as good as Monk's.

My initial efforts, guided by traditional sourdough techniques, were based on the use of "natural" yeast. I poured 1 cup of whole milk into a crockery bowl, covered it lightly with a tea towel, and set it in a warm, cozy corner of the kitchen for more than 24 hours. It clabbered, taking on a thickened, separated look and a somewhat sour smell. Then I stirred 1 cup of plain all-purpose flour into it, covered it again, and left it sitting out for 5 or 6 more days, stirring it once a day. Slowly, it became more bubbly and yeasty smelling—more like the starter that Monk gave me.

Part of this process involves the attraction of natural yeast from the surrounding air—so-called wild yeast. If the weather outside is warm and nice—say, 80 degrees and fair—you can set your milk-flour mixture out and see a noticeable difference in how well it works, simply because it will draw more wild yeast from the air outside the house than inside.

From that point on, I refrigerated it, fed it, and used it to make bread, and with each feeding it became more and more like Monk's starter. But even after half a dozen or more feedings, the bread I made from it still didn't measure up in every way (taste, texture, sweetness, lightness) to Monk's original loaf, or to all the ones we had made from her starter.

Just when I was about to give up hope of making a satisfactory starter on my own, one of the many readers who reacted to my first column, Gladys Koonce of Goodlettsville, Tennessee, sent me some new directions that have proved to be just about perfect.

When I read Mrs. Koonce's directions for feeding the starter and making bread with it, I saw that they were almost identical to Monk's. That gave me confidence that her starter recipe would be just what I had been looking for—and sure enough, it was. Mrs. Koonce's starter preparation, which she developed herself through trial and error, produces a finished loaf that is virtually the same as Monk's bread. I'm pleased to pass it on now to all who asked for it:

To Make Starter

Peel a raw Idaho **potato** and scrape it with a spoon to get **3 rounded tablespoons of real potato "flakes."** Combine with **1 cup of water** in a saucepan and stir over medium heat until the mixture becomes a smooth paste. While still warm, stir into it **3/4 cup of sugar** and **1 cup of plain all-purpose flour.** Let this mixture sit at room temperature in a covered container for 7 days, stirring once each day. On the eighth day, feed it with sugar, instant potato flakes, flour and water, the same as Monk feeds hers. On the following day, take out 1 cup to make bread and refrigerate the rest.

To those of you who sent instructions, tips, variations and queries, let me say thanks. I'm especially grateful to Gladys Koonce for showing us how to start the starter—a gift as generous as the key to a bakery. And to those who haven't tried the bread yet, let me tell you it's easy to make, satisfying in every way, and not as time-consuming as it may seem. Here again is the recipe for making bread:

In a large mixing bowl, combine 6 cups of wheat (or other) flour, 1/4 cup of sugar and 1 tablespoon of salt (more or less of both, as you prefer), 1/2 cup of vegetable oil, 1-1/2 cups of warm tap water, and 1 cup of starter. When well mixed, put in a greased bowl and turn to coat with oil. Cover and let sit overnight. Divide into 2 or 3 equal parts, knead lightly, shape into loaves, and place in well-greased pans (2 large or 3 medium). Let sit several hours in a warm place to rise above pan rim. (A sure-fire warm spot: inside a cold oven with the light turned on.) Bake 30-35 minutes at 350 degrees.

Every morning over my toast and coffee, I remember Monk Baird and Gladys Koonce, and I think: A friend in knead is a friend indeed.

Main Dishes

EGGS CREOLE

It doesn't seem at all outlandish to me to speak of New Orleans as the cookery capital of the United States. There must be more great restaurants, cooks, recipes, cookbooks, markets, and avid eaters per capita in the Crescent City than in any other place, with the possible exception of New Iberia, over in the Louisiana Cajun country.

Traditional New Orleans Creole foods and their more contemporary variations represent some of the finest Southern cooking to be found anywhere. It's impossible to say in a few words what makes Creole dishes so distinctive and superlative, so I won't try; I'll just tell you about one of them, and let it speak for itself.

Ella Brennan, the senior sibling among four who own and operate Commander's Palace, one of the truly great restaurants of New Orleans, added a soulful, spicy dish called **Eggs Creole** to the brunch menu a few years ago, and I offer this rendition of it in evidence as proof of the Creole genius. Whether you order it there or prepare it at home, you'll recognize it as a rich gem for special occasions only—but I guarantee you won't forget how wonderful it is.

The day before you intend to serve it (these instructions are for four), cook **1/2 cup of quick grits** in **2 cups of boiling water** according to directions on the box. Turn off heat and stir in **a pinch or two of salt, 1/4 cup of grated sharp cheddar cheese, 2 tablespoons of unsalted butter,** and **2 or 3 cooked patties of spicy hot sausage,** crumbled fine. Pour this mixture about 1/2 inch deep into a shallow cake pan or into 3-inch round molds (anything from which you can get 4 disks about that size) and refrigerate.

COMMANDER'S
PALACE
EGGS CREOLE

Next, make your **Creole sauce.** Finely chop enough **onion, bell pepper,** and **celery** to make a generous **2 cups total** (the ratio of each to the others as you prefer) and sauté in **2 tablespoons of butter.** When the vegetables begin to soften, add **2 cloves of garlic,** finely minced, and cook a little longer. Then add **2 cups of chopped tomatoes** (fresh or canned) and **their juice, a bay leaf, 1 teaspoon of paprika, 1 tablespoon of Worcestershire sauce,** and **1 teaspoon of hot pepper sauce.** Simmer over low heat, stirring occasionally, for about 10 minutes. Combine **1 tablespoon of cornstarch** with **1/4 cup of cold water** and stir this into the pot. Add **1 or 2 tablespoons of minced fresh parsley,** if you like. Stir until well thickened, adjust the seasonings, and then pour the sauce (about 3 cups) in a jar and refrigerate.

Next day, in preparation for serving, warm the sauce. (If it's too thick to suit you, add a small amount of tomato juice.) Cook some more sausage to serve alongside, and prepare your bread and coffee. Then take the firm grits rounds and dust them with flour, dip them in a beaten mixture of **1 egg** and **1/4 cup of milk,** coat them with bread crumbs, and fry them in hot fat until well browned on both sides. When done, drain on paper towels and keep warm in the oven.

Finally, poach **4 eggs** in hot water (an art in itself, but easier to master than it looks). To serve, put a grits round on each plate, followed by an egg, and spoon a generous serving of warm Creole sauce over the top. Serve at once with the rest of breakfast (nothing but coffee is really essential), and you'll understand after one bite why Creole cookery has been the pride of New Orleans and the South for generations.

Sure, I know—it's time-consuming, complicated (or at least involved), and literally too rich for your blood. But look at it this way: Suppose it's a holiday, or the birthday of someone very special to you, someone who loves a fine breakfast and a little free time to linger over it. If you want to mark the occasion with something memorable—and you can't make it in to Commander's Palace—invest in your own presentation of Ella Brennan's Eggs Creole. It's a labor of love, and a work of culinary art.

Some things are worth a little trouble. In my book, this is certainly one of them.

Bean Soup

Marjorie Kinnan Rawlings is best remembered as a novelist (*The Yearling*), but I think of her first as the author of *Cross Creek Cookery*, one of the most entertaining of the South's many fine cookbooks.

In that book, written in 1942, she observed that the poor make a meal of soup, while the rich only dabble in it. "Soup comes into its own as a main course," she added, and she went on to describe the pleasure of stopping in one of the authentic Spanish restaurants of Tampa, Florida, and eating her fill of Spanish bean soup with Cuban bread and butter.

That classic soup, made with garbanzo beans (sometimes called chick peas), has been closely identified with Tampa's Spanish restaurants since they first appeared in the city almost a century ago.

Another hearty and delicious soup from the same menu is made with black beans (also called turtle beans). Both recipes call for soaking the beans in water overnight and then combining them with sautéed vegetables and pork and seasonings. There are many variations from cook to cook.

Mrs. Rawlings' black bean soup recipe, which she says she got from the wife of the mayor of Tampa, is easy and delectable. This is it:

Put the soaked **beans (1 pound)** in a large pot with **2 quarts of fresh water**, bring to a low boil and let simmer for 1 hour or more. Cut up **3 onions, 3 garlic cloves, half of a bell pepper,** and **4 strips of bacon** and sauté them in olive oil. Add this mixture, together with **2 bay leaves** and **1 tablespoon of vinegar,** to the beans and continue cooking for another hour or more, until the beans are tender. Season to taste with salt and pepper. Shut off heat and let stand for about an hour, then reheat and serve, with bowls of **cooked rice** and **chopped onions** available for each diner to combine with the beans to their individual taste.

Mrs. Rawling's
Black Bean
Soup

With bread and a green salad and a drink, that's a full meal. It's also a bit exotic if you live upcountry in the interior South, where turtle beans and chick peas are not commonly seen. When people speak of bean soup and soup beans in these parts, they're generally talking about great northerns (a.k.a. white beans), or perhaps navy beans.

Whether you serve them slightly drained as a side dish or puréed as a soup, white beans are a basic and essential staple of traditional Southern cookery. They'll warm your body and soul, and leave you full and satisfied. They're also very easy to prepare, as this standard recipe demonstrates:

WHITE BEAN
SOUP

In a large pot, boil a **ham hock** or a piece of seasoning meat in **2 quarts of fresh water** for 30 minutes or so, skimming off any grease. Add **1 pound of soup beans** (great northern, navy) and boil vigorously for 2 minutes. Shut off heat and let the pot stand covered for 1 hour or more. Then reheat, adding **1 pod** or more of **dried red pepper.** As the beans cook, season to taste with **salt, black pepper,** and **other flavorings of your choice.** Cook until the beans are soft and tender (30 minutes to 1 hour). Add more water if necessary to maintain the consistency you want—pourable like soup, or thick enough to eat with a fork.

Some cooks use thyme, oregano, and other herbs in their white beans, but I've always preferred the simple flavor combination of beans, ham hock, salt, and red and black pepper. The taste takes me back to a childhood of good country eating.

This is what some people call field-hand food—hearty, nutritious, filling, flavorful, satisfying, and delicious. You're not likely to see white beans or bean soup on menus at elegant and expensive restaurants—more's the pity—but any good Southern cafe or plate lunch diner worth its grits will frequently feature them. (So does the dining room in the U. S. Capitol, where Senate Bean Soup has been a daily fixture on the menu for decades.)

All you need with a bowl of soup beans is a little relish or chow-chow, perhaps a green onion or two, a glass of buttermilk, and plenty of hot-water cornbread to hold opposite your spoon hand. That may well be the least expensive meal you can get in the South, in a restaurant or at home—and it may also be one of the best.

GAZPACHO

In any good Southern summer, with just the right mix of sun, rain, temperature, and humidity, there comes a time when a gardener's kitchen is almost overwhelmed with tomatoes, cucumbers, and green peppers.

I'm no great shakes as a gardener myself, but I recognize the time and welcome it eagerly. Sacks of vegetables begin to appear at the back door as if some invisible army of elves had left them. When my cup runneth over like that, my gratitude knows no bounds.

This peak of the season is the time for gazpacho, a cold soup made with fresh vegetables. The name is Spanish and so is the history, going back to the early settlement of Florida and no doubt beyond. Californians, who love their gazpacho, may scoff at this little history lesson, but we should forgive them that and understand that it's only human to want to claim a dish as delicious as this.

Along the Gulf Coast of Florida, Alabama, Mississippi, and Louisiana, where Spanish explorers first ventured four centuries ago, a salad of Spanish origin known as gaspacha or gaspachee is still served. It combines some form of bread (originally hardtack) with tomatoes, cucumbers, onions, peppers, and a basic oil and vinegar dressing.

Mary Randolph, in her great 1824 cookbook, *The Virginia House-Wife*, gave this recipe for what she called GASPACHA—SPANISH:

"Put some soft biscuit or toasted bread in the bottom of a sallad bowl, put in a layer of sliced tomatas with the skin taken off, and one of sliced cucumbers, sprinkled with pepper, salt, and chopped onion; do this until the bowl is full, stew some tomatas quite soft, strain the juice, mix in some mustard and oil, and pour over it; make it two hours before it is eaten."

In Spain, gazpacho is found in the Andalusian region along the Mediterranean Sea, and there too it is a salad with a long history and a popular reputation.

As a soup it goes back to the 1840s, and the South appears to be the place of its greatest popularity, if not its origin. (Californians brought it back into vogue only within the past twenty years or so, but contrary to popular belief, they didn't invent it.)

There are numerous variations, of course, both in the vegetables and the seasonings, but I prefer the one below. It has a chunky consistency—the opposite of a purée. The chopping is best done by hand (not with a food processor) to retain the flavor and texture of the tomatoes and other vegetables, and the end result is certainly worth the effort.

Here's the simple formula for a quart or so. You can easily double or quadruple the amount, because it keeps well chilled; in fact, it seems to gain a fuller, deeper flavor after a day or two in the refrigerator.

Peel and chop **4 large tomatoes** and put them in a mixing bowl. Add **l large cucumber,** peeled and diced; **1 medium-sized onion,** finely minced; **1 green bell pepper,** diced; and **1 or 2 cloves of garlic,** finely minced. Pour in **1 cup of tomato juice.** Season with **salt** and **pepper,** and with **vinegar and oil.** If more liquid is needed, add **tomato juice.** Adjust seasonings, refrigerate, and serve cold.

GAZPACHO

It's a good idea to experiment with various kinds of vinegar and oil until you've found the combination you like best. Balsamic vinegar is an especially strong and flavorful variety, and olive oil, which has enjoyed a surge of popularity in recent years, has its own distinctive taste too. There are some milder alternatives as well.

However you individualize it, gazpacho is a salute to the great summer gardens of the South, than which there are none better. And, it's also a graceful bow to history, particularly to the Spaniards who sailed the Gulf many long years ago and subsequently found that summer vegetables grown in these parts are something to remember.

BURGOO

In the time of youthful innocence before television made worldly cynics out of 13-year-old kids, few events in the rural South were more eagerly awaited than the annual county fair.

It was a production that flooded the senses with a multitude of rare pleasures: mule pulling contests, harness racing, livestock judging, carnival rides and sideshows and other midway attractions, gospel and country music performances, horse shows, beauty contests, and competitions to choose the best cooks and canners and bakers.

The fairs that I attended on Frank Clark's farm in Trigg County, Kentucky, in the late 1940s are still sharply etched in my memory. To a town boy like me, the wonders of farm life were endlessly fascinating and appealing, and the fair was a week-long showcase of those wonders. From the front gate to the oval racetrack at the rear of the farm, the sawdust-strewn pathways were lined with one magnetic enticement after another. But of all the activities assembled there, none was more irresistible to me than the cookery that took place at the barbecue pit and the burgoo pot.

The pit was a long trench filled with smoldering hickory coals and topped with wire-covered racks on which dressed pigs and goats and sheep were slowly roasted. The pot was a huge iron kettle suspended over a hardwood fire; in it bubbled a spicy, aromatic meat-and-vegetable stew known to all fairgoers as Kentucky burgoo.

For all I knew, everybody in the world ate barbecue and burgoo, especially at fair time. Not until much later did I learn that barbecue had been a particular specialty of the South for at least two centuries— and, under other names, may have been included in the cookery of the region's Indian natives back before the time of Columbus.

As for burgoo, it had ancient roots too. The origin of the name was a complete mystery, but the stew itself closely resembled what seaboard Southerners from Virginia to Georgia called Brunswick stew, and the Indians before them were known to have enjoyed similar hunter stews made with wild game and assorted vegetables.

"Burgoo" is still a term of mysterious birth. Raymond Sokolov claims in *Fading Feast,* his book about disappearing American regional foods, that the word was used as early as 1740 to describe a porridge eaten by British sailors. He also quotes a sailor in an English novel of the 1830s calling one of his low-life companions "a burgoo-eating . . . trowsers-scrubbing son of a bitch!" The French, the Turks, and various other nationalities have been credited with the invention of burgoo by one writer or another, but the fact remains that Kentucky is virtually the only place where it still exists under that name.

Kentucky burgoo history is filled with colorful characters such as Gus Jaubert, a famed Civil War-era chef, and J. T. Looney, whose stew-making prowess brought both him and a thoroughbred racehorse the name Burgoo King. (The horse rose to the top of its class by winning the 1932 Kentucky Derby.) Jaubert and Looney commonly made hundreds of gallons of burgoo at a time, cooking it in enormous vats.

As the acknowledged granddaddy of all burgoo chefs, the legendary Jaubert was remembered as a culinary saint by Confederate Rebels and Yankees alike. He is said to have served his stew to General John Hunt Morgan and his band of Confederate raiders during the Civil War—and then to thousands of Union veterans of the Grand Army of the Republic at a celebration in Louisville in 1895. The quantity of burgoo ladeled out at that reunion was reported to be 6,000 gallons, which means that if each soldier consumed a quart—a prodigious feat in itself—the multitude numbered some 24,000. Any way you spoon it, that is one hell of a mess of burgoo.

James Tandy Ellis, in a newspaper column he called "Tang of the South," brought burgoo-cooking down to manageable proportions back in the 1940s when he drew upon the collective wisdom of Jaubert and Looney and other masters of the burgoo art to concoct a recipe for about one and a half gallons—enough to serve fifteen to twenty people.

In modern versions, the game meat that used to distinguish traditional Kentucky burgoo has given way to mutton, beef, pork, and chicken. Squirrel and rabbit hunters can still enjoy something akin to the original flavor, but others must be content with commercially available meats.

Except for a few restaurants around Owensboro, Kentucky, burgoo is rarely found on menus. Mutton is the principal barbecue meat in the Owensboro area, and thus it is mutton that gives the main flavor to the burgoo—it and the many seasonings that permeate the spicy stew.

The recipe created by Tandy Ellis has been published so often in Kentucky that it has entered the public domain and left its author with a permanent monument to his memory. Drawing on my own recollections of the Trigg County Fair and on some knowledge gained in Owensboro, I have made a few modifications in the Ellis recipe and come up with the following version of historic **Kentucky burgoo.**

**KENTUCKY
BURGOO**

In a large, heavy kettle (2-gallon capacity or more), put **2 pounds of lean beef** (cubed), **1/2 pound to 1 pound of mutton** (or lamb, if you can't get mature sheep), **1 medium-sized chicken** (cut up), and **1 dressed squirrel** or **rabbit** (if available). Add **4 quarts of water,** bring to a hard boil, reduce the heat, and simmer the meat for about 2 hours with the pot covered. Remove the chicken and game, discard the bones and skin, cut up the meat, and return it to the pot.

Continuing to simmer, add the following ingredients one at a time, stirring them in well: **2 cups of diced potatoes, 2 cups of diced onions, 2 cups of small green butterbeans or lima beans, 2 green bell peppers** (diced), **2 carrots** (diced), and **2 cups of fresh** (or canned, or frozen) **corn kernels.** Keep simmering for about 3 more hours, stirring occasionally; add more water from time to time if the stew seems too thick. For seasoning, put in **2 or more red pepper pods, 1 teaspoon of cayenne pepper,** and as much **salt** and **black pepper** as you prefer, and simmer for another hour or so.

After the burgoo has been on the stove for at least 6 hours, add **2 cups of cut-up okra** (fresh, if available, or frozen), **1 dozen medium-sized fresh tomatoes** (peeled, cored, and cut up) or **1 quart of canned tomatoes, 2 or 3 cloves of garlic** (minced), **1/4 cup of cider vinegar,** and **1/4 cup of fresh lemon juice.** Continue simmering for about 3 more hours, stirring and tasting occasionally and adjusting the seasonings. The stew will continue to thicken, so add a little more hot water if you like.

For the best texture and blend of flavors, a good burgoo ought to cook a minimum of 9 hours. Like many great soups, stews, gumbos, and other pot foods, burgoo improves with age, whether it's on the stove or in the refrigerator or freezer. The ingredients must surrender their individual character and take on a rich and hearty new identity that is unique and distinct unto itself.

Hot with pepper and hot from the stove, a bowl of burgoo with a thick slice of homemade light bread or a corn muffin is a meal by itself, but it's also well-matched with a fresh-from-the-pit barbecue sandwich. The recipe above will serve a dozen very hungry people, and as many as twenty with more moderate appetites. You'll need plenty of cold drinks to accompany this highly seasoned eating experience.

Duck and Sausage Gumbo

In their definitive restaurant guide, *The New Orleans Underground Gourmet,* Richard and Rima Collin use the term "platonic" to describe certain meals and dishes that seem to attain what the Greek philosopher Plato spoke of as the perfect realization of an intended objective.

I can't recall whether the Collins found a platonic bowl of duck and sausage gumbo in their tour of New Orleans restaurants, but I have recently devoured such a dish created by my wife Ann, and it was, to borrow the words of a good country song, close enough to perfect for me. Ann is an all-around whiz of a cook, but she is absolutely unbeatable as a maker of what I call spoon dishes—soup, stew, gumbo, burgoo, and such. She made a Louisiana-style duck and sausage gumbo for us once before, and it was so good I wondered if it could ever be repeated. Now, sure enough, she's done it again.

It was one of those rare occasions where all the necessary pieces just fell into place. We had two Arkansas mallards in the freezer, courtesy of our duck-hunting next-door-neighbor, Benny Bell; a sack of smoked country sausage from Kentucky pork curer Doug Freeman; and some of Louisiana's best cookbooks for reference. Ann's Tennessee kitchen skills completed the Southern square. I watched, and took notes. Here, as best I can tell, is how she did it.

First we had a **roast duck** dinner, cooking the birds in a well-seasoned basting sauce of **vegetable oil** and **red wine.** The rich pan leavings, when simmered with enough water to make three or four cups of liquid, became a thin but intensely flavorful gravy-like stock.

Ann then stripped off the leftover meat and boiled the duck carcasses, including the skin and gristle, with plenty of cut-up **onion** and **garlic,** a couple of **bay leaves,** some **celery tops,** and enough **water** to end up with two more quarts of stock when strained. It was weaker and less rich than the first, but still flavorful.

**Duck and
Sausage
Gumbo**

Next, the **duck meat** was chopped into small pieces, making about **2 cups.** (We got an extra bonus—another 1/2 cup of prime meat—from a slice of country ham I happened to have in storage.) Then Ann sautéed **1 pound of the smoked sausage,** crumbled it, and set it aside with the other meat.

In the skillet grease and dregs, she sautéed **2 cups of chopped onion, 2/3 cup of chopped bell pepper, 1 cup of chopped green onions** with their tops, and **1 tablespoon of minced fresh garlic.**

When the vegetables were soft (and still in the skillet), she sprinkled in about **6 tablespoons of flour,** stirring as she went. After the mixture was well browned, she poured in all of her first stock (the darkest and richest). This was a short-cut roux, the saucy basis of many a fine Louisiana dish. It thickened nicely as she stirred it for about 10 minutes over low heat.

She transferred the skillet contents to a big 2-gallon stew pot and continued to simmer it. Then she poured about half—1 quart—of the second stock into the pot and seasoned the mixture with **1/2 teaspoon of cayenne, 1/2 teaspoon of dried thyme,** and enough **salt and black pepper** to suit her taste. **Two tablespoons of chopped fresh parsley** also went in at this point.

The rest of the stock was added a cup at a time, followed by the duck, ham and sausage, and the finished pot was covered and simmered for about an hour. We stirred and tasted it frequently, adjusting the seasonings, and found to our delight that the great virtues of a classic gumbo were already manifest therein—and they would increase as it aged a bit. With fully a gallon of it to warm us, I felt as undeservingly rich as a lottery winner.

All that remained was to make a salad, warm a fresh loaf of French bread, cook some rice, and pour the drinks. When the gumbo had simmered and thickened sufficiently, Ann turned off the heat, ladled enough for first servings into a separate pan, and stirred in about **3 teaspoons of filé powder.**

(Instructions concerning the addition of filé indicate that reheating may make the dish stringy or gummy, so we only stir it into as much gumbo as we can eat at one sitting. Filé powder, made from **dried sassafras leaves** and available in most specialty food stores, is an ancient Indian herb that found its way into Louisiana cookery centuries ago and has remained as a basic thickening ingredient for gumbo. Some gumbo cooks prefer okra as a thickener, and indeed, it was an African word for okra—*gombo*—that gave this dish its name, but both the cooking method and the flavor of okra gumbo have distinctions of their own.)

Ann spooned generous helpings of rice into wide, shallow bowls and topped it with an elegant sufficiency of her rich, spicy, utterly distinctive duck and sausage gumbo. There in two beautiful bowls was a medley of flavors from a multitude of culinary cultures, all united in a perfectly harmonious balance. It was truly a platonic meal.

Carolina Oyster Roast

Mel McLaurin vividly remembers fall and winter weekends after World War II when his father would drive the family from Fayetteville, North Carolina, to Wilmington on the coast—a three-hour journey in those days—for a feast of roast oysters at Henry Kirkum's place.

Uncle Henry, as he was called, was an old-time oyster roaster, one of several then operating in the Wilmington area. Since 1924, he had been steaming fresh oysters over wood fires until the shells popped open, and rushing them straight from the heat to tables where eager eaters waited.

A historian by profession, Mel McLaurin has more than just a gastronomic appreciation for this popular coastal ritual. He knows that it is an ancient custom, centuries older than Henry Kirkum's enterprise.

European explorers who first encountered native Americans along the Eastern Seaboard in the sixteenth century reported that the Indians offered them, among other foods, an abundance of succulent oysters roasted over open fires. Throughout the colonial era, newcomers to the continent took up this hot alternative to raw-oyster eating with great enthusiasm.

By the time Uncle Henry came along, roast oysters were about as common a dish in some coastal areas of the South as fried chicken and ham were in the region's interior.

Times have changed now. Oysters are not as large or as abundant as they once were, and other seafoods have grown in public favor, and the old oyster roast is now largely confined to occasional community fund-raising events and to a relative handful of restaurants scattered along the coast.

One of those survivors, appropriately enough, is Uncle Henry's Oyster Roast & Seafood Restaurant. Henry is no longer living, of course, but Harlee Kirkum, his 83-year-old son, is still there tending the fire, and the restaurant itself is still located where it always was, at the confluence of Whiskey Creek and the Inland Waterway, a short drive from the center of Wilmington.

When McLaurin took me there for conversation and dinner, we found Kirkum tending the fire in an outbuilding. A genial man in a plaid shirt and khakis and a baseball cap, he seemed to welcome having someone to talk to.

"We used to cook with wood, and then crankcase oil," he said. "Now we use gas. It's the best." Without a doubt it makes a cleaner fire, and one easier to maintain and regulate.

"This isn't the original restaurant," he went on. "Hurricane Hazel tore it down in 1954, and we built back. There used to be seven or eight of these places out here on the water, but this is the last one left. They all died out but us. Oysters got scarce."

I asked him what is causing the scarcity.

"Factories on the water," he replied without hesitating. "Pollution. Too many people. Industrial waste, and all the boats, and all the houses being built on septic tanks. There's no more clean water left. You have to go a long way now to get oysters, and they're not big and plentiful like they used to be. One day there won't be any more left."

Oysters grow and reproduce in beds found in the shallow bays, inlets, sounds and coastal waterways—the same places where the heavy hand of development is so apparent. From Chesapeake Bay clear around the horn of Florida to the Texas coast, oyster harvesters tell the same gloomy story: One day they'll all be gone. Uncle Henry's is now operated by another Henry Kirkum, the founder's grandson, who is also Harlee's son. His kitchen is sparkling clean, as sanitary looking as an operating room. He offers an array of fresh seafoods— shrimp, crabs, clams, scallops, fish—but roast oysters are the main attraction.

They're served by the dishpan full—six to eight dozen, if you're counting—and a waiter assists by finishing the shell-opening process and serving the bivalves with drawn butter and spicy sauces on the side.

The diners devour them, praising the flavor. But as Mel McLaurin and Harlee Kirkum both observed, remembering the plump, juicy, salty-sweet wonders of yesterday, these are not in the same league.

Roast oysters have been a part of the food heritage of Wilmington for all of its 250-year existence, and no doubt they were the pride of colonists and Indians for at least 250 years before that. But if you want a good taste of that history yourself, you'd better hurry. Time is running out.

GRILLED SHRIMP

The last time I splurged on a couple of pounds of jumbo shrimp, I was staggered by two things: the astronomical price, and the scaled-down size of the biggest shrimp available.

Jumbo has taken on a new dimension that approximates what used to be called *medium-sized*. The really big guys, those pinkish-gray crustaceans that looked to be about the size of a clenched fist and counted only about a dozen to the pound, are now either unavailable or out of reach of my wallet.

The golden age of shrimp from the Gulf of Mexico, the most fertile harvesting bed in the world, had to have been in the 1950s and '60s, or so it seems to me. Before that, mechanized trawling equipment and portable refrigeration were still being perfected, and afterward, the same technology was so refined that overharvesting was the inevitable result.

My knowledge of shellfish history may be distorted by the memory of jumbo feasts I savored during a five-year sojourn in Florida back in the 1960s. In those days, ten bucks would get you all the shrimp a foursome could gorge on, and we devoured them like they were going out of style—which, as it turned out, they were.

We ate shrimp fried and boiled, hot and cold, in stews and gumbos, with rice, in scampi dishes, in poor-boy sandwiches, in pastries. We probably would have eaten them raw, had we known about sushi.

But if I had a preferred way of eating shrimp, it was none of the above. My favorite method of cooking jumbos was barbecued—or, to be more precise, marinated and grilled. The marinade recipe came from a friend in Tampa, a woman whose love of cooking and recipe-collecting made her a great source of menu ideas and methods. She called this **barbecued shrimp;** by whatever name or description, it was superb—and it still is.

For each **2 pounds of jumbo shrimp,** washed but left in the shells, prepare a marinade by finely chopping and combining **3 garlic cloves, 1 medium-sized onion,** enough **fresh parsley** to make 1/4 cup, and **1 teaspoon of fresh or packaged basil.** Add **1 teaspoon of salt, 1 teaspoon of dry mustard, 1/2 cup of vegetable oil,** and **the juice of 1 lemon** (about 1/4 cup).

When the mixture is well blended, cover the shrimp with it and marinate overnight in a tightly covered container in the refrigerator. Build a well-distributed charcoal fire in your grill. Cover the cooking rack with aluminum foil and poke holes in it with an ice pick or fork.

GRILLED
SHRIMP

Spread the shrimp over the rack and cover it to hold the smoke in. You can turn the shrimp with a slotted spoon if you like, but it's not essential. Baste them generously with the marinade. In about 20 minutes, the smoky, spicy jumbos ought to be about ready. (Watch the shells; when they harden and begin to crack, it's time to remove from the fire.)

This is a peel-and-eat meal, a hands-on job that calls for plenty of paper napkins, a few side dishes (baked potatoes, green salad, rolls), plenty of cold drinks, and a pungent, sinus-clearing dunk sauce. You can make one of those in a hurry simply by combining **catsup, horseradish, lime or lemon juice,** and **minced garlic** in proportions and quantities sufficient to suit your taste and meet your need.

Or, if you prefer something a bit more elaborate, here's a great **cocktail sauce** recipe from a 35-year-old Florida Department of Agriculture bulletin: Blend **1/2 cup of chili sauce, 1/4 cup of horseradish, 1 teaspoon of Worcestershire sauce, 1 teaspoon of minced onion, 1/2 teaspoon of salt, 1/2 teaspoon of garlic salt, 1/8 teaspoon of black pepper, 2 dashes of hot-pepper sauce, 1 tablespoon of vinegar, 1 teaspoon of celery seed, 1 teaspoon of celery salt,** and **2 tablespoons of sugar.** Refrigerate for a day or two, giving the flavors time to unite. Serve cold.

Straight from the grill, the shrimp will be almost too hot to handle, and messy besides, but never mind—just keep licking your fingers and press on, peeling and dunking and eating until the jumbos are gone. Even if they're only half the size of the Jumbo Jims of your dreams, they'll still be delicious.

CROPPIE

There used to be signs on the outskirts of my hometown of Cadiz, Kentucky, proclaiming it the "Crappie Capital of the World." That always struck me as an ill-considered bid for glory. The title worked only for the relatively small segment of the population who knew that the crappie (pronounced "croppie") is a highly favored catch among sport fishermen. It didn't work for all the others, many of whom no doubt wondered if the sign was a misspelled putdown of Cadiz as a bummer of a town—a crappy place to live.

As a play on words, the "Crappie Capital" title may have brought the town some media attention, calling to mind the observation of P. T. Barnum or W. C. Fields or someone similar that it's usually better to have your name called in vain than not to have it called at all.

But Cadiz (pronounced KAY-diz) is too nice a place to be branded as crappy, and in any case, fishermen not just there but throughout the waterlands of western Kentucky and Tennessee now claim the popular crappie as their own, so the signs are gone, and Cadiz has surrendered its notoriety and resumed its former status as a quiet and pleasant little town. (Cadiz and surrounding Trigg County have a more legitimate claim to fame as Kentucky's preeminent center of salt-cured, hickory-smoked country hams.)

All the same, the crappie is a fine little fish that deserves a capital, and that would no doubt help it to get the respect it's due. First, though, it might be smart to launch a campaign to change the spelling of crappie to croppie, just as the Cajuns have succeeded in changing crayfish to crawfish. The crayfish used to be just a little mudbug that nobody outside the state of Louisiana paid much attention to—but now, as crawfish, it's in demand all over the country. Maybe a change like that would have a similar effect on the finny pride of Kentucky and Tennessee sport fishermen.

One thing's certain, though: No matter what you call it, the croppie (I think I'll stick with the phonetic spelling) is one sweet little fish. Whether pan-fried whole or deep-fried as fillets or oven-baked with lemon juice and butter, it makes a delicious meal, one of the absolute favorites of fresh-water fish lovers wherever it can be found.

Because they congregate in schools to spawn in the protected shallows of lakes, croppie have long been popular with fishermen (and women) at Kentucky Lake and Lake Barkley near Cadiz and at Reelfoot Lake near the Mississippi River in northwest Tennessee.

Loyd Northington of Paducah, a fisherman in Kentucky for more than half a century, has never lost his taste for croppie—the sport or the platter. "They spawn in April and May," he says, "and that's the best time to fish for them. They used to be so plentiful that you could take your boat out around the underbrush in the shallows and pull them in as quick as you got your hook baited."

Flashing silver in the sunlight, a croppie weighing two pounds or so and measuring about a foot and a half in length is a joyful sight to any sport fishing enthusiast with rod and reel in hand.

But, says Northington, "It's getting so they're harder to find. There's more fishermen now, and less underbrush in the lakes. The state has put a limit on how many croppie you can catch. I still like to fish for them, though. They're a mighty good eating fish. Most people like to fillet and deep-fry croppie, but I think it's better to scale and clean them, cut off the heads but leave the tails, wash them and pat them dry, roll them in stone-ground cornmeal, and pan-fry them whole—in lard, if you've got it. They have more flavor that way."

One of the best-known anglers and all-around outdoor sportsmen in western Kentucky is Harold Knight, co-owner of a game-call and hunting/fishing equipment business in Cadiz that has clients nation-wide. "Croppie is one of my favorite fresh-water fish to eat," he says. "It's as good as a walleye, and similar to a small bass. I like to fry the little ones whole—from about a half-pound up to about a pound and a quarter. Bigger than that, I prefer to fillet them. I've tried just about everything to roll them in or coat them with—cracker crumbs, flour, egg, beer—but nothing beats plain old cornmeal with black pepper.

"I wish I could fry them in lard, but vegetable oil is healthier. Whatever you use, you need to get your oil real hot, and fry the fish quick. They have a nice, soft meat and a mild flavor—not oily. A mess of croppie is some real good eating."

Both Kentucky and Tennessee have now imposed catch limits of 30 croppie per day. That may seem like a lot, but in prior times, fishermen often brought them in by the hundreds. Because of its designation as a game fish, croppie can't be harvested and sold commercially in Kentucky, and thus you won't find them on restaurant menus.

Tennessee, on the other hand, allows limited commercial harvest-ing of the fish, and there are a few restaurants in the Reelfoot Lake area that serve them. One of these is The Pier, on Lakeview Street in Samburg, a small village in Obion County. J. T. Spicer and his wife, Jerry, have owned and operated the place for the past six years or so, but it has been a popular fish house since the years right after World War II.

"To tell you the truth," says Spicer, "I wish croppie was still strictly a sport fish. We serve a croppie dinner for those who insist on it, but it's not our main item by any means. To me, it's superior as a sport fish and a pan fish, something you catch for the fun of it and cook at home."

On that point, Loyd Northington and Harold Knight would heartily agree. "There's an old saying," remembers Knight. "'When the dogwoods are blooming, the croppie are spawning.' That's my favorite time to fish for them, and to take them home and cook them."

The frying methods differ little from cook to cook, but baking or broiling gives croppie a somewhat different taste and texture (and, no doubt, so would grilling or smoking, though I haven't tried those meth-ods). Drawing on Knight's ideas—and with the additional benefit of four nice croppie from his string—I came up with this lemon-butter broil that was the talk of the table:

First, make a simple lemon-butter sauce such as this one out of the New Orleans Creole tradition: Melt **1 stick of butter** in a saucepan. Add **3 or 4 tablespoons of fresh lemon juice, 2 tablespoons of finely chopped fresh parsley,** and as much **salt** and **black pepper** as you prefer. This should make a little over a half-cup of sauce. Blend well over low heat.

BROILED "CROPPIE"

Next, rub your scaled and cleaned whole croppie with a little salt and pepper, score them with X-shaped slits on one side, and lay them in a broiling pan, scored side up. Baste well with the warm sauce. Preheat the oven to broil and run the fish in on the top shelf, about 4 inches from the heat, for 5 minutes. Remove and check for doneness. If it flakes easily with a fork, it's ready; if not, broil for another minute or so.

Remove the fish to a warm platter, pour as much of the remaining sauce on them as you choose, and serve immediately. Everything else that goes with this dinner—hush puppies or other bread, slaw or salad, potato or other vege-table, drinks—ought to be ready and waiting when the croppie comes sizzling out of the oven. A delicacy like this is not meant to be dallied with or lingered over. Like their season of spawning, the cooked croppie's moment of glory is brief; be prepared, and seize the moment.

BARBECUE

We fuss a lot in a friendly way about barbecue in the South—about pork versus beef, about finger etiquette, about basic bread and side dishes and the sauce mystique. There are more barbecue factions and smoked-meat sects around here, each with its own hair-splitting distinctions, than there are denominations in the far-flung Judeo-Christian establishment.

But some things are too important to be left in disagreement, and so true that even infidels and heretics cannot deny them convincingly. Among these universal verities is this absolute declaration: You can't reach the highest pinnacle of true barbecue without hardwood smoke, a slow fire, and time, precious time.

No matter how you cut it, slice it, chop it, or pull it, you can't make real barbecue in a hurry. "If you can hear it sizzling," a wise apostolic brother once told me, "your fire's too hot." To do it right requires time in the pit— twelve, fifteen, eighteen hours or more. The ritual of the all-night vigil beside the glowing coals has been repeated so many times from the Rappahannock to the Rio Grande that it has long since taken its rightful place in Southern mysticism and folklore.

It is in these shank-of-the-evening hours of care and waiting that the greater truths and myths of barbecue and the meaning of life are passed on from elders to the younger generation. Transcending as they do the boundaries of race, class, age, sex, religion, politics, and place of birth, these communions of the spirit are a blessed tie that binds and bonds and unifies all who partake.

And finally, in the golden light of a Southern dawn, there comes an exhilarating moment of truth when every message of the senses is saying in unison, "It's ready," and the first charred, crusty, tender, smoke- and sauce-anointed taste of the meat confirms it. Truly, there is nothing quite so fine as genuine barbecue at the instant of its readiness.

And yet, as superior as it is, barbecue in these parts is ever so much more than just the meat; it's also the preparation, the ritual, the social occasion, the fellowship, the anticipation, the realization, the memory. Clear to the bone, barbecue is a savory slice of Southern history, a pulled chunk of the region itself, at its ever-loving best.

◇

Straying from the private pits into the highly competitive commercial world of barbecue sales and marketing, I feel the ground shifting ominously beneath my feet. This is dangerous territory; the pit wars rage from eastern North Carolina to the western tip of Texas, and if you don't think it's serious business, try asking for tomato-based sauce out east of Raleigh, or telling a Texan how you really prefer pork. I'd sooner stroll unarmed through downtown Beirut.

So I'll keep my personal preferences to myself for the time being— except to say that in the restaurants and barbecue stands no less than the private cooking grounds, there's still no substitute for slow cooking over a real fire. Some abominable so-called meat, masquerading as barbecue, is being peddled out there, and the perpetrators need to be called to account. Using liquid smoke, gas heat, store-bought sauce and the good Lord only knows what other sacrileges, these unscrupulous peddlers are hastening the death of real barbecue by giving it such a bad name that only good riddance offers any promise of relief.

Such outrageous behavior makes me appreciate all the more those dwindling few practitioners of true pit artistry. They would sooner go out of business than offer anything less than genuine pit barbecue to their loyal clientele. Pride, more than anything else—more, even, than profit—is what keeps them standing watchfully over the fires. Pride and honesty and stubbornness compel them to do it right or quit doing it.   When I go into, say, Bozo's, on the western edge of Mason, Tennessee, and ask for a plain brown pig—that's a pulled pork sandwich on a warm bun, no sauce, no slaw—I can be confidently assured that what I'll get is a straight-from-the-pit mound of succulent shoulder meat, a perfect combination of dark, crusty outside and light, tender inside pieces near the pinnacle of their truest calling.

The Bozo folks and the precious few like them are the remnant, the last of the smoke people. When they are gone, there won't be any more real barbecue left. I hope *I'm* gone before that happens.

COUNTRY HAM

"We will sell no ham before its time."

Now there's a perfect slogan for the folks who cure and age country hams the old-fashioned way. Too bad Paul Masson thought of it first, and put Orson Welles on television to repeat the message.

Any winemaker worthy of the appellation knows instinctively that you can't rush a good wine. The principle also applies to hams—but sad to say, the major commercial producers of this most enduring of Southern culinary delights have long since abandoned the proud standard of quality in favor of higher volume and quicker profits.

For nearly four centuries, farmers in the upper South have passed on and kept alive a traditional methodology of ham-curing that has made their product unsurpassed. Particularly in certain sub-regions of Virginia, North Carolina, Kentucky, Tennessee, and Arkansas, this reputation for excellence attracts praise from around the nation, and even from overseas.

But the very popularity of traditionally cured hams has prompted many meat-packing companies to simulate and speed up the process. Aided by scientists in the state colleges of agriculture, these firms now do in as little as six weeks what those devoted to the old ways insist can't be done right in less than nine months.

The U. S. Department of Agriculture appears to have thrown its weight behind the mass producers. In new regulations governing meat inspection and safety, the department has in effect made it possible for the producers of quick-cure hams—so-called "42-day wonders"—to put these ersatz meats on the market as bonafide country hams.

At the same time, the USDA regulations make it virtually impossible for small farmers to gain approval of their time-honored and obviously superior curing methods without an investment in new facilities and inspection devices that can fairly be described as punitive.

The ironic consequence can be seen in television commercials for "genuine, old-fashioned country hams" that are artificially salted, cured, smoked, and aged—and in the dwindling number of true country hams that are technically subject to being branded by the government as illegal products, the same as bootleg whiskey.

The ancient art of ham-making was already fading from the scene when the mass producers found their confirming allies in the universities and the USDA. For decades it has been clear that in this age of speed, fewer and fewer farmers would take the time to butcher hogs in sub-freezing weather, pack the hams in salt for a month or more, finish curing them with hickory smoke or some other approved application, and hang them up to age through the spring and summer.

From hog-killing in December to ham-selling the following October is a minimum nine-month rite of passage that can only be shortened at the cost of quality and basic authenticity. Amazingly, a handful of Southern farmers still observe the rite. Like the great winemakers of France, there are subtle differences of technique among them—but as a group, they are the true artists, the last of the masters.

You won't see them advertised on TV or in the slick magazines. But if you go to them—to such places as southside Virginia, eastern North Carolina, western and central Kentucky, middle Tennessee, northern Arkansas—you can still buy hams prepared the way they were centuries ago, when America was a new colonial possession of the British.

In mid-October of every year, for example, you can go to Cadiz in western Kentucky and find at the Trigg County Ham Festival about two dozen local farmers competing in a formal contest to select the grand champion traditionally cured country ham.

Some of the farmers in Cadiz and elsewhere in the Southern "ham belt" will gladly sell their products directly to you—a practice that the USDA, curiously enough, has never seen fit to discourage. (It is shipment of those same products through the mail that the department apparently objects to.)

Regardless of the technical—and political—fine points of regulation, it is still possible to locate and authenticate real country hams, worthy descendants of the cured pork of old.

And in that regard, it seems appropriate once again to paraphrase Orson Welles: If you can find a better ham, buy it.

HAM AND BEATEN BISCUITS

When I was a boy, my grandparents introduced me to country ham and beaten biscuits, and my life was immeasurably enriched thereby. More than a mere taste for these delicacies, more than an appetite, they gave me an ancient ritual and a deep cultural experience.

It was in the little town of Cadiz, the county seat of Trigg County, Kentucky, that I received my initiation into the fellowship of country ham and beaten biscuit devotees. My grandfather had a backyard smokehouse there in which he cured and aged and stored hams and other pork cuts. He also kept in fine running order for my grandmother a contraption called a biscuit brake, a kneading device designed to transform a ball of dough into a slick, glossy ribbon of raw pastry.

The smokehouse stood just a few steps from the back porch of their home—close enough that the heady fragrance of its contents subtly touched the senses of anyone who passed. I was strongly attracted to that aroma, and still am. The smokehouse was an olfactory temple that I entered with hushed reverence—and then only when invited. The walls were of red brick, smoke-darkened to a deep burgundy. Dripping pork fat and spilled salt and the tread of heavy boots had packed the dirt floor and crusted it over. Air holes around the edge of the tin roof allowed smoke to escape. Hams, bacon, sausage—the bounty of that perennial winter ritual known as hog-killing—hung there in all their glory, having been united with the coarse curing salt and the dense green hickory smoke to produce a smell and a flavor of unique distinction in the realm of cookery.

In the upper South—in Virginia, where it all started, in North Carolina and Kentucky, in Tennessee and Arkansas and the hilly sections of north Georgia and Alabama—smokehouses used to be commonplace outbuildings on almost every farm. The weather in those states was ideal for curing pork: cold enough for butchering in December and January, mild enough for salting and smoking in late winter and early spring, hot enough for the insect-killing summer sweats. Those essential seasons made a country ham what it was (and, in a precious few places, still is): the epitome of pork, a tender and delectable work of comestible art, a gastronomical wonder of the world. The great hams of the rural upper South, like the great wines of provincial France, thus were sustained and perpetuated by a centuries-old tradition in which the wisdom and the secrets of the fathers were handed down from generation to generation.

Just as the curing of the hams was my grandfather's responsibility, the making of the beaten biscuits belonged in my grandmother's domain. Her biscuit brake consisted of a marble slab mounted like a table top on a wrought-iron sewing machine base; to the slab was affixed a set of nickel-plated rollers, one above the other, and an oak-handled hand crank to turn them. At first glance, the machine looked like a cross between a Singer and a wringer, a device for both sewing and washing clothes.

But this was no Rube Goldberg invention. I thought my grandfather had made it—he was a very creative fellow, and a mechanical whiz—but it turned out that a machinist in St. Joseph, Missouri, had marketed such machines for years after the Civil War. Joseph DeMuth, while serving in the Union army, had seen women in Kentucky and Tennessee struggling to make a certain kind of hard, unleavened biscuit that required repeated pounding of the dough with a heavy mallet. These so-called beaten biscuits had the virtue of lasting for days without becoming stale, and thus made good pocket bread for people on the move. DeMuth, noting what a labor they were to make, went home after the war and, borrowing ideas from earlier inventors, assembled his first dough-kneading machine and put it on the market.

I like to imagine that Percy White and his young bride, Berta Crenshaw—my grandparents—were the first Kentuckians to own a DeMuth machine, theirs coming as a wedding gift in the mid-1890s. Whether or not that is so, they certainly were model owners. In the 1940s, when my brother and I were finally old enough to turn the crank, the old machine was still running like a top. With frequent regularity—especially in the winter, when country ham was often served—Grandmother made up a batch of dough and we dutifully manned the crank, dreaming all the while of paper-thin slices of aged ham heaped high between halves of a smooth and tender biscuit. Then, as now, I recognized that inspired combination as a marriage made in culinary heaven.

There are ham lovers on the East Coast, from Maryland to Georgia, who insist that their country ham is the best and truest rendition of a centuries-old art form. I have deep respect for those good folks, and for their products. But in all candor, I submit that nothing can beat a Trigg County ham that has been cured and smoked and aged for a year or more and then cooked by a method to be described below. And if the ham is served with real beaten biscuits, the tandem easily soars above any and all competitors.

COUNTRY
HAM

Starting with a genuine **country ham** weighing, say, **15 pounds,** you can follow these steps of preparation. First, scrub it with a stiff brush in lukewarm water to remove mold (a harmless but telling sign of age). Then, using a handsaw (or with your butcher's help), cut the hock into several pieces (to be used for seasoning pots of beans, cabbage, etc.). Stir about a **cup of vinegar** into a large kettle with some **tap water,** put in the ham, cover it with more water, and let it soak overnight. Next day, remove and rinse the ham, return it to the kettle fat side up, cover it with fresh water, and bring it to a low boil. Simmer uncovered for 1 hour.

Pour that water off, rinse the ham, and cover it again with fresh water, to which **2 cups of apple juice** and **1 cup of sugar** have been added. Return to the heat and cook uncovered at just below the boiling point for about 3-1/2 hours, or about 15 minutes per pound. Then, turn the heat off and leave the ham immersed in the water for about 2 hours. When you pour the water off, the ham should be cooled enough to handle. With a sharp knife, trim off the hard skin and most of the fat, debone it if possible, and pat it with paper towels before placing the ham on a large serving platter.

Next, mix equal parts of **dark brown sugar** and **bread crumbs** (about 1 cup of each) with **2 teaspoons of black pepper** (more or less of these ingredients, to suit your taste) and gently pat this sweet/hot/spicy topping all over the warm ham. As the ham continues to cool, the topping will form a crust. Cover the finished dish with a tea towel and set it aside to cool through and through.

Now about the biscuits. Until recently, only those who owned a biscuit brake or who had the patience to pound the dough several hundred times with a heavy instrument could create them. The dough has to be somehow pressed and folded and layered repeatedly to achieve the desired result. But now, thanks to food processors, a reasonable facsimile of silky smooth beaten biscuits can be made quickly and easily. Here's how:

Sift together **3-1/2 cups of plain all-purpose flour, 1/2 teaspoon each of baking powder and salt,** and **2 tablespoons of sugar.** With a pastry blender, work in **1/2 cup of lard** (vegetable shortening will do in a pinch, but it's a poor substitute). To this coarse, meal-like mixture, add **3/4 cup of very cold** (almost icy) **light cream** (half-and-half), and then knead the dough into a cohesive ball. Seal it in a plastic bag and leave it out on the counter to rest and stabilize for a few hours, or even overnight.

BEATEN BISCUITS

To make the biscuits, divide the dough in half, subjecting each in turn to a 2-minute whirl with the dough blade in the food processor. Then recombine it, roll it out to a thickness of about 1/2 inch, fold it and roll again, and continue folding and rolling until the dough seems quite smooth and silky. Cut the biscuits about

1/2 inch thick and 2 inches in diameter, place on an ungreased cookie sheet, and pierce each one two or three times with a fork (this allows air to escape from the layers during baking).

In a preheated 325-degree oven, bake the biscuits for 5 minutes on the bottom rack and 25 minutes on the middle rack. Remove one and open it to make sure they're done in the middle. They should be smooth, lightly tanned, firm (even hard) on the outside, dry and flaky and pastry-like in the center. Turn out on a rack to cool. They're delicious warm, but almost as good cold, and they keep extremely well in a tightly-sealed tin.

Now comes the moment. The ham, when sliced tissue-thin, yields fragile cross sections of the spicy topping, a tiny ribbon of fat, and a tender portion of the rich red meat. These are folded and piled generously on the bottom half of a warm beaten biscuit and then crowned with the top half. The consuming pleasure must be experienced to be fully appreciated. This is what the months of work and waiting and preparation, and the years of tradition, are all about. Wars have been fought for less.

Supporting Dishes

FLORIDA CITRUS

One of my fondest memories from a five-year sojourn in Florida back in the early 1960s is the pleasure I got from going out in the yard on a sunny winter morning and picking my breakfast off a citrus tree.

Fresh-squeezed orange juice, tangarines, juicy grapefruit halves— they were all part of the daily standard at our house, and the fruit seemed to be everywhere, abundant, and inexpensive if not free for the taking.

We get grapefruit and oranges in the supermarket now from Texas and Arizona and California as well as Florida, but whenever I think of citrus, I still think of the sweet blossom fragrance, the gold-on-green colors, and the juicy abundance in that Southern citadel of endless groves.

Citrus goes back a very long way in the Sunshine State. Historians say that oranges were first found in the Orient in about 50 B.C., and Columbus supposedly brought them to the West Indies five centuries ago; then, according to legend, the Spanish settlers of St. Augustine planted orange seedlings there in 1565. From that beginning, the Florida citrus industry has grown to enormous proportions.

The growth has been phenomenal but not steady. Periodic ravages of nature—freezes, hurricanes, plant diseases, insect invasions—have decimated groves and driven up prices. Even so, the 1988-89 crop totaled more than 220 million boxes (a box contains 1-3/4 bushels), and that compares favorably to the 1979-80 record of 283 million boxes. When the crop size was first recorded in 1886, the count was just over a million boxes.

A few more statistics underscore the magnitude of the industry in Florida. The state has about 70 million citrus trees covering 700,000 acres. From these come 70 percent of this country's oranges and half of the world's grapefruit. The wholesale value of Florida citrus in 1988 was $3.3 billion.

Oranges have always had a strong appeal to the buying public, and particularly to snowbound Northerners who associate the fruit with sunshine and balmy tropical breezes. It was not the fruit, though, but a by-product of it that catapulted citrus to the top of the all-American menu.

The by-product was frozen orange juice concentrate. Scientists at the Florida Citrus Commission research center in Lake Alfred are credited with discovering the method by which orange juice is now concentrated. The method was patented in 1945 in the name of three of the researchers, who in turn assigned their discovery to the U. S. Secretary of Agriculture for free use by the public. Frozen orange juice not only became the mainstay of the citrus business; it also helped to make the entire frozen food industry commercially viable. Today, more than 90 percent of all Florida oranges are processed for juice, whether concentrated or single-strength.

Dr. Edward L. Moore, one of the three holders of the patent, was still working at the research laboratory in late 1988. At the age of 72, he had been there since he moved to Florida from Massachusetts during World War II.

"We didn't so much discover concentrated juice," he said modestly. "What we did was develop the chemistry for fixing the right strength of the concentrate, and the proper ratios of sugar and water and citric acid. We overconcentrated it, you might say, and then cut it back with fresh juice."

According to Dr. Moore, the so-called "cutback" in most frozen orange juice now comes primarily from peel oil, pulp, and other flavor essences. "I've never thought it gives as good a taste as we used to get when we added fresh juice," he says.

When I told him I frequently boost the flavor of frozen juice by adding one or two fresh-squeezed oranges to the mix, he laughed and said, "Well, that's the way we did it back in the forties."

As a low-calorie food high in Vitamin C and other nutrients, citrus has always enjoyed favor among health-food advocates. To me, though, its principal virtue—aside from great taste—is its evocative power.

I'll show you what I mean. On a cold, gray winter morning, take a nice grapefruit and cut it in half. Carefully cut around the sections and remove the core. Fill that center cavity with honey and put a small pat of butter on top. Sprinkle a mixture of sugar and cinnamon over the surface and run the fruit under the oven broiler for a couple of minutes—just long enough to warm it up, melt the butter, and brown the sugar and cinnamon.

Now sit down and enjoy that with a cup of coffee and a piece of toast, and see if it doesn't make your winter day a little brighter—almost as if you were basking in the warmth of a sunny south Florida citrus grove.

STRAWBERRIES

Of all the continental wonders the European explorers encountered when they reached these shores centuries ago, none was more ubiquitous than wild strawberries. All along the East Coast and into the interior they grew in sweet profusion, bright as scarlet blankets in the woods and fields.

"Wee can not sett downe foote but tred on strawberries," wrote one Englishman. Another, though he knew the plants were cultivated back in the mother country, reported that "This berry is the wonder of all the fruits growing naturally in these parts."

Sweet, juicy strawberries have remained an American favorite ever since, and though California now raises most of the commercial berries (with Florida the next most productive state), they can be found in season in all the Southern states and many others as well.

In the flat fields around Plant City, Florida, east of Tampa, local growers have been harvesting berries since the 1930s, and early each March they celebrate the season with a festival. In 1988, the 54th annual Florida Strawberry Festival attracted close to 750,000 visitors during its 11-day run. Even more impressively, they consumed a half-million pints of berries in every conceivable form, from milk shakes to shortcakes.

In the old days, Florida berries were, like those in other Southern states, primarily a fresh-market crop for local consumption. But in the mid-1970s, the state began to follow California's lead and develop "shippers"— larger, hardier varieties with longer growing seasons and bigger yields. Most important of all, these new berries were far less perishable, and thus could be shipped to distant markets without spoiling.

Today, the Florida season lasts from late November to mid-April (still only about half as long as California's), and the crop is more important to the growers and shippers—and to Florida agriculture generally—than it has ever been before.

Meanwhile, upcountry Southerners from south Georgia to Kentucky still grow and market strawberries in the more traditional manner as a short-season crop primarily for local markets and pick-your-own consumers.

These local growers can't compete with the big boys on volume or durability, but virtually all of them insist that their smaller, more delicate and fragile berries are also juicier, sweeter, and more intensely flavorful than any of the commercial varieties.

Tennessee Beauty, Cardinal (developed in Arkansas), Early Glow, and other fresh-market varieties—some of long-standing popularity, others newly hybridized—are indeed the favorites that my mid-South palate craves, though the late-season crop around festival time in Plant City certainly has great virtues of its own.

Some year, I'd like to follow the crop—Florida in March, south Georgia and Alabama in April, Tennessee and Kentucky in May, Indiana and Illinois in June, Wisconsin and Minnesota in July, Canada in August. Unless I'm badly mistaken, the local growers all along the way would declare persuasively that their berries were the very best.

I wouldn't dare argue with them. I would just relax and enjoy each and every bite, making note of the subtle differences and concluding that there's really no such thing as a bad strawberry.

In jams and jellies, pies and parfaits, shakes and sundaes, syrups and shortcakes, strawberries are an eternal blessing almost everywhere—and especially in the South.

Here's a **jam/preserves recipe** that will let you keep that authentic strawberry flavor on your pantry or freezer shelf for year-round enjoyment:

STRAWBERRY JAM

Wash and cap enough firm, ripe, **sweet-tart berries** to make **4 cups** (whole or sliced). Put them in a large saucepan with **1 tablespoon of vinegar.** Cover and boil for 1 minute; then remove from the heat and stir in **3 cups of sugar,** taking care not to mash the berries unnecessarily. Return to the stove and boil uncovered until the syrup begins to thicken noticeably (about 20 minutes). Remove again, skim off any foam that may have formed, and pour the preserves out into a large flat container. The jam will thicken as it stands overnight, but it should retain its rich red color. Next day, pack it into sterilized jars or freezer containers. Four cups of berries should yield two pints of jam. It's best not to cook more than four cups at a time; larger amounts are apt not to thicken sufficiently.

WILTED LETTUCE SALAD

Bettye Elizabeth Campbell—Grandma Bettye to the little ones—was a miracle worker in her farmhouse kitchen near East Fork in rural Amite County, Mississippi, back in the bleak and barren days of the Great Depression.

Little Dave, one of the grandchildren, never imagined that his family could be poor and hungry, not with two grandmothers regularly turning short rations into full meals for their numerous descendants.

Though he is now a 65-year-old man with a farm of his own, Dave Campbell still can summon a vivid recollection of the kitchen and dinner table at Grandma Bettye's house, and of the seemingly endless parade of dishes she made from memory or created as if from thin air.

Listen to his soliloquy on wilted lettuce salad:

"The tender spring lettuce and other greens were called salet. Not salad—salet, or maybe sallet, or salat. Some grew wild, like poke weed, and some we planted in the garden. Leaf lettuce, for example. We would pick it very young, when the leaves were small, pale green, extremely tender, and almost sweet.

"Grandma would wash and drain the lettuce. Then she'd take a slab of bacon from the smokehouse and slice it kind of thick, and fry it up real crisp. Then she'd crumble it real fine and set it aside.

"She'd put a mound of lettuce on your plate, and lay a few long, slender green onions beside it—those first little thin ones, tops and all, right out of the garden—and maybe a few radishes too.

"Then she would heat up the bacon grease that was left in the big black skillet, and just before it was hot enough to smoke, she'd pour some of it right on top of the lettuce. Real quick, then, you'd add some of the crumbled bacon, sprinkle on some black pepper and a little salt, and you'd eat it while it was still hot.

"That's a unique combination of flavors—hot, smoky bacon and cool, tender lettuce, in a fleeting moment of togetherness. I've never forgotten it."

By whatever name—salad, salet—wilted lettuce is a sensational taste experience that probably predates the depression by at least a generation or two. Without knowing for sure, I'd be willing to bet that John Bibb, the amateur horticulturist who developed a leafy variety of lettuce (Bibb, we now call it) in Frankfort, Kentucky, before the Civil War, was acquainted with the tandem taste of fresh greens and hot bacon drippings.

Such Southern cookbook writers as Marion Flexner of Kentucky and Eula Mae Stratton of Arkansas have extolled the virtues of wilted lettuce salad. They and others have also refined the dressing. Flexner, for example, included this recipe for **bacon and vinegar dressing** in her 1949 collection, *Out of Kentucky Kitchens* :

Fry **4 slices of bacon** in a skillet. Drain on paper towels and crumble. To the hot fat in the skillet (removed from heat), add **2 hard-boiled egg yolks** and **2 tablespoons of water.** Mash with a fork and stir until the yolks make a smooth paste. Add **1/3 cup of cider vinegar,** then season to taste with **salt, sugar, cayenne,** and **black pepper.** (Some recipes also call for dry mustard and lemon juice.) Reheat the mixture, taste for seasoning, and then pour over fresh lettuce or other greens in salad bowl. Sprinkle crumbled bacon on top, and serve at once.

WILTED LETTUCE SALAD DRESSING

"That sounds about right to me," says Dave Campbell, who still makes a few wilted lettuce salads when his garden onions and lettuce are at their spring peak. "I'm not so sure about the sugar, but everything else in that recipe goes well in a hot bacon dressing.

"Grandma Bettye might be a little suspicious of all the refinements, but I've got a feeling that if you could serve her a wilted lettuce salad like that, she'd find it very much to her liking."

Turnip Greens

There is a Greens Line that runs through the South. Like the Mason-Dixon Line, it's difficult to plot and subject to dispute, but it's there, and it has its own purposes and its own mystique.

South of the Greens Line, in the lower reaches of Louisiana, Mississippi, Alabama, Georgia, South Carolina, and all of Florida, the dominant winter staple among greens lovers is collards. North of the line, stretching to the Ohio River and sometimes even beyond, the leafy vegetable of preference is turnip greens.

Collard greens, though they grow thick and hardy-looking, are actually best suited to the shorter and milder winters of the deep South. Turnip greens, on the other hand, appear more delicate and more vulnerable to snow and ice, when in fact they are at their best after a hard freeze.

Once they're cooked, these two quite different vegetables end up looking and tasting very much alike. If I have a preference, it's turnip greens—but only because they were so commonly served at the Kentucky table of my boyhood. (We also ate lots of fresh spinach and mustard greens.)

In the mountains of Appalachia and some other parts of the upper South, wild greens are very popular, especially in the spring. Dandelions, watercress, and pokeweed yield tender and delicious greens; so do some less familiar shoots, among them creases (a dry-land variety of watercress) and lamb's quarters.

When he was growing up in rural middle Tennessee in the 1920s, Ben Hutcherson watched his elders sow turnip green seeds in the garden in the early fall and then harvest fresh greens throughout the winter.

"I still do it the same way," he says. "There's two main varieties of seeds: purple-top and what they call seven-top. The seven-tops come up smaller and not as thick, but they're a lot more tender and better tasting."

Purple-tops take their name from the purple and white turnips the seeds produce. Their greens are best when very young and tender; when mature, they have a stringy toughness and a strong, bitter flavor.

Seven-tops, so named because they grow in seven-stem fronds, are hybrid greens not meant to produce turnips (though they do yield tiny nubs that can be eaten). Their higher mission is to make tender, mild, pleasantly flavorful greens—and they answer admirably to that calling.

Hutcherson clears a patch in his garden the first week in September. He broadcasts the seed by hand and then rakes the area lightly. Within a few weeks, his crop shines like a bright green carpet in the morning dew.

"I get plenty of greens from early November right on through the winter," he says, "unless we have a long spell of below-zero days. They don't mind some cold weather, though. Seems like they're tenderest right after a hard freeze."

Using a sharp knife, Hutcherson cuts the shoots at ground level, "just above the turnip," and trims off only the heaviest part of the stem. He seldom eats the turnips themselves. "A grocery sack full of greens will cook down to a nice mess," he says, "plenty for four to six hungry people." (A "mess," in Southern parlance, translates roughly to "an ample amount.")

After he has washed his bag of greens thoroughly and culled the biggest stems and wilted leaves, he cooks them quickly. This is his method:

Fill a **2-gallon** kettle half full of **cold water** and set it over high heat. Put in a piece of **ham hock** or other seasoning meat (or **bacon drippings**, or whatever flavoring element you prefer), a **dried pod of red pepper,** and enough **salt** to suit your taste. Cover the pot and let it boil hard for about 10 minutes. Next, stuff the **greens** into the pot, stirring and poking them down with a wooden spoon. When all the greens are immersed and the water is boiling rapidly again, re-cover and keep at a rolling boil for 8 minutes, by which time tenderness should be assured. Taste and adjust seasonings, then shut off the heat and leave the greens covered until ready to serve.

TURNIP
GREENS

The bonus in any mess of greens is the pot likker, that clear, flavorful, nutritious, and delicious broth in which the vegetables have cooked. A warm mug of it with a piece of cornbread is almost a meal in itself.

Ben Hutcherson recognizes that many Southerners prefer to cook their greens a lot longer than he does--and sometimes, he says, that may be necessary: "In other seasons of the year, turnip greens probably need more cooking. But in the dead of winter, they're almost tender enough to eat when you bring them in from the garden."

With plenty of good Southern cornbread to accompany it, a steaming bowl of turnip greens is one of the signature dishes of home cooks in the region. You'll probably want something to drink, too—iced tea, buttermilk, coffee, or even water will do nicely—and the rest is pure enjoyment.

CABBAGE

On almost any given day in October, travelers driving past Milepost 192 on the Blue Ridge Parkway in southwest Virginia will find encamped there a mountain farmer by the name of Donald Brady.

He'll be easy to spot. His mode of transportation is a covered wagon drawn by a team of oxen, and his principal cargo is cabbage—hundreds of heads of it, freshly harvested and weighing three or four pounds each.

This stretch of the Virginia mountains southwest of Roanoke—and particularly Carroll County, on the North Carolina line—is known near and far as "the cabbage capital of the world." With allowances for some slight exaggeration, the title seems to fit.

They grow about 3,000 acres of cabbage in Carroll County each summer—and at 34,000 heads to the acre, that's a gross yield of just over 100 million heads. About 80 percent of the crop goes directly to market all over the South and Southwest; the rest is processed for slaw and kraut.

"Yep, this is the place," says Donald Brady. "The soil is just right and the climate's perfect up here in these mountains—ideal conditions for growing cabbage. That's why it's been going on here for so long."

Brady remembers from his childhood the sight of ox-drawn wagons hauling cabbages to Hillsville, the Carroll County seat, and to the little ridgetop communities of Fancy Gap and Meadows of Dan.

His parents and grandparents grew cabbage, says Brady. Now, at the age of 62, he is the king of the patch himself, not only producing several million heads on his farm but also serving as president of the Southwest Virginia Vegetable Producers Association.

Like most modern agriculture, cabbage-growing is much more of a scientific and technological undertaking than it used to be. The hybrid seeds, developed especially for the "no till" method of farming now used in these mountains, were produced in upstate New York; they yield "supermarket cabbages" of uniform size, color, firmness, and weight.

Brady and the other Virginia farmers plant every seven inches in parallel rows that are exactly eighteen inches apart. "We start setting about the fifteenthth of April," he says, "and keep at it steady until the fifteenth of July. By then we're already cutting, and the harvest continues until mid-November. It's an everyday thing—you don't ever let up until you're done."

Now, in place of wagons, refrigerated eighteen-wheelers transport a thousand fifty-pound boxes at a time—about 18,000 cabbages—and the trucks are a common sight on the region's highways through the summer and fall.

This one small area supplies most of the fresh cabbage to be found in Southern markets. "Yankee cabbage," says Donald Brady with a chuckle, "is mostly grown in New York, Pennsylvania, Ohio, Wisconsin. Of course, we like to think ours is superior in quality."

Superior or not, it's certainly the equal of anybody's cabbage—a pretty shade of green, firm to the touch but tender when cooked, crisp and crunchy in slaw, intensely flavorful any way you fix it.

My favorite way to eat it is as a traditional Southern vegetable. That involves boiling in water with a slice of seasoning meat, adding red and black pepper and salt for flavor, and using the kettle juice—the pot likker—as a nourishing and appetizing soup.

Purists who want to avoid the pork and salt seasonings can grate the cabbage, season it with vinegar, and eat it raw. I like that, too.

And then there's creamy **cole slaw,** a universal side order in modern American restaurants. If you enjoy throwing together a quick and satisfying dish, seasoning to taste as you go, try this one:

Finely grate **half of a medium-sized head of cabbage** by hand or in a food processor, and by the same method mince **a carrot, half of a bell pepper, a few sprigs of fresh parsley** and, if you like, **a green onion or some chives.** Stir together in a bowl and season to taste with **salt, black pepper, red pepper, sugar, paprika, garlic salt, celery salt, wine vinegar, half-and-half or cream,** and **mayonnaise.**

COLE SLAW

The only reliable guide to quantities of seasonings in a freehand concoction like this is self-restraint; you can always add more salt, vinegar, or whatever, but you can never take out anything once you've stirred it in. Mountain-grown cabbage from southwest Virginia makes all these methods of preparation taste as fresh and delicious as you could ever hope to have them. Donald Brady and the other Blue Ridge farmers have proudly seen to that.

Sweet Potatoes

I have long since given up any hope of understanding the differences between sweet potatoes and yams.

Both are tubers—fleshy, root-like vegetables that grow underground—and there are so many varieties, all similar in taste and appearance, that it's impossible to tell them apart.

Never mind that the sweet potato belongs to the morning glory family, and is not even distantly related botanically to the yam. Never mind, either, that the white potato, another tuberous look-alike, is an altogether different vegetable with a taste that could never be mistaken for a sweet potato.

What we're talking about here, regardless of its label, is that hard, oddly-shaped supermarket produce item with a thick brown skin and a firm flesh of pale yellow to bright orange color that cooks up nicely into a soft, moist, sweet, and delicious side dish or pie.

The Louisiana Cajuns call their sweet potatoes *bon bon du close*—candy from the field. In North Carolina, a region of abundant yam growth and consumption, they are widely thought of as one of the most basic of staple vegetables.

And in Alabama, where they were popularized by the research of Dr. George Washington Carver of Tuskegee Institute almost a century ago, you'll find them on the menu wherever traditional Southern cooking is served.

By whatever name, sweet potatoes are to the soul food and country cooking of the South what beans are to Boston: a signature dish of symbolic importance and great public favor.

Considering how versatile and tasty they are, it's a little bit surprising that sweet potatoes aren't served in the South even more frequently than white potatoes and rice. In the fall-winter holiday season, though, they're almost certain to show up on Southern tables in one form or another.

The earliest recipes for sweet potato pudding specified grated raw potatoes as a base (and then baked, of course), but Southern tastes gradually came to prefer casseroles in which the vegetable had been first boiled in its jacket until tender and then mashed and seasoned with spices.

A Thanksgiving or Christmas feast without such a dish just wouldn't seem Southern to me. Like turkey and dressing and cranberry sauce, sweet potatoes are an essential menu item.

One fall a few years back, I encountered at a dinner party a sweet potato soufflé of such distinction that I went back to the kitchen to find out how it was made. The caterer, Wilma Parker of Gallatin, Tennessee, generously offered me the recipe, and I quickly scribbled it down.

Less than a month later, at another dinner in Adams, Tennessee, some 35 miles west of Gallatin, I was served an almost identical sweet potato dish by a talented cook and hostess named Lorena Owens.

After I had compared the two recipes and found them to be so similar, I couldn't help inquiring if Mrs. Owens and Mrs. Parker had ever met. They had not, and furthermore, the recipe had come to each of them via routes that never could have crossed.

All of which goes to prove that great cooking, like other kinds of creativity, sometimes originates in more than one place at the same time.

There are some fine old casseroles made from raw sweet potatoes that I still enjoy sometimes, but nothing that I've ever found is any better than the one I associate with Wilma Parker and Lorena Owens. Here is my less perfect but reasonably close approximation of theirs:

First, boil **3 or 4 large sweet potatoes** in their jackets until tender. Peel and mash the potatoes while still hot, and melt **1 stick of butter** in them. (If the mixture seems too thick and dry, add some sweet milk a tablespoon at a time.) Season to taste with **sugar** and **spices**; a combination I like is **1/4 cup of dark brown sugar, 1/4 teaspoon of ginger,** and **1/2 teaspoon each of cinnamon, allspice, cloves,** and **nutmeg.**

SWEET POTATO SOUFFLÉ

Beat **2 whole eggs** with a wire whisk and add them to the potatoes. Then pour the mixture into a lightly buttered oven-proof dish. On the top, sprinkle a blend of the following: **1/4 cup of packed brown sugar, 1/2 cup of crushed corn flakes, 1/2 cup of chopped pecans,** and **1/4 stick of melted butter.** Bake for 30 minutes in a 350-degree oven.

This is one of those standard dishes that seems destined to return again and again by popular demand. When I think of holiday dinners, it's one of the first menu items to pop into my mind.

RICE

Of all the staple vegetables that have characterized Southern cooking, from beans and peas to greens and potatoes, none except corn has been more basic—or less celebrated—than rice.

It probably wouldn't be stretching the case too much to say that rice has been largely unappreciated, even maligned and scorned, in these parts. Even its true identity is misunderstood; technically speaking, it's not a vegetable at all, but a cereal grain.

And, contrary to popular belief, almost none of the rice on our grocery shelves is imported from the Orient. Instead, it is a home-grown product of the South, with California chipping in a modest percentage.

Rice has been grown commercially in the South for three centuries, and now it's a bigger domestic crop than ever. Not only does the region produce 90 percent of the rice eaten in this country; it also exports about half its annual crop to other nations. Even in some of the most traditional rice-consuming centers of the world, such as Hong Kong and Indonesia, a portion of the modern daily ration originates here in the American South.

There are conflicting stories about how rice became a Southern crop in the first place, but all of them point to South Carolina in the late 1600s. The most oft-repeated tale concerns a sea captain named John Thurber who sought shelter from a storm in the port of Charleston in 1685. While there, he gave a small bag of Madagascar rice to a local planter, and from that beginning grew the vast rice plantations of the Carolina-Georgia lowlands.

After the Civil War, rice-growing migrated around the coast to Louisiana and Texas and then into the Mississippi Delta country. Today, Arkansas is the largest rice-producing state, with 1.2 million acres—about 30 percent of the national total. All except California's 10 percent share is grown in the South (including Texas).

Most of our rice is the long-grain variety, and most of it is planted in the spring and harvested in the late summer and early fall. The low-lying fields must be irrigated to supply the crop's great need for water.

Because the Delta is located along the flyway for migratory waterfowl, the rice fields of the region are magnets for duck hunters in the post-harvest season. Around Stuttgart, Arkansas, ducks and rice are supremely important to the local economy—as much so as tobacco in Kentucky or seafood in Florida.

Many of the Creole and Cajun dishes of Louisiana and the combination dishes of beans or peas with rice that have long been popular favorites in Southern coastal locales are a testament to the enduring presence of this ancient food in the regional diet.

Curiously, though, the interior South—including the rice-growing areas of Arkansas and Mississippi—has never taken to rice with much gusto. In South Carolina, where rice hasn't been grown commercially for nearly a century, cookbooks still clearly reveal an abiding love for the grain, while in the recipe collections of the upper South it's just another vegetable, and a minor one at that.

And then there is Louisiana, where rice is both a major crop and an indispensable staple of the cookery. A Creole or Cajun feast without rice in one form or another is as rare as a Tennessee summer country dinner without corn.

The persistence of food habits and images is always strong. Rice makes us think of China and Japan and Southeast Asia, not of Arkansas and South Carolina and the Gulf Coast. Yet here it is, a presence in our diet for 300 years—and in Hong Kong at this very moment, no doubt someone is reaching for a steaming bowlful that came out of a field in the wetlands of Louisiana or the prairie of Texas or the delta of Arkansas.

Whether they cook it the same or not I can't say, but our standard method is always printed on the box: Bring **2 to 2-1/2 cups of water** to a boil, stir in **1 cup of rice**—and, if you like, **1 teaspoon of salt** and **1 tablespoon of butter or margarine.** (I prefer to season it after it's cooked.) Cover tightly and simmer for 20 minutes. Remove from the heat and let it stand, still covered, until all the water has been absorbed (about 5 minutes).

RICE

Then serve it up with whatever else the menu features, and you've got yourself a Southern side dish—and a universal one—that's rich in flavor and history.

RED RICE

From the time I was about twelve and my family was down to two kids in the house, we generally ate supper at a sturdy old painted wooden table in the kitchen. My usual place was on the end nearest the wall, where I was free to exercise left-handed fork action without fear of locking elbows with my right-handed brother.

If we got to the table early, while our mother was still fixing supper, I could usually tell what was coming simply by sniffing the aromas that mingled in the warm kitchen air. Fresh-baked bread, for example, offered an unmistakably yeasty smell that I found irresistible. If a pot of turnip greens or white beans sat simmering with a meaty chunk of ham hock on a back burner, I could easily pick up the scent. And all the desserts, of course, I knew by heart, from the array of pies and cakes to the incomparable banana pudding. Even on the rare occasions when a food I didn't like was on the menu—liver, for example—I could still rely on my nose to tell me what was in store.

Then one day Mom threw my senses into delirious confusion. With pot holders in each hand, she brought a bubbling-hot dish out of the oven and set it before us. It looked and smelled like nothing I had ever encountered before, but I knew instantly that I was going to like it.

"What is it?" I asked in a hushed voice that bespoke my awe.

"It's Spanish rice," she replied somewhat casually, as if it were nothing more than just another bowl of macaroni and cheese.

I might as well have been in Madrid, or Mexico City, or Havana, so impressed was I with this foreign delicacy that my own small-town, landlocked Kentucky mother had created.

That's how it is with Spanish rice (a.k.a. red rice, Savannah rice, Creole rice, tomato pilaf, etc.). If you've ever had the pleasure of eating it, you'll surely remember its aromatic powers, its rich colors, and most of all its irresistible flavor: the onions and peppers and garlic, the tomatoes, the bacon, the seasoning spices, and of course the rice, all blended and intermingled to complement one another and elevate the whole to a medley of so much more than the sum of its parts.

Pat Zurales of Mobile remembers red rice. "When I was growing up," she says, "we used to visit my grandparents in High Springs, Florida. My grandmother was from Savannah, and she was a great cook out of that old coastal Georgia-Carolina tradition. She made red rice regularly, and my father loved it so much that when he was courting my mother, who was from the North, he told her she'd have to learn to cook it before he would marry her—he practically made it a condition. It was all in good spirit, of course, but she did it. I'm happy to say she learned."

When her turn came, Pat learned too, and now she makes it "pretty often—I'd say at least once or twice a month. It's good with just about anything. It's especially good with pork chops."

Food habits tend to be very durable, as we've seen in the example of the contrasting rice histories of South Carolina and Arkansas—the former with a centuries-long affection for the grain, even though it hasn't been grown there since the beginning of this century, and the latter leading the nation and much of the world in rice production, but trailing just about everybody in rice consumption.

Coastal Southerners are major rice eaters—not in the same league with Orientals, maybe, but probably ahead of any other group in this country. If their cookbooks are a fair measure, the diners of South Carolina and Louisiana are in a rice class by themselves, domestically speaking. *Charleston Receipts*, the classic Junior League recipe collection, leans far more heavily on rice than potatoes as the primary staple in its pantry, and the same is true for many of the best Louisiana cookbooks.

But sometimes a great dish such as red rice manages to fly free from its native environment and take root elsewhere. That must have been what happened at my house. My mother, who as far as I know never went to Savannah or Charleston or New Orleans and had no cookbooks from those places, still managed somehow to prepare some excellent coastal and Creole foods, not the least of which was that memorable Spanish rice/red rice dish.

It might have been a variation on a casserole called Spanish rice in an old *Progressive Farmer* cookbook, or perhaps someone traveling through our little town gave the recipe to her, or maybe it had found its way into her mother's repertoire long years before. In any case, it is pressed into my memory so indelibly that when I speak the name of it, I begin to salivate.

Practically every recipe I have ever seen for red rice differs slightly from the others; like the name, its formula never seems to stay put. All the more reason, then, for you to experiment with combinations until you get one you treasure. This is mine, gathered from my recollection of the dishes my mother created and from my own trial-and-error cooking. Like Pat Zurales and countless others from one end of the South to the other, I consider this to be one of my basic comfort foods.

Begin by frying **4 or 5 strips of bacon** until crisp; drain on absorbent paper, crumble, and set aside. Put **3 or 4 tablespoons** of the **dregs and grease** into a heavy pot (I use an aluminum dutch oven, but the same large black skillet I fry the bacon in might do just as well). Chop **1 large onion** coarsely and sauté it in the fat over medium heat for about 5 minutes. I sometimes include some **chopped bell pepper** with the onions, and **a teaspoon** or more **of minced garlic.**

When the onions have begun to get soft and translucent, add **2 cups** of peeled and chopped **tomatoes** (fresh or canned), reserving the juice. Season the pot with **1/2 teaspoon of salt, 1/4 teaspoon of black pepper, 1/8 teaspoon of cayenne,** and **1 tablespoon of Worcestershire sauce.** Simmer and stir the mixture; adjust the seasonings to suit you. Add **1 cup of long grain raw rice** and continue cooking, uncovered, over low heat for about 10 minutes, stirring occasionally. If it seems too dry, add some or all of the tomato juice or a little hot water; the mixture should be quite moist, but not standing in liquid.

RED RICE

When the consistency and taste are to your liking, transfer the contents to a 1-quart baking casserole with a top, stir in the crumbled bacon bits, cover the dish, and bake it for about 45 minutes in a preheated 450-degree oven. Once or twice during that time, lift the lid and stir the rice gently with a spoon, so it won't get dry and hard on the bottom or around the edges. As soon as the rice is tender, it's ready to serve.

This should be enough for four generous servings. The recipe can be doubled if your pot and baking dish are large enough.

Speaking for myself, I could make a meal of my Spanish/red rice, a green salad, a loaf of french bread with butter, and a cup of coffee or a glass of iced tea. I could do that, in fact, every week or two for a long time without tiring of it.

I could even get up from my desk and go do it right now.

Hmmm. Let's see—bacon, onions, tomatoes, rice . . . .

GRITS

I've thought about this a lot, and I've finally concluded that what makes grits important to Southerners has more to do with symbolism than it does with flavor or anything else.

Grits are (I prefer the plural) a ceremonial offering, a historic dish in the South's presentation of breakfast—and, as it turns out, their association with symbolic rituals goes far back into the pre-Southern past.

Grits come from corn, the most ancient and elementary of all our vegetables, and in almost mystical ways they seem to stand for the Southern will to endure and prevail against heavy odds. With grits, we get down to the nitty-gritty. After a bowl of grits, we half expect to find the day brighter, the load lighter, the road straighter and wider.

Our poets, notably Roy Blount, have penned odes to grits. Our scribes and scholars have sung their praises too. Southern troubadour Gamble Rogers tells a wonderfully funny story about some enterprising Floridians who supplement their income by bleaching their coffee grounds and selling them to the tourists as grits.

There is even a documentary movie on the divine dish—simply called *It's Grits,* if I remember clearly—put together by a small band of stone-ground-grain aficionados in South Carolina, itself a veritable cauldron of the grits culture.

Grits are an all-purpose symbol for practically anything of importance to Southerners. They stand for hard times and happy times, for poverty and populism, for the blessings and curses of a righteous God. They stand for custom and tradition, for health and humor, for high-spirited hospitality. They also stand for boiling, baking, and frying.

They belong to the South almost exclusively; no one else in this country pays much attention to them. People eat a lot of cornmeal mush elsewhere in the world, but that's not the same thing as grits.

There's still some confusion, even among Southerners, about exactly what grits are, so this may be the appropriate place for a clarifying definition.

Grits are a food product—some would say a cereal—made from dried corn kernels. When these hard kernels are soaked in a solution of water and lye to remove the husks or hulls, the resulting pea-sized kernels are called hominy, or big hominy. Hominy that is dried and then ground up like coffee becomes grits (some say hominy grits or small hominy). This is essentially what you get when you buy a box of grits in the supermarket.

Another old-fashioned way to make grits is to grind hard corn kernels with a water-turned stone, after which the coarse particles are bolted, or sifted, to remove the husks. This is what you get when you buy a sack of grits at a country grist mill such as you find here and there in the South.

The late Turner Catledge, whose Louisiana sensibilities used to lend intelligence and grace to the pages of *The New York Times,* once wrote that grits were "the first truly American food," because the Indians who met the first English sailors at Jamestown in 1607 offered them servings of "a steaming hot substance consisting of softened maize seasoned with salt and some kind of animal fat, probably bear grease."

The Indians called it "rockahominie," said Catledge, and the sea-weary Englishmen reportedly took to it deliriously, as happy as hogs in slop. By most accounts, the Southern affinity for grits has continued to this day. Our grits heritage spans nearly four centuries, from the Powhatan Indians and Captain John Smith to the grits brigade of President Jimmy Carter.

With so much history to draw from, it's no wonder to me that a rich deposit of myth and legend and folklore has attached itself to grits. The very word itself is rooted in an ancient ceremony of sacrifice in which victims were sprinkled with holy corn meal and set on fire. (The word *immolate* means literally to sprinkle with meal or grits prior to sacrificing.)

I have also heard it claimed by South-Country sages that you can eliminate an infestation of ants, even dreaded fire ants, simply by pouring a box of dry grits directly onto the anthill or colony. The ants will devour the grits greedily, they say, and then miraculously self-destruct.

It's not clear to me whether the ants are reduced to ponderous immobility as the dry weight absorbs their body fluids, or whether their thirst after eating causes them to drink so much water that the grits swell up inside them and their bloated little bodies finally explode.

At the very least, grits are good for a few laughs—and if you happen to love the taste of them, as I do, then you've got yourself a basic comfort food that'll do you good and help you too.

In the coastal areas of the South, you'll hear people talk about grits and grunts (grunts being a type of fish), and the phrase translates into a combination of boiled grits and almost any type of fresh fish.

Upcountry, in the mountains of Appalachia and the Ozarks, a favorite breakfast dish is fried grits, arrived at by slicing the leftovers (they set up hard when cold) and frying them in bacon drippings.

At almost any Southern Junior League or yuppie brunch, you can count on finding cheese grits, a baked dish of post-World War II origin that blends the flavor of grits with cheddar and garlic. I have yet to meet anyone—even a hater of conventional grits—who can resist such a casserole.

Some people think grits consumption is decreasing in the South. Columnist Charlie Robins, one of my favorite Southern humorists, has declared himself "alarmed over the grits situation." Speculating that the people's devotion to them may be eroding, he notes that nowadays, "you have to ask the waitress to bring you grits. Previously, you only had to ask the waitress not to bring you grits."

Worse, he says, "At some restaurants, you not only have to ask for grits, but have to pay for them as well. I consider this a sacrilege, as I am quite sure that the Lord never intended for grits to be sold."

Whether sold or bestowed, store-bought or homemade, true grits are a veritable embodiment of the Southern spirit at its best, an all-souls porridge that knows no barriers of race, class, age, sex, religion, ethnic origin, political persuasion, or zip code.

Anybody can cook them. The directions are on the package. A word of warning: Commercial grits come boxed in two varieties. There's Quick (5-minute cooking) and Instant (practically a stirred combination of dry grits and boiling water). For better flavor, stick to the Quick.

If you can find stone-ground or water-ground grits in a sack, you'll get better flavor still, but they have to cook longer—25 to 30 minutes.

Finally, for something uncommon and unforgettable, here's a recipe for **Nassau grits,** a Caribbean/Spanish dish that folks around Pensacola, Florida, have been enjoying for generations:

NASSAU
GRITS

Fry **4 strips of bacon** until crisp; drain, crumble, and set aside. Leaving about **2 tablespoons of drippings** in the skillet, sauté **1 small bell pepper, 1 medium onion,** and **1 large clove of garlic,** all finely chopped, for about 5 minutes, or until somewhat softened. Then add a **1-pound can of tomatoes** (cut up), reserving the juice, and simmer the mixture for 20 minutes. Next, add **1/2 cup to 1 cup of cooked ham** (chopped) and simmer for about 10 minutes more. If too dry, add some or all of the tomato juice.

While this mixture is cooking, pour **1 cup of grits** into **1 quart of boiling water** and cook as directed on the package. When the grits are done, stir the vegetable mixture in with them and simmer for a few more minutes to let the flavors mingle. Ladle into a serving bowl, sprinkle the bacon on top, and rush to the table, there to join the biscuits, eggs, and coffee already prepared. The recipe will serve 6 people generously.

There you have it, a repast fit for anyone and everyone. And if that's not a genuine pleasure, then ducks don't waddle, fish don't swim, and grits ain't groceries.

CORNBREAD DRESSING

To be as tiny as she was, my Kentucky grandmother threw a lot of weight around in the kitchen. It wasn't her physical presence that commanded attention and respect; it was her cooking knowledge. She seemed eternally wise to me, as if she had been born knowing. I grew up believing in her infallibility.

She returns to my memory every year at turkey and dressing time, simply because the cornbread dressing she made to accompany the big bird was a world-class side dish. I can't imagine anyone making it better.

All manner of dressings and stuffings can be found in old Southern cookbooks dating back to the early 1800s. Non-Southern cooks picked up the habit too (though few of them ever understood cornbread), and the dish came to be spoken of in the same breath with cranberry sauce as an essential accompaniment on the holiday table.

Now you're apt to run across dressing almost anywhere you find roast turkey. The cornbread base may be missing, but the dish might include biscuits or white bread, pecans or chestnuts, giblets, sausage, oysters, or some other exotic ingredient. There are even some store-bought mixes for making dressing, but they bear a faint resemblance to the real thing.

Whether stuffed inside the bird or baked separately, dressing belongs with turkey like bacon with eggs or crackers with chili. We prefer ours shaped by hand into oval patties about the size of eggs and then baked to a deep brown crispness on a cookie sheet.

The original recipe in Grandmother White's cryptic shorthand has been our guide for more than 30 years. Now, having worked on perfecting our own version of it, I think we've finally attained a close approximation of her masterpiece. Here's the step-by-step method:

The day before the big feast, make the cornbread base by sifting together 1 cup of plain white cornmeal (not self-rising), **1 cup of flour, 3/4 teaspoon of baking soda, 2 teaspoons of baking powder,** and **1-1/2 teaspoons of salt.** Beat **1 egg** with a whisk and stir it into the dry mixture, followed by just enough **buttermilk— about 1-1/2 cups—**to give the batter a thick pouring consistency.

Preheat the oven to 350 degrees. Put **2 tablespoons of bacon grease** in your bread baker (a large black skillet is best for this) and let it get smoking hot in the oven. Then pour in the batter, set it on the bottom shelf for about 5 minutes, and move it up to the middle shelf to bake 20 minutes more, or until it's crispy brown.

CORNBREAD
DRESSING

When done, turn the cornbread out on a rack to get cold, and then transfer it to a large pan or bowl and thoroughly crumble it.

Next day, while your turkey is in the oven, make a stock by stewing the giblets, neck, and other scrap pieces in water, adding seasonings and pan juices. Most of this will go into your gravy, but save a little—say, 1 cup—for the dressing. Mince **1 medium-size onion** and **1 or 2 ribs of celery**—enough to make about 1 cup of each—and saute them in a skillet with about **2 tablespoons of bacon grease.** When the vegetables are soft, add them to the cornbread crumbs, along with **1 teaspoon** (more or less, to suit your taste) **of poultry seasoning or sage.**

When well blended, moisten the mixture with broth a little bit at a time to get it just sticky enough to hold shape when you mold it by hand into patties. Taste and adjust the seasonings just before you begin molding. Lay the egg-sized ovals (you should have 15 to 20 of them) snugly side by side in a 9-inch square cake pan or on a larger cookie sheet and bake them just before dinner at 350 degrees for about 25 minutes. Serve hot alongside the turkey, gravy, mashed potatoes, and cranberry sauce.

We find that a single recipe is barely adequate for four people—and that's with no leftovers, which is unthinkable for a long holiday weekend. Be prepared, then, and double or triple the formula.

As far back as I can remember, which is all the way to Grandmother White's heyday in the Forties, not a single crumb of cornbread dressing has ever gone begging at any house in our far-flung family network. It may be the single most coveted item on our Thanksgiving table, and that's saying a lot. Forced to a choice, I'd take the dressing over the turkey any day.

Sweets

Coconut Pie

Here's a little trivia quiz for you. What do these classics of Southern cookery have in common: iced tea, café brûlot, banana pudding, pineapple sherbet, coconut cake.

Answer: They all depend for their primary ingredients on foods imported from outside the continental United States.

It's a curious paradox. For all our widely heralded successes with home-grown foods, from grits and okra to catfish and country ham, we still must look to far-away producers for some of our most celebrated dishes.

Imagine our breakfast tables without coffee, our summer lunches without iced tea, our Thanksgivings and Christmases without ambrosia. For a century or more, tea, coffee, bananas, pineapples, and coconuts have played a significant role in the culinary history of the South—and virtually all of those foods have come to us from overseas.

(There's a little bit of tea grown in South Carolina, and some of the tropical fruits and nuts can be found here and there in the lower reaches of Florida, but the volume is commercially insignificant.)

And not only have these imports influenced Southern cooking in and around the points of entry; they long ago penetrated to the interior heart of the South as well, and there they have remained.

The coconut is a perfect example. Nut-bearing palm trees literally live a world away from, say, Arkansas or Kentucky, but grocers in those states have been marketing shredded coconut meat and even the curious-looking whole nuts themselves for generations.

There's no telling how long this has been going on. I have a 150-year-old Kentucky cookbook with a coconut cake recipe in it. "Having removed the hull and dark skin from a cocoanut," the instructions begin, "weigh a pound of it and grate it fine." That's still the best way to do it.

One obvious reason you could get coconuts in the nineteenth-century South was the fact that they traveled well; hard to break and slow to spoil, they could be shipped with little or no waste. And so, a portable treasure of the tropics found its way to the farthest reaches of the landlocked South.

That must explain why so many country cooks in the region do such wonderful things with coconut. Dovie Gentry is one of them. In her farmhouse kitchen near Lewisburg, Tennessee, she makes a memorable coconut pie with all the effortless grace of a true master of the art, and I consider myself blessed to be served an occasional slice of it.

I have eaten some world-class coconut pies in my time—rich, light, custardy blends of sugar, cream, butter, eggs, and shredded fresh coconut in flaky shells of pastry. I recall them all fondly, with admiration and appreciation for their creators.

But for basic simplicity and ease of access, not to say taste, I can think of nothing more satisfying than Mrs. Gentry's sweet confection. She calls it Coconut Chess Pie. I call it quick, easy, and just plain good.

In transcribing her recipe, I may have missed a couple of the fine points, because the reality of mine has never quite matched the memory of hers. What's missing may simply be her magic touch—and you can't put that in a recipe.

But I'm still trying, and the people who help me eat my failures keep asking for seconds. One of these days I'm going to get up the nerve to try a slice on Mrs. Gentry.

This is my practiced attempt at her pie, which to distinguish from hers I'm calling **Country Coconut:**

Sift together **3 tablespoons of cornstarch (or flour), 1 cup of sugar,** and **1/4 teaspoon of salt.** Stir in **3/4 cup of sweet milk, 3 tablespoons of melted butter or margarine, 3 well-whisked egg yolks, 2 teaspoons of vanilla extract,** and **1/2 cup or more of grated coconut.** When well mixed, pour into an unbaked 9-inch pie shell and bake 50 to 60 minutes in a preheated 350-degree oven, removing as soon as it's firm in the center.

Country Coconut Pie

That's all there is to it. If you like, you can beat the left-over egg whites with a little sugar and cream of tartar to make a meringue and spread it atop the pie for the last 10 minutes of baking. And, for looks as well as taste, you might want to sprinkle a little more grated coconut over the meringue.

With or without a crown, though, this is a sweet queen of a pie. It's a song of the faraway tropics, expertly composed by a gifted Southern cook.

FRIED PIES

One of the fascinating things about food, over and beyond the eating of it, is the way it gets around. When you start asking why a particular dish or concoction is found where it is, you may end up with a long and winding tale of social history that is as appealing as the food itself.

Why are Italians so closely identified with pasta? How did rice get to be so basic in all Oriental diets? Is there a particular reason why Mexicans eat tortillas and not cornbread, or why Germans drink beer and not iced tea?

To get even closer to home and more specific, consider why collard greens are far more popular than turnip greens in, say, South Carolina or the Florida Panhandle, while in Tennessee and Kentucky the opposite is true.

I don't know the answers to all these questions, but I do enjoy trying to find them. One I've been chasing lately is this: What is there about fried pies that makes these fruit-filled pastries so popular in the upper South but hard to find in the lower reaches of the region?

People in Arkansas seem to eat more peach or apple fried pies than anyone else, judging from the large number of cafes that serve them, and Tennessee and Kentucky eaters aren't far off the pace. Along the Atlantic and Gulf coasts, though, the sight of fried pies in a cafe or home kitchen is uncommon to say the least.

It couldn't be that Arkansans like fried foods better than South Carolinians, or that Kentuckians raise more peaches than Georgians. What's more likely—and this is just a guess—is that mountain people learned long ago to preserve their modest harvest of peaches and apples by drying them in the sun, and these dehydrated fruits, when properly stewed and seasoned, make the very finest fried pies.

Look in almost any good Kentucky or Tennesee or Arkansas cookbook and you're likely to find one or more recipes for this delicacy. *The Foxfire Book of Appalachian Cookery* calls them half-moon pies (because they're made with a circle of dough folded in half). That's the same descriptive term my mother used in her western Kentucky kitchen.

Back during the depression, dried apples and peaches were a mark of frugal stewardship in many a Southern country home. Even with only a couple of fruit trees in the yard, a bumper crop couldn't be eaten fast enough to prevent substantial waste. The alternative was to peel and core the surplus, spread them out to dry, and save them to eat throughout the year.

With home-dried fruit thus so common and so popular in the upland South, half-moon pies followed as naturally as winter follows autumn. They differed according to each cook's use of sugar and spices, and some who fried the pies (or, in rare instances, baked them) gained local renown for their mastery of the technique.

There was, for example, Vernie Stephens of Portland, Tennessee. Until she died a few years ago in the tenth decade of her life, Mrs. Stephens made dozens of fried pies every week and sold them out of her home. And now in Hohenwald, another middle Tennessee community, Geneva Grover and Nell Barber have developed a thriving business with the pies they fry and sell at fairs and festivals in a fifty-mile radius of their kitchen.

Whether as a cottage industry, a cafe specialty or simply for home consumption, fried pies have been a pride of Southern cooks for the past half-century or more. If you live in Arkansas, Kentucky, Tennessee, or the higher elevations of Virginia, North Carolina, or Georgia, chances are there's a fried-pie cook within hailing distance of you.

If, on the other hand, you want to make them yourself, here's a typical recipe from *Kentucky Hospitality*, a bicentennial collection of all-time favorites published by the Kentucky Federation of Women's Clubs in 1976. It's credited to Mrs. Earle Combs of Richmond, who won the praise of scores of relatives by taking her **fried apple pies** to the Combs family reunion, an annual affair that started in 1960 and now draws more than 2,000 people.

Cover **1 pound of dried apples** (or peaches) in water and soak overnight. Drain and add a small amount of fresh water and cook slowly until tender. Mash the fruit. Add **3/4 cup of sugar, 2 tablespoons of butter or margarine,** and **2 teaspoons of cinnamon** (more or less, as your taste dictates). Stir well and let the mixture cool.

FRIED PIES

Make your favorite pie crust, using only half the regular amount of shortening. Roll out on a floured board to a medium thickness (about 1/8 inch). Cut into circles 4 to 6 inches in diameter. Place a generous tablespoonful of filling on one side of each circle. Fold the other side over and seal firmly along the edge with your fingertips or a fork. Fry in about **1/2 inch of hot lard,** turning once. When pastry is browned, remove and drain on paper towels. While the pies are still warm, sprinkle lightly with sugar.

A pound of dried fruit will make about 16 pies, so be sure you've got enough pastry. Also, you can use another shortening besides lard if you prefer, or you can bake the pies in a 400-degree oven. (For a crisper pastry when baked, brush first with melted margarine.)

LEMON PIE

It may come as something of a surprise to pecan and chess pie lovers to learn that those two quintessentially Southern confections are relative newcomers to the region's dessert tables. It certainly did shock me to find that out. Pecan and chess are so popular in these parts, and so little known elsewhere, that I always assumed they had been here forever.

But when I started looking for them in the Southern cookbooks of the nineteenth century, I got nowhere fast. *Housekeeping in Old Virginia* (1879), one of the most prominent collections of its time, contained several recipes for molasses pies and transparent pies and cheese cakes that were similar to what we know as pecan and chess pies, but it had nothing by those names.

Even more recent comprehensive collections such as the *Picayune Creole Cook Book* (1901) and *200 Years of Charleston Cooking* (1930) had no chess or pecan recipes among their many pies.

Somehow, those two current champions among our contemporary pies made a late entrance onto the menu and a rocket-like climb to the top. One of these days, I'd like to find out how and when that happened.

But for the moment, I'm mainly interested in the forerunners to chess and pecan, and particularly in what appears to have been the first filling a Southern cook ever baked in a pastry.

There's no way to be certain about this, so I'll hedge a little and say that *probably* the first Southern pie (as we now think of pie) was flavored with sugar and the juice of a tropical fruit: the potently acidic lemon.

You might be able to make a case for apple or sweet potato or some kind of milk-and-egg custard, but there's no doubt that lemon was right up there with them in early colonial times when pastries began to appear.

Food historians say that Columbus and the early explorers brought lemon seeds to the Caribbean islands and Florida from Spain, where the tart citrus had been thriving for centuries. Lemon trees like hot, humid weather without heavy rainfall—the very sort of climate that prevails in much of the Mediterranean and Middle East regions—and so the fruit has been common there for more than a thousand years.

The trees took root in Florida, but they never have proliferated there; too much rain to suit them. (They do much better in dry, sunny southern California, where 80 percent of our lemons now originate.)

Even so, what Florida could supply and what came by ship from the Caribbean to ports along the east coast was enough to make lemon-flavored drinks and desserts popular in the first century of the American colonial era. There was something irresistibly appealing—then and now—to the combination of lemon and sugar.

So lemon pie got here early, and it has held its own ever since. Lemon tarts, lemon curd, lemon pudding, lemon meringue, lemon icebox, lemon soufflé, Shaker lemon—the list goes on deliciously, knowing no regional or seasonal limits. Say what you will about all-American apple pie, or chocolate, or even chess and pecan; the sour little lemon may actually be the most beloved of all.

By whatever name—**lemon curd** (very British), lemon pudding, lemon filling for cakes and pies—there are some time-honored recipes that vary little from one to the next. Here's one that never fails, whether you want a dozen tarts or one big meringue pie:

LEMON CURD

In the top of a double boiler, melt **1 stick of butter or margarine** over boiling water. Stir in **1/2 cup of fresh lemon juice** and **1 teaspoon** (more if you like) of **finely grated rind,** followed by **1 cup of sugar.** Stir until well blended. Beat together **3 whole eggs** and **3 egg yolks** and add them to the mixture. Continue cooking and stirring until the pudding is quite thick (10 minutes or more), then remove it from the stove. Chill thoroughly (overnight if possible) before using.

The leftover egg whites can be used to make a meringue for one pie or several tarts. Or, the chilled filling can be spooned into prebaked tart shells and topped with whipped cream. Or, you can spread the cool, thick custard between layers of a cake.

Or . . . or . . . or. It takes a while to run out of uses for a great lemon mixture like this. Once you've made it and put it in the refrigerator, it'll stay there quietly waiting for a call to service, and age won't diminish its powers. That's a comforting thought, isn't it?

BLACK BOTTOM PIE

First-time experiences often carve a permanent niche in the memory, like initials etched in a schoolroom desk. The first time you stayed away from home, the day you learned to swim, your first romance—these are the stuff of permanent recollection.

For many a lover of chocolate and other sweets, the first encounter with a black bottom pie no doubt qualifies as such a memory-maker. Duncan Hines, the pathfinding American travel guide and food critic of the 1930s and beyond, recalled with pleasure in his later years the profound first impression this spectacular confection made on him. He was vague about the time—probably 1938, give or take a year—but the place he remembered precisely: a cozy little diner called Dolores Drive-In at 33 N. E. 23rd Street in Oklahoma City.

Hines was a native Kentuckian who traveled extensively throughout the United States from the time he first published his *Adventures in Good Eating* guidebook in 1936 until his death in 1959. In two other books as well—*Adventures in Good Cooking* and *Duncan Hines Food Odyssey*—he repeated his praise of the Dolores pie. Of all the Southern desserts he had ever eaten, he declared, his favorites were pecan pie and black bottom pie. The former, of course, is universally known as one of the South's greatest culinary gifts to humanity; the latter Hines described as "one of those marvelous creations that has somehow managed to keep its light under a bushel."

Meanwhile, in another part of the forest, Florida novelist Marjorie Kinnan Rawlings (*The Yearling*), who loved to socialize over a good table almost as much as she loved to write, weighed in with her testimony on the miraculous qualities of this pie. In *Cross Creek Cookery*, an appealing gastronomic narrative she wrote in 1942, Rawlings proclaimed black bottom to be "the most delicious pie I have ever eaten." She first made it, she said, from a recipe sent to her by "a generous correspondent" who claimed that it originated at "an old hotel in Louisiana," its name and location unrecorded. Rawlings later came into possession of another, somewhat different recipe, and combined the two to make her own version—which, curiously, was almost identical to the one published by Hines.

We may never know the true source of black bottom pie, but we do know how much Marjorie Rawlings thought of it. Here, she declared, is "a pie so delicate, so luscious, that I hope to be propped up on my dying bed and fed a generous portion. Then I think that I should refuse outright to die, for life would be too good to relinquish." (Alas, she died at the age of 57 in 1953, presumably without a slice of black bottom pie at her bedside.)

The first of these intricately layered custard classics to enter my life didn't exactly set off a wild celebration in the streets, but it certainly was the talk of the table when it was served as the climax of a great Florida dinner about twenty-five years ago, and it has remained one of my prime favorites ever since. I still associate it with Florida, perhaps because of that evening—or perhaps because its cool, light, rich qualities seem so compatible with Florida cuisine and climate.

I have subsequently discovered that the pie is equally at home with all manner of food styles, in all regions and seasons. The basic recipe that Duncan Hines and Marjorie Rawlings first heralded to the nation some fifty years ago is still the most widely accepted method of preparation. To make it in these frenetic times requires a certain tranquil patience, which no doubt explains why it is so seldom seen. Nevertheless, what it returns in appearance and flavor and overall satisfaction is far greater than its cost in money and time. In fact, I doubt if anyone but an unappreciative grouch with weak eyes and anesthetized taste buds could pass up a slice without an admiring glance and a salivating surge of deep longing.

What follows here is the Hines-Rawlings rendition of **black bottom pie,** slightly modified and updated but not significantly changed. In its purest essence, this is the one and only, now and forever, amen.

Black Bottom Pie

First, crumble about **2 dozen ginger snaps** and moisten the fine crumbs with **6 tablespoons of melted butter.** Transfer to a 9-inch deep-dish pie plate and press against the bottom and sides with thumbs and fingers to make an evenly distributed crust. Bake in a preheated 325-degree oven for 10 minutes and set aside to cool.

The filling consists of two distinct layers topped by whipped cream. To prepare the layers, begin by soaking **1 tablespoon of unflavored gelatin in 4 tablespoons of cold water,** and set aside. In another bowl, combine **1/2 cup of sugar, a pinch of salt,** and **1 tablespoon of cornstarch.** Next, separate **4 eggs,** beat the yolks well with a wire whisk, and set the whites aside.

In the top of a double boiler over gently simmering water, melt **2 squares of unsweetened chocolate,** stir in **1 teaspoon of vanilla extract,** and set off the stove but still over the hot water. Scald **2 cups of milk** in another saucepan, stir the sugar and cornstarch mixture into it, let it cool a bit, and then slowly add the egg yolks, beating steadily to make a smooth union. When this custard is well blended, pour it into a heavy pot and cook it over low heat, stirring constantly, for about 10 minutes, or until it begins to thicken and coat the stirring spoon. Remove from the heat, set the pot in cold water, and stir in the softened gelatin. Keep stirring until the custard is completely smooth; it will thicken more as it cools.

This custard is the base for both layers of pie filling. Pour about half of it, or about 1-1/4 cups, into the melted chocolate and mix together well. Let the other half cool some more while you beat the **4 egg whites** with **1/4 teaspoon of cream of tartar** and **1/2 cup of sugar;** then fold this stiff meringue into the remainder of the custard. Finally, fold in 2 tablespoons of white rum.

Now you're ready to assemble the pie. Pour the chocolate custard into the crust and distribute it evenly with a spatula. Then pour the other custard on top and smooth it out. Chill the pie thoroughly in the refrigerator (overnight is ideal, but not essential). When ready to serve, beat **1 cup of whipping cream** to stiff peaks, adding **2 tablespoons of powdered sugar** and **1 teaspoon of vanilla extract** while beating, and spread it over the pie. For both color and flavor as a finishing touch, grate a little unsweetened chocolate on top.

When sliced and served, the cross sections of the pie will reveal the crumb crust, chocolate custard, rum custard, whipped cream, and shaved chocolate in a bottom-to-top display of culinary beauty. Even more impressively, the blend of flavors is so perfectly complementary that the overall taste will seem much more delicious together than the unassembled ingredients ever could be if consumed separately. In other words, the makings of a black bottom pie bring their separate strengths together in one crust to form a more perfect union, almost as if they were destined for each other.

You can't beat destiny. Never mind all the dirty pans and dishes, or all the time this creation required. Works of art take time. This is the sort of pie you'd love to have in the refrigerator if someone important happened to drop in, like Julia Child or Craig Claiborne. Or someone unimportant, for that matter. Or better yet, if no one dropped by. Then you could eat it all, and not even mind washing the dishes.

But such a classic confection begs to be admired and shared. So take my advice, and remember the wisdom of Marjorie Rawlings and Duncan Hines: Don't hide this delight under a bushel. Serve it with generous love, and you'll know that life is too good to relinquish.

PINEAPPLE SHERBET

The blowtorch heat and humidity of a Southern summer can drive even the most dedicated sun worshiper to seek relief in something cool. A swim may do the trick, or a tall and frosty drink. But for me, nothing is quite as effective as a big, slushy bowl of homemade pineapple sherbet.

I grew up on that good stuff. My mother used to start making it in ice trays as soon as the temperature reached 90 degrees, and with four young sherbet lovers standing by to scarf it up, she practically had to incorporate the preparation of it into her daily routine. It was an easy task, though, and because of that, she rarely let the supply run out before Labor Day.

Now, many years removed from that satisfying boyhood experience, I still partake of the summer blessings of Beck's pineapple sherbet, and along with it I have taken a special liking to a cranberry ice recipe that has similar qualities.

As I have rotated these two refreshers in and out of the freezer, I've pondered the irony of these two prime Southern sherbets being made from faraway fruits and berries—Hawaiian pineapples and Michigan cranberries.

You might think that something as delicious as pineapple sherbet would be the toast of Honolulu, but no. I have it on no less an authority than *The Taste of Aloha* , the definitive cookbook of the Honolulu Junior League. In that collection of more than 500 recipes is one for strawberry ice (Southern, perhaps?), but not a line about the virtues of pineapple sherbet.

I haven't checked any cookbooks from the cranberry bog regions of the Midwest and East, but my hunch is that the homemade sherbet/ ice syndrome is not strong there either. Maybe you have to experience a few summers of Southern humidity to develop a craving for freezer desserts. When you reach the point where a sauna bath reminds you of Mobile in August, you're ready for **Beck's Pineapple Sherbet** and **Bo's Cranberry Ice.**

And so, without further delay, here they are in all their Southern simplicity. Freezer buffs in Ann Arbor and Oahu may copy.

BECK'S PINEAPPLE SHERBET

First the pineapple: In a saucepan, dissolve **1 cup of sugar** in **3 cups of water.** Bring to a boil, then simmer 5 minutes and set aside to cool. To **1/2 cup or more** of freshly squeezed **lemon juice** in a mixing bowl, add enough **water** to make 1 quart of unsweetened lemonade as tart as you wish. (Limes, of course, can be used in place of lemons.) Add **1 teaspoon or more of the grated zest,** or outside skin, **of the citrus,** followed by a **15-ounce can of crushed pineapple** (or an equal amount of fresh pineapple).

Combine the sugar syrup with the fruit, pour the mixture into a deep pan (a bread pan is ideal, but ice trays will do), and freeze it to a stiff mush. Then, in a large bowl, break the sherbet up into a slushy mass (an electric mixer is helpful for this) and fold into it the stiffly beaten **whites of 3 eggs.** Refill the pans and return to the freezer, there to become a soft, frothy ice, sweet but tangy—and delicious.

And the cranberry: Boil **1 pound of berries** in **3 cups of water** until the skins pop. Strain through a colander or ricer, pushing against the sides to force the pulp through. Discard the skins. To the pulp and juice add **2 cups of sugar,** and stir over low heat until dissolved. Remove from heat and add the **juice of 1 large orange** and **1 large lemon or lime.** When well mixed, freeze to a stiff mush in pans or trays. Break up into slush with a mixer and when it's soft and fluffy, refreeze it. This fluffing and refreezing can be repeated to keep the mixture soft, or beaten **egg whites** can be folded in to accomplish the same thing. Another way to assure softness is to add **1 teaspoon of unflavored gelatin** (dissolved in 1/2 cup of water) to the liquid cranberry and citrus mixture.

Bo's Cranberry Ice

And there you have it—two light and tangy antidotes to the Southern summer sultries. That's almost enough to make you wish for an August heat wave.

BLACKBERRY COBBLER

The telltale signs were out there in the fallow fields and gullies of the rural South back in May. It was blackberry winter, that perennial late-season cold snap when blossoms cover the thorny bushes and the fruits first appear as knobby little specks of green.

Now it's July, and the blackberries have swelled to a deep purple plumpness, and their tart acidity has finally been transformed into a sweet, ripe, juicy flavor that's distinctly their own—and almost irresistible.

Looking out over all that wild thorniness, I have a hard time deciding whether this year's crop is far too large or too small.

Even when the yield is abundant, it's a chore to claw your way through the thickets of briars and brambles and the red tide of chiggers in order to pick a gallon of blackberries.

No wonder they sell for three or four dollars a quart at the farmers' markets and roadside stands. I used to pick them as a kid and sell them for fifty cents a gallon—big money in those days—but I don't ever remember thinking the compensation was anywhere near adequate.

The Indians had plenty of blackberries to eat long before the English came to Virginia—and, for that matter, there were plenty of them in England too at that time, known then and now as brambleberries.

I wonder if they also had chiggers back in those days. It's hard to imagine a country thicket of berry canes without a few million chiggers attached.

Cultivated blackberries, thornless and often chiggerless, are all the rage these days, and I'd be the first to admit that they're a lot easier to pick. The taste is not as vivid, it seems to me, but I'm not knocking them. The combination of cultivation and freezing has made it possible for you to get blackberries just about any time you want them, and that's nice.

Still, nothing can quite match a jar of jam or a cobbler made from wild berries, and the taste is all the sweeter and more satisfying if you've picked them yourself.

As something of a celebration of that once-a-summer occasion when a gallon bucket of freshly picked black beauties stands waiting by the sink, I've got a cobbler recipe that's so good you'll want to hoard it—and so rich that once a summer is all you can justify. I received it third-hand from Kathleen Cannon, a woman of long experience and high achievement in Southern food, who was described to me as "the best cook in Franklin, Tennessee."

BLACKBERRY COBBLER

Start by making the pastry with **2 cups of all-purpose flour, 1 teaspoon of salt, 1-1/3 sticks of real unsalted butter** (no substitutes), and **6 or 7 tablespoons of ice water.** Sift the flour and salt together, cut in the cold butter with a pastry blender until the pieces are as small as rice grains, and add the water a tablespoonful at a time until the dough is thoroughly moistened and combined. Gather it into a ball, wrap it in wax paper, and chill it in the refrigerator. Grease a large baking dish, about 12 by 6 inches or the equivalent. When the dough is cold and firm, divide the ball into two pieces, one slightly larger than the other. Roll out the larger portion on a floured surface. When it's thin, like pie pastry, press it into the dish, taking care to cover the sides and corners.

Next, measure **6 cups of washed blackberries.** Combine **1-1/4 cups of sugar** with **2 tablespoons of cornstarch** and carefully stir this dry mixture into the berries. Pour the sugared berries into the pastry and distribute them evenly. Roll out the remaining pastry, cut it into thin strips, and lay them criss-crossed over the top. Finally, cut up **2/3 stick of butter** and dot it all over the top of the cobbler.

Bake on the bottom shelf of a preheated 425-degree oven for 15 minutes, then reduce the heat to 375 degrees and continue baking for 45 more minutes, by which time the crust should be nicely browned and the berries a bubbling-hot mass of sweet juiciness.

It would be hard to make a case for this dessert as a cholesterol-buster because of all that butter, but you could certainly classify it as a memorable special-occasion treat—and as such, I heartily commend it to you.

I also note in passing that the master baker, Kathleen Cannon, and her friend Mattilee Reese, who gave me the recipe, are both well past 80 and still enjoying this classic cobbler.

BANANA PUDDING

On the face of it, a banana festival in the landlocked agricultural belt of western Kentucky and Tennessee sounds like a colossal mismatch. After all, the fruit comes almost exclusively from the tropics of Latin America. Why would it be celebrated a thousand miles or more from there, in the state-line-straddling towns of Fulton, Kentucky, and South Fulton, Tennessee?

As it happens, there is a perfectly good explanation for this unlikely event, which has been taking place in September for over twenty-five years. What is more, no one in the know any longer questions the Fulton-South Fulton identification as "the banana crossroads of the United States."

Back in 1880, the Illinois Central Railroad put its newly developed "icebox" cars to use in the shipment of tropical bananas out of New Orleans to most of the middle and eastern sections of the country. Bananas soon became an all-American favorite, and they've held favor ever since.

By the turn of the century, when Fulton had become a major railroad switching center and cargo redistribution point, the banana connection was firmly established. Eventually, most of the bananas bound for mid-America stopped there for fresh supplies of ice (or heating, if the weather called for it) before being sent on to their scattered destinations.

Eighty-plus years of close identification with bananas thus created a whimsically offbeat image that the Fultonians came to like, and in 1963 they formalized it by starting their festival to celebrate the fruit.

Now, besides the usual attractions associated with outdoor food festivals, you and 10,000 others can have a taste of the world's largest banana pudding, a one-ton colossus that's bigger than a bathtub. (The recipe: 3,000 bananas, 250 pounds of vanilla wafers, 950 pounds of store-bought creme pie filling).

All this festive activity underscores the banana's long and exalted status in the storehouse of Southern cookery. Though it was largely confined to such port cities as Charleston and New Orleans prior to the Civil War, the fruit since then has been a kitchen staple and a recipe headliner even in the most remote corners of the region.

Along with pineapples and coconuts, bananas have transcended their tropical origins to become as common as strawberries, peaches, and other native fruits in our diet.

Southern cookbooks over the past century have featured bananas in breads and cakes, in pies and ice cream, in drinks, salads, pancakes, and baked dishes, as well as in puddings.

Martha McCulloch-Williams, who was born in the Tennessee-Kentucky border region in the middle of the nineteenth century, extolled the versatility of bananas in her classic narrative cookbook, *Dishes & Beverages of the Old South,* published in 1913.

Brennan's Restaurant in New Orleans has for decades been serving a spectacular flaming dessert called Bananas Foster (named in honor of one Richard Foster, a regular customer), and the recipe has been published widely. This is the essence of it: butter and brown sugar combined in a chafing dish or skillet, a banana sliced lengthwise and sautéed in the mixture, a sprinkle of cinnamon, a taste of banana liqueur and a measure of rum, all touched with a flame to ignite.

It can be served as is, basted with the hot sauce, once the fire is out—or, even more impressively, the heat can be countered with a side scoop of French vanilla ice cream. Either way, this is a top banana presentation.

If I had to name my all-time favorite dessert—or at least the first choice from my childhood—it would probably be my mother's **banana pudding.** Everyone ought to have an heirloom like this. In my mind's eye I can see one now, cooling in an ovenproof glass baking dish on a wire rack beside the stove: a layer of vanilla wafers on the bottom, the bananas sliced lengthwise and nestled in a thick and bubbling cauldron of bright yellow custard, and arching above it all a golden-brown mountain of meringue. So eagerly awaited was that confectionary delight that we generally dished it up before it was cool, and risked burned tongues for the divine pleasure of its sweetness.

I have the recipe, and once in a while I try to recapture the splendor of it as it appears in my memory and imagination. That may be an impossible quest, but I like challenges—and besides, even the failures are delicious. Here's the time-honored method:

Separate **6 eggs,** beat the yolks until smooth, and stir in **1 rounded tablespoon of flour, 3/4 cup of sugar, a pinch of salt,** and **1-1/2 cups of whole milk.** Pour the mixture into a double boiler and stir constantly over boiling water until it thickens into a custard (5 to 10 minutes). Set the pan aside to cool a bit. Beat the **6 egg whites** with **1/2 teaspoon of cream of tartar** and about **1/4 cup of sugar** until stiff peaks form.

BANANA PUDDING

Cover the bottom of an 8-by-12-inch baking dish with a single layer of vanilla wafers and lay on top of the cookies several peeled bananas sliced in half lengthwise. Spread the custard evenly over the bananas, followed by the meringue. Bake in a preheated 350-degree oven for about 15 minutes, or until the custard is bubbling hot and the meringue is nicely browned.

Now there's a dessert worthy of a festival in its honor. A warm dish of it with a cold glass of milk is a blessing of the first order. It's also the highest calling of the noble banana, foremost adopted fruit of the South and the nation.

Huguenot Torte and Ozark Pudding

The Huguenot torte, a delectable nut and apple pudding-cake topped with whipped cream, is widely appreciated in the South Carolina low country as a classic Charleston dessert of historical significance.

Like the great English trifles that have been served at Virginia dining tables for almost four centuries, Huguenot tortes are often touted as original confections from the mother country.

Huguenots—French Protestants seeking religious freedom—were among the earliest and most influential of Charleston's seventeenth-century settlers. That the rich and irresistible dessert bearing their name dates back to that period makes a believable story. The promotional materials extolling the city's historic and contemporary virtues as much as say so, and modern cookbooks from the region do too.

But John Taylor, the irrepressible owner of Hoppin' John's, a cookbook specialty shop in Charleston, has come up with information indicating that the beloved torte is a mid-twentiethth-century creation strikingly similar to an Arkansas-Missouri mountain sweet called Ozark pudding.

Writing in *Omnibus,* a Charleston-area monthly, Taylor declares that "Charleston's famous 'torte' is not a torte at all," not 200 or more years old, and not even French; *au contraire* , it is "probably a twentieth-century conceit" borrowed from the landlocked upper South.

He backs up this bold assertion with impressive facts. First, there are no Huguenot torte recipes in South Carolina cookbooks prior to World War II. Second, a recipe for Ozark pudding very similar to the standard formula for Huguenot torte was served at a dinner in honor of Winston Churchill and Harry Truman in Fulton, Missouri, in 1946.

Third, Taylor interviewed Evelyn Anderson Florance, whose Huguenot torte recipe was published in the 1950 Junior League classic, *Charleston Receipts,* and learned that her inspiration for the dessert had come from an Ozark pudding she ate at a church supper in Galveston, Texas, in the 1930s.

"I got a recipe for it," said Mrs. Florance, "and worked with it until it was the way I liked it." She named it Huguenot torte in about 1942, she added, when she was asked to make desserts for a Charleston restaurant called the Huguenot Tavern.

So, it wasn't seventeenth-century French Huguenots who gave Charleston its celebrated tortes; it was Evelyn Florance, a contemporary Junior Leaguer, borrowing from an Ozark Mountain tradition in another part of the South.

Or was it? For the question still remains: Where did the Ozark pudding recipes served in Texas and Missouri come from, and also the one in *The Progressive Farmer's Southern Cookbook* (1961), which is the earliest one I can find in print?

Though *The Progressive Farmer* book calls it "an Arkansas favorite," I could find almost no mention of Ozark pudding in the old cookbooks of that state—or, for that matter, in Missouri's. Apparently, the dessert was as uncommon in yesterday's Ozarks as Huguenot torte was in the Carolina low country of long ago.

So if Huguenot torte was inspired by an Ozark pudding recipe in the 1930s, what or who inspired the first Ozark pudding?

It may be impossible to answer that question with any assurance, but I have a candidate to nominate. *Southern Cooking,* by Mrs. S. R. Dull of Atlanta, first published in 1928, includes a recipe called Apple Torte that contains exactly the same ingredients (in slightly different proportions) as the Huguenot torte in *Charleston Receipts* and the Ozark pudding in *The Progressive Farmer's Southern Cookbook.*

Not from the mother country, then, but from good old Mother Dull. If she does in fact deserve credit for having put both Huguenot torte and Ozark pudding into the South's culinary repertoire, that's hardly news; Henrietta Stanley Dull and her classic cookbook gave much that is original and lasting to Southern cookery.

Here, for the record, is **Mrs. Dull's Apple Torte,** a confection worthy of the best tables from Charleston to the Ozarks:

Beat **2 eggs** well and add **1 cup of sugar, 3-1/2 tablespoons of flour, 1-1/2 teaspoons of baking powder, 1/8 teaspoon of salt, 1 teaspoon of vanilla extract, 1/2 cup of chopped nuts** (ideally, black walnuts), and **1 cup of chopped apples** (use firm, tart apples, peeled). When thoroughly mixed, pour into a well-greased shallow pan or dish (about 8 by 12 inches) and bake at 350 degrees for 30 minutes.

Serve warm with **whipped cream.** And while you're eating it, say a little silent word of thanks for the Huguenots and the mountaineers—and especially for dear old Mother Dull, who was a pretty sharp lady.

MRS. DULL'S APPLE TORTE

PLUM PUDDING

You can't get much more British than plum pudding. There are many conflicting accounts of its origin, but as far as the South's culinary history is concerned, it seems safe to associate this rich ceremonial dessert with the Jamestown settlers.

Curiously, it contains no plums, and apparently never did. The name may have been a generic term for dried fruits in general, or it may have meant raisins, or *plum pudding* may have simply meant *good pudding.*

In any case, it joined many other British desserts—custards, trifles, syllabub and such—in the Southern kitchen in the 1600s, and in some parts of the region even now, the holiday plum pudding ceremony is a command performance at which attendance is required.

Here's a good story for you about the persistence and success of a plum pudding tradition. Back in the 1920s, when an Italian music teacher named Gaetano De Luca was director of the Nashville Conservatory of Music, his wife Nancy gained fame among their friends and associates for the excellence of her plum puddings.

Mrs. De Luca was descended from a family of seventeenth-century Virginia settlers, a family in which the plum pudding recipe had been passed down from generation to generation like a cherished heirloom. Using that precious formula, she made the dessert her signature recipe, and people from Tennessee to New York raved about it.

After the death of her husband, Nancy De Luca began in 1936 to sell her plum puddings, calling her cottage-industry enterprise Warrenton Old English Plum Pudding, Ltd. (Her Warren ancestors had founded Warrenton, Virginia, before the Revolutionary War.)

In addition to plum puddings, she also made fruit cakes, and the business prospered. In 1959, when in failing health, she sold it to four young mothers—customers of hers—who were looking for a way to make money with part-time work.

Three of the four women, now grandmothers, still own and operate the Warrenton mail-order business in a warehouse-kitchen in Nashville. Working from August until Christmas, they and upwards of 20 employees turn out an incredible *tonnage* of plum puddings, golden fruit cakes, and bite-size rum cakes.

"The plum pudding volume alone is a hundred times greater than it was in 1959," says Rose Brown, one of the owners, "but the rum cakes are even more of a success. They're now our most popular item."

Twenty-eight rum cakes wrapped separately and packed in a round tin sell for about $16. They're angel food cake squares thickly coated with rum icing and rolled in finely chopped pecans.

The light-colored fruit cakes, another of Nancy De Luca's prize recipes, are made with real butter and eggs, dried fruits and nuts, sherry, and brandy. A two-pounder also costs about $16.

And the plum puddings—a heady blend of milk, eggs, raisins and other dried fruits, bread crumbs, beef suet, spices, and whiskey—come in three sizes (one, two, or three pounds) and are priced in the $12-$22 range. There's also a hard sauce available for topping.

The Warrenton ladies make 155 pounds of plum pudding batter at a time. The cakes are then shaped, steamed, dried, and packed for shipping. "They'll keep forever in the refrigerator or freezer," says Rose Brown.

When the time comes for the plum pudding serving ceremony at home, the heavy confection must be resteamed for about an hour (a rice or vegetable steamer is ideal for this), inverted onto a serving platter, and brought to the table hot.

The crowning touch, as ancient as the pudding itself, is to ignite a small quantity of brandy, rum, or whiskey and pour the flaming liquid over the pudding. The blue flame soon flickers out, and a small serving of the dessert with its rum hard sauce makes a memorable climax for a special holiday feast.

There are numerous mail-order fruit cake businesses scattered around the South. In fact, Southern cooks sell a wide variety of food specialties through the mail, from country ham and barbecue sauce to she-crab soup, gumbo, and poke sallet greens.

The Warrenton sweets represent an outstanding success story in that venerable home-cooking, mail-marketing tradition. And the plum puddings, echoing as they do the food history of Virginia and England, clearly show the enduring value of cookery in our remembrance of things past.

Holiday Candy

Just about the only time anyone ever makes candy around our house is in the fall holiday season. Sometime between the middle of November and the end of the year, you can at least count on finding a tin of fudge.

In a really good year, there might also be Martha Washington candy, bourbon balls, caramel chewies, divinity, or peanut brittle stashed away in a cupboard somewhere. Or maybe some of that great chocolate toffee.

But the rest of the year is a candy-bare desert, a wasteland. I wouldn't exactly liken it to bread-and-water rations, but I would say we spend ten months without candy, recovering from two months' indulging.

There was a time when making candy was a much more regular homefront activity, and Southerners, who seem to have a weakness for things sweet, certainly produced their share of it.

Now you don't see so much of that, partly because people just don't eat as much candy as they used to—but mainly, I think, because they don't hang around home as much, and certainly don't spend as much time in the kitchen, making candy or anything else.

There's probably a microwave fudge. I haven't bothered to look. Half the fun of candy is in the making, and the socializing that goes with it. Instant candy is sort of a contradiction in terms, an oxymoron.

That doesn't mean candy-making has to be a long and complex task, though. The ideal is to have a recipe that's fairly simple, takes enough time to highlight an evening of light entertainment, and tastes wonderful.

By those standards, a whole candy counter full of great old Southern confections would easily qualify. I offer in evidence two to prove the point.

The first is those chewy little **caramels** that you wrap individually in squares of wax paper. Whether hard or soft (they can turn out either way), they're apt to be tough going for denture wearers, but the saving grace is that they melt in the mouth deliciously.

Louise Richards of Elizabethtown, Kentucky, has always made them better than anyone I know. Her recipe and the one offered by the Darden sisters, Norma Jean and Carole, in *Spoonbread and Strawberry Wine*, a most entertaining collection of family cookery and history, are almost identical. Here's the method:

CARAMELS

Combine **1 cup of sugar, 3/4 cup of dark corn syrup,** and **1/2 stick of butter** in a saucepan. Blend over low heat, then add **1 cup of light cream** (half & half) and **a pinch of salt.** Continue cooking and stirring until it heats to 250 degrees on a candy thermometer (the firm ball stage).

The candy may appear curdled during the cooking, but don't worry—it will eventually come together smoothly.

Remove the pan from the heat and stir in 1 teaspoon of vanilla extract and 1 cup of chopped pecans or walnuts. Pour the hot candy into a well-buttered shallow pan about 6 inches square (or round) and let it cool. Then cut it into small squares and wrap the pieces individually in wax paper. They keep well in tins, and can also be frozen.

The second holiday candy is on my must-make list, and has been since we saw the recipe in a Southern newspaper more than twenty years ago. The clipping has long since disintegrated, but we saved the formula.

It's quite similar to one published in the mid-1950s in a cookbook of the Women's National Press Club in Washington. Mamie Eisenhower, the president's wife, contributed the recipe, saying she had been making it since she and her husband-to-be were courting in the 19-teens. Ike supposedly named it **"Million-Dollar Fudge."**

It may not be Southern by birth, but if you love your adopted recipes as much as your native ones, as we do, you'll happily welcome this sweet treat into the family circle.

If ever there was a fail-safe fudge, this is it—no temperature test, no soft-ball stage, no double boiling. The recipe makes five or six pounds of superlative candy, enough to satisfy a big household and a whole passel of passers-through from Thanksgiving to Christmas.

Million-dollar Fudge

Into a large, heavy cooking pot, put **4-1/2 cups of sugar, a 12-ounce can of evaporated milk, 1 stick of butter,** and **1 teaspoon of salt.** Bring the mixture to a gentle boil and cook it for 8 to 10 minutes, stirring occasionally. Then turn off the heat and add the following: **1 12-ounce package of semi-sweet chocolate drops, 1 8-ounce bar of milk chocolate, 4 4-ounce bars of German's sweet chocolate,** and **1 large jar of marshmallow creme.** Stir until all the chocolate is melted and well mixed, then add **2 teaspoons** of **vanilla extract** and **4 cups** of **pecans** or **walnuts,** coarsely chopped. When all the ingredients are thoroughly combined, pour the fudge onto a buttered cookie sheet and spread it out to a thickness of about 1 inch. Cut it in squares when it cools, and store it in tins.

You're looking at ten to fifteen bucks' worth of candy here, but what the heck—Christmas only comes once a year. And besides, where else can you get world-class chocolate these days for $2 a pound?

POUND CAKE

When you encounter a confection with a formal name as imposing as the Bishop Asbury Pound Cake, you're bound to sit up and take notice.

Bishop Francis Asbury, after all, is one of the founding fathers of American Methodism, and the English-born preacher's circuit-riding exploits in the South and elsewhere in America were an important part of our colonial past. Furthermore, pound cake was an English culinary invention of the mid-1700s, which happens also to be the time of Asbury's birth. Could it be that the Bishop Asbury Pound Cake is a facsimile of the first such creation, made from the original recipe?

Well, no it isn't. As a matter of fact, this particular cake is only traceable to the 1930s, and to the rural countryside around Elberton, Georgia. It was then and there that Beverly Asbury was introduced to the favored pound cake of his family (who were Baptists and Presbyterians, as well as Methodists), and it was he, Bev Asbury, a minister himself, who later gave it a formal name.

"Bishop Asbury did indeed travel and preach near our homeplace," says Bev Asbury, "but there's no family connection between us, as far as I know. He may have eaten pound cake on the circuit, but it wasn't ours. This cake takes its name from my family and from the fact that it's fit for a bishop—or anyone else who loves a good Southern pound cake whenever and wherever it's available."

With or without upper-case identity, pound cake in all its many manifestations is one of the most basic and venerable of Southern sweets. Mary Randolph, who in 1824 wrote the first authentically American—and Southern—cookbook (*The Virginia House-Wife*), had a pound cake recipe that compares favorably to the best traditional versions since recorded. (In addition to the standard blend of butter, eggs, sugar, and flour, hers was spiced with grated lemon peel, nutmeg, and brandy.)

In every Southern state from Virginia to Texas, old cookbooks can be found extolling the virtues of pound cake. The *Williamsburg Art of Cookery*, a historical collection, includes a pound cake recipe that supposedly was served to a Virginia church congregation in 1754. Henrietta Dull and Marion Brown, whose cookbooks are generally regarded as twentieth-century Southern classics, paid respectful homage to the confection, and so did numerous others.

Like Bev Asbury and his Georgia family, most Southerners tend to associate pound cake with Christmas and other holidays or special occasions. "We didn't have it any other time," says Asbury, "except perhaps when a bunch of birthdays coincided in February."

The reason it was considered special, he now concludes, is that in the days before electric mixers, it was a tedious chore to blend the batter. The ingredients are heavy, and if they aren't thoroughly mixed, the cake shows streaks. "The adults always admired a cake that wasn't streaked," he recalls, "but the kids didn't care one way or the other, because they all tasted great."

And well they should, for traditional pound cakes such as the Bishop Asbury are essentially an amalgam of one pound each of butter, sugar, eggs, and flour (hence the name), with perhaps small amounts of vanilla, spices, citrus, or liquor to add distinction. (Cupcakes, in case you're wondering, are said to be so named because the teacup is the basic unit of measure for the principal ingredients.)

The one-pound quantities of main ingredients translate literally to 2 cups or 4 sticks of butter, 2-1/4 cups of sugar, 2 cups of eggs (about 10), and 4-1/2 cups of flour, measured after sifting. The **Asbury recipe** modifies those amounts slightly. Here it is:

ASBURY POUND CAKE

Cream together **4 sticks of real butter** (softened to room temperature) with **4 cups of sugar,** using a heavy-duty electric mixer. Add **10 whole eggs** (also warmed to room temperature) one at a time and, with the mixer running continuously at medium speed, add **2 tablespoons of fresh lemon juice** and **2 teaspoons of pure vanilla extract.** Finally, add **4 cups of sifted cake flour** a little bit at a time. Grease and flour a 10-inch tube pan and pour the thoroughly mixed batter into it. Bake in a preheated 325-degree oven for 1-1/2 hours, or until a straw test shows that it's done. Remove to a rack to cool a bit, and then turn out onto the rack.

In Bev Asbury's words, "A warm slice is a delight, almost like a fine pudding—but for a pound cake's true consistency to set up, wait and slice it one or two days later. And if there's any left after you serve it, there's nothing in the world better than a piece of it toasted for breakfast."

Fat chance. Pound cake generally disappears like it was going out of style—which, of course, it never does.

Given the ease with which the cake can be made using a mixer, it has become more of an all-seasons dessert (with fresh berries and whipped cream, for example, it's an excellent variation on strawberry shortcake). Such versatility is part of the tradition with pound cake around New Orleans. Rima and Richard Collin, authors of *The New Orleans Cookbook,* a Louisiana classic, call it "the favorite local cake," whether topped with fruit and whipped cream, filled with candied fruit and rum, iced for birthday cakes, used in puddings and Creole-style trifles, or simply eaten plain.

Modern Southern cooks and bakers have further enriched the pound cake with such additional ingredients as sour cream, cream cheese, whipping cream, chocolate, coconut, and other tasty elements—

as if more were needed. Here, for example, is a **contemporary pound cake** recipe of proven worth, the basic addition being heavy cream.

CONTEMPORARY POUND CAKE

Cream together **2 sticks of softened butter** and **3 cups of sugar.** Add **6 whole eggs** one at a time, blending thoroughly with an electric mixer. Sift **3 cups of flour** and add it a little at a time to the batter, alternately with **1/2 pint** (1 cup) of **heavy cream.** Finally, blend in **2 teaspoons of vanilla extract.** Pour the thoroughly mixed batter into a greased and floured 10-inch tube pan and bake for 1 hour and 25 minutes in a preheated 325-degree oven, testing for doneness with a straw after 1 hour and 15 minutes, and every few minutes thereafter. Cool on a rack for 10 minutes or so, then turn upside down and remove from the pan.

A slightly different flavor and texture is obtained by substituting 1 cup of sour cream for the whipping cream. Some recipes also call for small amounts of salt, baking powder, or baking soda. With or without these minor modifications, a well-baked pound cake in the old or new Southern style can bring joy to any household. Bishop Asbury, itinerant Southerner that he sometimes was, would no doubt say amen to that.

SPICE CAKE

So many rich and fancy cakes show up on Southern holiday tables that it's refreshing sometimes to encounter a plain and simple confection like old-fashioned spice cake.

It's not that I'd ever turn down a slice of classic coconut, or a delicate sliver of Lady Baltimore or Lane Cake, or even a wedge of homemade fruit cake or jam cake. I couldn't do that unless I was sick.

It's just that after all the richness of holiday dining, a little square of an all-purpose confection like spice cake, served straight from the pan, may seem like a sensible alternative.

You might see this cake just about anywhere in the South, at any season of the year, on almost any occasion—at a picnic, a party, a weekend supper, a wake. It travels in the pan, keeps its shape and its freshness, stays moist—and of course it's always delicious.

Four of the best Southern cake bakers (and cookbook writers) of this century—Jennie Benedict of Kentucky, Henrietta Dull of Georgia, Betty Lyles Wilson of Tennessee, and Marion Brown of North Carolina—all had strikingly similar recipes for spice cake.

Variations on the basic theme can be found in several nineteenth-century cookbooks from Virginia and the Carolinas. Even earlier than that, people in the South had developed a fascination with exotic spices from Central and South America and the Far East.

Sailing ships calling at the Atlantic ports of Charleston and Savannah and the Gulf Coast docks of Mobile and New Orleans found waiting markets for cinnamon, cloves, nutmeg, ginger, allspice, and other intensely flavorful seasonings. From very early in the region's history, its cooks were adept at building recipes around the treasures of the spice trade.

Cakes and cookies were especially enhanced. A wide variety of these confections still rely heavily on spices to define their flavors. As for the particular item known as spice cake, it seems to have evolved in the nineteenth century into a sheet or pan cake, usually iced but otherwise rather plain.

The basic combination of ingredients varies only slightly from baker to baker. Most use butter, sugar, flour, eggs, and milk, flavored by some combination of molasses, vanilla extract, cinnamon, cloves, allspice, ginger, and perhaps another spice or two.

Regardless of the slight differences among them, they all make a reasonably light, unpretentious, but very satisfying Southern cake that has found its way into the repertoires of cooks both near at hand and far removed from the region.

This recipe draws from the Benedict-Brown-Dull-Wilson school of spice cake making, with perhaps a closer nod to Benedict than the others. In Louisville back around the turn of the century, she was justly famed for her great confections. It's easy to understand why.

Benedict Spice Cake

Sift together **2-1/2 cups of plain all-purpose flour, 1 teaspoon of baking soda, 1 teaspoon of baking powder, 1/8 teaspoon of salt,** and the following spices: **2 teaspoons of cinnamon, 1-1/2 teaspoons of cloves, 1-1/2 teaspoons of allspice.** In a separate bowl cream together **1 stick of softened butter** and **1 cup of sugar,** and when well blended, add **3 beaten egg yolks** and **1/2 cup of molasses** to the mixture. In a third mixing bowl, combine **1 cup of buttermilk** and **2 teaspoons of vanilla extract.**

Combine about 1/3 of the dry mixture with the creamed mixture, followed by about 1/3 of the milk, then repeat the alternate blending until the batter is smooth and complete. Pour it into a well-greased 9-by-12-inch cake pan and bake at 325 degrees for about 30 minutes, or until a toothpick inserted in the center comes out clean.

An old and popular icing for spice cake is called brown sugar meringue. To make it, beat **3 egg whites** until stiff, adding **1 teaspoon of vanilla extract** and **1 cup** (packed) of **light brown sugar.** Fold in **1 cup of broken pecan pieces.** Spread over the cake in the pan, and it's ready to eat. And you should be ready to savor an old Southern standard.

Culture

Traditions

THE ROOTS OF SOUTHERN FOOD

Imagine being in charge of a kitchen somewhere in the South when word is received that the United Nations General Assembly is coming to dinner—more than 1,500 delegates and guests altogether, representing a panoramic spectrum of cultural backgrounds and palates.

A daunting prospect, to say the least—but not too much for a team of world-class Southern cooks. Such a challenge arose in Nashville, Tennessee, back in 1976 when the UN, for the first time in its history, made an *en masse* excursion away from its headquarters. The local planners of a Nashville summer-afternoon banquet for the world body considered and dismissed a multitude of menu proposals highlighting various international gourmet cuisines. Finally, wiser heads prevailed and the designated hostess-caterer, Phila Hach of Clarksville, Tennessee, was asked to prepare and serve a classic and traditional Southern country feast.

And so it was that in the shadow of the Parthenon in the city that for more than a century has called itself "the Athens of the South," envoys from 125 nations of the world came to dine on country ham, catfish and hush puppies, fried chicken, green beans with ham hock, corn on the cob, potato salad, cole slaw, home-grown tomatoes, cucumber pickles, deviled eggs, cornbread, yeast rolls, beaten biscuits, watermelon, cantaloupe, iced tea, sweet milk, buttermilk, orange juice, mint juleps, pecan pie, chess pie, and various other assorted treasures of Southern culinary history.

If such an occasion had arisen in 1876 or even 1676, many of the same foods might have been served—the ham, the fish, the chicken, the corn and beans, the melons, the bread. Throughout most of the five centuries of life here since the time of Columbus, the South has evolved a distinctive cookery that has consistently reflected its culture. Here, perhaps more than anywhere, the old maxim surely applies: We are what we eat.

◇

Right from the first, Spanish and English explorers both introduced and discovered good things to eat when they came ashore in present-day Virginia, the Carolinas, Georgia, Florida, and the islands farther south, and that process of exchange and cross-fertilization continued with the later arrival of other Europeans and Africans. Together with the native American populations of the coastal region, the emigrants from other lands sowed the symbolic and literal seeds from which sprang the roots of a diverse cuisine now widely known and loved as Southern cooking. Under that broad umbrella, numerous styles of food preparation have thrived—Creole and Cajun, coastal and mountain, country and soul, ethnic and indigenous, traditional and modern, plain and fancy, uptown and down-home.

Corn was already here when pork arrived on the hoof by ship from Spain. The Indians also had beans, peas, squash, onions, greens, and various kinds of fruits, nuts, and berries to offer, as well as woods that teemed with wild game and waters that abounded with seafood. Over the span of a century or more, the newcomers contributed livestock, wheat and oats, cabbages and yams, okra and black-eyed peas, peanuts, potatoes, tomatoes, oranges, rice, melons, chocolate, coffee, tea, and countless other foodstuffs.

And in this fertile atmosphere, where plentiful rain and sun and the turning of the seasons combined to create an ideal environment in which almost anything could grow, the South became primarily an agricultural land, the garden of a young nation. With all the necessary native and imported raw materials at hand, it was but one step further to the creation of an eclectic and richly distinguished regional cuisine. All that was needed to make great cookery was great cooks—and, as it turned out, the South had those too.

Cooking is a creative talent, an art, a science—and, some would say, more a gift than an acquired skill. Great cooks are commonly described as "natural born," not made. Somehow, as if by an unwritten formula of apportionment, the South seems to have received more than its share of kitchen virtuosos. Natives and immigrants, blacks and whites, women and men, they have all brought to the kitchen enough wisdom and instinct and sure-handed control to make Southern cooking stand out above all the other regional culinary styles in the nation.

More than natural law accounts for this wealth of talent; there are some historical explanations as well, and some of them are ironic and troubling. Slavery was a major factor in the evolution of black cooks. The women and men of African heritage who did the lion's share of cooking and serving for generations on end were the primary creators of what we now celebrate as Southern cooking. It was they, more than any others, who transformed the rudimentary staples of a pioneer culture into the refined dishes of the plantation and the sumptuous feasts that came to epitomize Southern hospitality.

Poverty was another historical condition that influenced the evolution of Southern food. At least twice in American history, in the traumatic eras of the Civil War and the Great Depression, the masses of Southern people, whatever their race or class, experienced hunger first hand. Often, their very survival depended on the inventive and improvisational talents of fishers and hunters, gardeners and foragers—and most of all, cooks.

Out of these somber and often shameful periods of Southern history—periods of slavery, segregation, poverty—came legions of great cooks and the classic dishes they created. This puzzling anomaly has a striking parallel in another of the region's indigenous creations: music. The original music of the South—the blues, spirituals, jazz, country, gospel—is a collective art form born of hard times. From the depths of pain and heartbreak, local musicians brought forth expressive sounds of beauty that lingered in the mind, and the quality of their music caused it to spread around the nation and around the world. Without in any way endorsing or condoning the conditions under which that artistic expression was born, we nonetheless celebrate both the people who originated it and the music itself.

And so it is with Southern food. It, too, was born out of strife and travail and suffering, tempered by servitude, flavored by poverty and injustice. But the black and white women and black men who created it, who took the little bit of latitude they had for inventiveness and produced divine dishes of the highest order, transcended the barriers of race and class and sex that surrounded them. Their food was delightful, memorable; like the music, it proved to have a timeless and universal appeal—and now, long years later, we still declare its excellence, and praise those who created it.

◇

These are the paradoxical roots of Southern food. No culture can cut itself off from its history; it is what it is, and no amount of romantic embellishment can change that. Divisions of race and class, the subordinate role of women, and the physical and psychological isolation of this region from the rest of the nation were all facts of life in the Southern past.

But it is also true that every culture is a complex amalgam of positive and negative parts—and in the South, food has always been one of the most positive and enduring reflections of the region's character. In practically every good and lasting memory any Southerner holds—of family and friends, of home and countryside, of school and church, of joyful and even solemn occasions—food is there, working through all the senses to leave a powerful and permanent impression.

No wonder, then, that Southern food is often celebrated in verse and song, novels and short stories, art and theater, serious essays and humorous expressions. Consider, for example, this declaration by the ladies of the Methodist Church in Maysville, Kentucky, in their 1884 cookbook: "Bad dinners go hand in hand with total depravity, while a well-fed man is already half saved." It is not altogether clear which was their most compelling mission—good dinners or salvation.

Soprano Leontyne Price is a world-renowned opera star far removed from her Mississippi roots—but, she says, images of home still are "rampant in my memories," and foremost among them are catfish, cornbread, turnip greens, and fried chicken. Living closer to home but similarly appreciative is author Reynolds Price. Drinking deep from his own North Carolina well of family dinner-table recollections, he etched this vivid scene in his recent novel, *Good Hearts* :

> It was Mama's usual light lunch—the turkey with cornbread dressing and cranberry sauce, country ham, corn pudding, snaps and little butterbeans she'd put up last July, spiced peaches, cold crisp watermelon-rind pickle, macaroni and cheese, creamed potatoes and gravy, then her own angelfood cake and ambrosia. Every mouthful made the only way, from the naked pot upward by hand. I hadn't eaten with her since the Fourth of July, and it was a real shock to my tongue—that many kind flavors, all happening at once like good deeds intended for me. Whenever I compliment her on it, she just says "It's the only way I know to cook. I know they've got a lot of fine speedy things now, but I haven't got the time to read all those instructions they put on the boxes, and anyhow my glasses are generally lost." Even when she and Rato are there right alone, she turns out three of those meals a day—every one of them simple and appropriate as the original patent-model Last Supper.

It takes a Southerner—and a writer of Reynolds Price's caliber—to construct a passage like that. As the saying goes, you have to have been there to grasp the full picture. Price's "Mama" and all the other Mamas of the South, town and country, white and black, have elevated dinners like the one he describes to the highest level of quality, and in so doing have earned for themselves a measure of immortality.

◇

In every great history there are larger-than-life characters, dramatic events, hallowed places, mythic tales of stirring adventures. By these measures, the story of Southern food and its place in the culture certainly qualifies as a compelling drama, an epic of pathos and humor with a cast of millions. Look back at the record and you can see how central this cook's-eye view has been to the larger story of Southern history.

It was food that brought native Americans and Europeans together, and it was food that drove them apart. They met at Jamestown in 1607 over pork and corn and roast oysters, and in the "starving times" of subsequent winters it was also corn—or rather the lack of it—over which they fought.

The plantations that rose up in the coastal South and later in the interior became temples of hospitality so lavish that visitors went away marveling at the gastronomic spectacle. France, with all its culinary renown, had nothing on the elegant feasts presided over by these Southern country gentlemen and ladies, and as for England, its bland cookery seemed hardly worth comparing at all.

Thomas Jefferson, the agrarian gentleman and gourmet who served as governor of Virginia and minister to France before his election as President, probably did more than any other Southerner in history to establish the importance of food in the culture. (In one of his least applauded acts as governor, Jefferson enraged the butchers of Richmond by sending his personal agents into the countryside to buy up all the market-bound hogs. When he later offered the animals for sale at a highly inflated monopoly price, the butchers marched to the home of their "Hog Governor" and festooned his picket fence with chitterlings.)

While serving in France in the mid-1780s, Jefferson traveled extensively in Europe and always showed the keenest interest in food. On his return to Virginia, he introduced Southern and American eaters to vanilla extract, olives and olive oil, wines from France, pasta from Italy, waffles (and a waffle iron) from Holland, and new recipes for such culinary treasures as ice cream, meringues, and oil-and-vinegar salad dressing. His garden at Monticello was the most extensive vegetable plot in the United States, an experimental farm where new varieties of plants were constantly being tried and their performance meticulously recorded.

Though his tastes encompassed far more than the cookery of the South, Jefferson did much to spread the popularity of this food by serving and savoring such regional specialties as Virginia ham, Chesapeake crabs, shad, sweet potatoes, black-eyed peas, turnip greens, and roasted Indian corn. In order to appreciate what a lasting contribution that was, consider this: Two centuries have passed since the age of Jefferson, and now most of the nation's hogs and corn grow in the Midwest, but if you're looking for genuine country ham and barbecue, or for roasting ears and cornbread—not to mention bourbon whiskey—the best place to find them (and in some cases the only place) is still here in the South.

◊

Even before Thomas Jefferson planted his garden, the first cookbook to be published in America was brought out by William Parks, a printer in Williamsburg, Virginia. That 1742 volume was actually a reprint of a London cookery book that had little applicability in the colonies, but it did pave the way for others to come, and it also established the South as the American leader in cookbooks, a position it has never relinquished.

The Virginia House-Wife, by Mary Randolph, was the first truly American—and Southern—cookbook. Published in 1824, it became a model for other "Housewife" books (one from Kentucky in 1839, another from South Carolina in 1847), and food historians now consider it the most influential American cookbook of the nineteenth century.

The Dixie Cook-Book, a comprehensive volume of more than 1,300 pages, was published in Atlanta in 1885 and dedicated "to the mothers, wives, and daughters of the 'Sunny South,' who have so bravely faced the difficulties which new social conditions have imposed on them as mistresses of Southern homes, and on whose courage and fidelity in good or ill fortune the future of their beloved land must depend." The Dixie was one of many postwar volumes that aimed to instruct white women in the basics of cookery, such elementary training having been necessitated by the "new social conditions" of black emancipation.

It was also in 1885 that Lafcadio Hearn, a journalist in New Orleans, anonymously wrote La Cuisine Creole , the first major cookbook from that leading food city of the South. By the turn of the century, when the editors of The Picayune, a New Orleans newspaper, issued the now-classic Picayune Creole Cook Book, the city's reputation for good food and good times had long since been established in the South and around the nation.

Names and places in the nineteenth-century history of food in New Orleans still resonate with meaning: Antoine's, a famous restaurant from 1840 to the present; the St. Charles Hotel in the French Quarter; Elizabeth Kettenring Bégué, the cook and hostess who for all practical purposes invented brunch; legions of entrepreneurs and cooks who made steamboat dining on the Mississippi and Pullman diners on the railroads so appealing; and, perhaps most important of all, the food itself—such mystical and wonderful creations as bouillabaisse, a delectable seafood stew of French inspiration; and filé gumbo, a magical union of Choctaw and African cookery; and pralines, a caramelized sugar and pecan confection that may be as old as New Orleans itself.

Creoles, contrary to popular belief, were not social aristocrats but simply the first-generation New Orleans-born sons and daughters of immigrants (French, Spanish, African, whatever). By that populist definition, the term embraced all that has come to be regarded as distinctly and uniquely New Orleanian—and that takes in generations of distinguished cooks and delectable dishes.

Louisiana, by all odds the most food-conscious and cuisine-rich state in the nation, has given us two of the most distinctive cooking styles to be found anywhere in the world. New Orleans-born Creole and bayou-born Acadian (Cajun) are like city and country cousins, the one rich and elegant and sophisticated, the other earthy, spicy, straight-forward—and both of them confidently, even arrogantly, superior. With all due allowances for oversimplification, Creole and Cajun styles of cookery are like non-identical twins in a family of gifted overachievers: obviously different, obviously kin, and obviously excellent.

◇

In the early decades of the twentieth century, New Orleans solidified its position as a dining mecca with the rise of such restaurants as Arnaud's and Galatoire's—both still thriving now. Elsewhere in the South, a host of other institutions dedicated to fine food were building solid reputations of their own. Hotels such as the Peabody in Memphis, the Hermitage in Nashville, the Seelbach in Louisville, the Tutwiler in Birmingham, and the Adolphus in Dallas often rivaled the best of New Orleans and cities outside the region. In recent years, all of these hotels have been restored to their original splendor, and once again their dining rooms offer excellent fare.

Southern inns were immensely popular too, from the famous edifice in Williamsburg and others in small-town Virginia to the Grove Park in Asheville and a host of little gems, among them Boone Tavern in Berea, Kentucky; House by the Road in Ashburn, Georgia; Inn by the Sea at Pass Christian, Mississippi; the Purefoy Hotel in Talledega, Alabama; the Sedberry Hotel in McMinnville, Tennessee; and the Old Stage Coach, a summer haven in the heart of Arkansas. Many of the old lodges are gone now, but some, such as the Williamsburg and Grove Park inns and Boone Tavern, have not only survived but seemingly improved with age.

Aside from hostelries, there were numerous Southern dining places that developed a loyal and far-flung clientele. Weidmann's in Meridian, Mississippi, was—and is—such a place, and the same can be said for Tampa's famed Spanish restaurant, Columbia, and for the venerable Bright Star in Bessemer, Alabama. The Morrison cafeteria chain got its start in Mobile in 1920 and still is headquartered there, and Krystal, one of the earliest of fast-food hamburger chains, was founded in Chattanooga, Tennessee, in 1932. Another trailblazer in the field of food was Piggly Wiggly, the store that pioneered the concept of self-service grocery shopping; it was established in Memphis in 1916, and remains a prominent Southern institution, one of several in the competitive supermarket field.

Clearly, the South has contributed more than its proportional share to the social and cultural unfolding of American food history. Of particular importance in this regard have been some outstanding individual contributions by natives of the region. Kentucky alone, to cite one notable example, has given us journalist-humorist Irvin S.

Cobb, who often wrote about food and drink; travel guide and restaurant critic Duncan Hines, who parlayed his guidebooks into a sprawling network of food-related enterprises; historian Thomas D. Clark, one of the few of his profession to treat food as a subject worthy of scrutiny; and a small army of excellent cookbook writers, from Jennie Benedict and Emma Allen Hayes (one of the nation's first black foodbook authors, in 1912) to Marion Flexner, Cissy Gregg, Lillian Marshall, and Camille Glenn.

Martha McCulloch-Williams came within a few miles of being born a Kentuckian; her plantation home was just across the state line in Tennessee. In 1913, when she was a 65-year-old writer long removed to New York, she produced from memory an account of her early years that survives now as a classic, one of the first narrative cookbooks ever written. Far more than a mere collection of recipes, *Dishes & Beverages of the Old South* is a revealing social history of everyday life in a particular place and time.

Numerous others have followed with outstanding narratives of their own, adding much to the public understanding of Southern history. The books of Richard and Rima Collin fit this description. So do the *Time-Life* "Foods of the World" volumes on Creole and Acadian cooking by Peter Feibleman and on Southern cooking by Eugene Walter; Marjorie Kinnan Rawlings's *Cross Creek Cookery;* Celestine Sibley's *A Place Called Sweet Apple;* much of the Foxfire series edited by Eliot Wigginton; Joe Gray Taylor's *Eating, Drinking, and Visiting in the South;* Edna Lewis's *The Taste of Country Cooking;* several books by North Carolinians Beth Tartan and James Villas; and a family chronicle of kin and cookery called *Spoonbread and Strawberry Wine,* by Norma Jean and Carole Darden.

These by no means exhaust the list. And as for straightforward recipe collections of the highest quality, there are literally scores, hundreds, of them, as the mere mention of a few authors will signify: Henrietta Stanley Dull, Marion Brown, Winifred Green Cheney, Mary Land, Lena Richard, Craig Claiborne, Jeanne Voltz, Lena Sturges, Kathryn Tucker Windham, Sallie Hill, Cleora Butler, Paul Prudhomme, Justin Wilson, Nathalie Dupree. The Junior Leagues shouldn't be overlooked, either; chapters in Dallas, Montgomery, and Charlotte were the first in the nation to publish cookbooks before World War II, and chapters in Charleston, Memphis, Baton Rouge, and Tampa have seen their postwar volumes stay in print for decades and sell tens of thousands of copies.

The entire *Southern Living* phenomenon—a steady stream of fresh contributions in magazine and book format to the food literature of the region—is a 25-year record that speaks impressively for itself.

All in all, this partial catalog of leading cooks and books, historians and journalists, hotels and inns, restaurants and other food-related institutions in the twentieth-century South is testimony to the region's continuing vitality as a creative center of American cookery. By and large, Southerners are keenly interested in food—in growing it, cooking and serving it, selling it, eating it, preserving it, talking and writing about it. In this region, food has always been much more than just a necessary fuel for the generation of human energy; for a multitude of reasons, it has permeated the culture right down to its core. Social scientists and nutritionists may ponder endlessly the consequences of that penetration (do we eat more, drink more, weigh more? does eating make us more sociable, more verbal? do we get sick more often, and die younger?). Devotees of Southern cooking, on the other hand, may simply consider themselves the fortunate residents and beneficiaries of a food-rich and food-conscious society, and thank their lucky stars for all the delicious blessings it brings.

◇

An endless succession of transforming changes has swept through the South since the end of World War II, and not least among them has been a series of major modifications in what and how people eat. This is not just a Southern phenomenon, of course; it's national, even international.

Fast-food chains, new technology, the movement of women into the workplace, the decline of the agricultural economy, the rise of television and other marketing tools, advances in medical science, concern about health and nutrition—these and other developments have combined to revolutionize eating habits. People eat out much more than previously, and what they eat is different—more highly processed, more chemically altered, lower in fat, higher in fiber, changed (and, overall, probably less appealing) in taste. Terms such as "natural" and "light" are often used to describe modern food, though their meaning is not always clear.

Change is inevitable and necessary; growth is not possible without it. More often than not, change is also unsettling, a mixture of positive and negative elements, of gains and losses. Again, Southern food is illustrative: Greater freedoms and higher living standards are certainly desirable improvements, one manifestation of which is the sharp increase in restaurant dining—but another is the decline of home cooking, and with it the fading importance of the dinner table as a family council site and of meals in general as a unifying ritual. Women cook less, and that's good news for them; men may actually cook more, and that's a gain too. But both combined have less time than ever to devote to one of life's most satisfying and civilizing pleasures: the preparing and sharing of food and drink with others who appreciate its many virtues.

In the years to come, there will no doubt be a continuing movement away from the home-grown, home-cooked, home-served meals that once were the South's only option. Over and beyond the time and trouble they require, the dishes themselves now raise caution flags among health-conscious eaters. Sugar and cream, butter and eggs, salt and pork seasoning produce richer and heavier foods than today's life-styles require, and increasingly, admonitions against such ingredients are being heard.

But food habits are powerful, and the positive traditions associated with eating in the South are too satisfying and pervasive to simply vanish. It's one thing to make sensible modifications in eating patterns and diet; it's something else altogether to throw out the heritage and the incomparable Southern dishes with the dishwater. The traditions that gave identity and character and quality to the foods of our foremothers and fathers have a staying power that has survived the centuries; it seems safe to conclude that they will endure for yet a while longer.

And even if the celebrated dishes themselves were somehow to vanish from our tables, the foodlore and folklore surrounding them surely would remain, for Southerners seem never to tire of table talk—and their tales, like choice wines and cheeses and country hams, grow better with age.

The mysticism in a mess of greens, the healing powers of pot likker, the good-luck qualities of benne seed, the transformation of North Atlantic lobsters into Cajun crawfish, George Washington Carver's peanut and sweet potato crusade, the invention of hush puppies, the disputed birthplace of Brunswick stew—these are inexhaustible topics of discussion and enlightenment. So are such weighty matters as how and where cocktails originated, how Charleston came to claim the Lady Baltimore cake, who Emma Rylander Lane was and why there is a cake named for her, where chess pie got its name, and what the true connection is between Huguenot torte and Ozark pudding.

Breakfast is one of the South's gastronomic traditions, brunch another, cafe plate lunches another (meat-and-threes, Tennesseans call them), Sunday suppers still another. Holiday feasts are not-to-be-missed occasions, and the same imperative applies to meals associated with such special events as football bowl games, Mardi Gras, the Kentucky Derby, and the Master's Golf Tournament. Churches often link food to worship (prayer breakfasts, brotherhood dinners, all-day singing and dinner on the ground), and food is also an essential element of comfort in wedding celebrations and in the grief and mourning that surround funerals. Political campaigns, school events, charity fund-raisers, homecomings, farewell parties, even the beginning of hunting season and the end of the harvest are invitations to feasting in the South.

◊

It may be that Southerners are inclined to live for the moment and to eat, drink, and be merry because in their tomorrows, historically speaking, too many of them have died—from war and other forms of violence, from hunger and want, from disease, from hard living. Or, perhaps natives of this region love celebratory occasions and big spreads and all-you-can-eat marathons because too often in their ancestry there was simply not enough to go around. Whatever the reasons, the pattern is predictable: Find an excuse for feasting, announce the plans, and a multitude of Southerners will answer the call.

A Southern feast is much more than the sum of its parts. Barbecue is not simply a piece of meat in these states (and different meat at that, from the Carolinas through the mid-South to Arkansas and Texas)—it's also an event, a ceremony, a social happening. The same is true of an oyster roast, a shrimp boil, a fish fry. Brunswick stew and burgoo are customarily cooked in quantities sufficient to serve scores, even hundreds of communicants, and no one can outdo the Cajuns of Louisiana in consuming crawfish, gumbo, boudin, and jambalaya. Virginia lays historic claim to the perfection of salt-cured, hickory-smoked, properly aged country hams, but plenty of people in North Carolina, Tennessee, Kentucky, and Arkansas argue passionately that theirs are just as good.

So closely has barbecue been identified with the South that countless books have been written on the subject, and Southerners often engage in good-natured but utterly serious debates on the relative virtues of pork versus beef versus chicken as the best meat, and on vinegar versus tomato versus mustard as the best base for sauce. There is a vast difference between whole-hog pork with vinegar-and-pepper sauce, as found virtually everywhere in eastern North Carolina, and beef brisket with tomato-based sauce, as found all over west Texas. Between those two poles, subtle differences manifest themselves from state to state, town to town, even pit to pit. Regardless of place or style, though, barbecue ranks in importance somewhere close to politics, religion, sex, and sports.

There are food festivals from one end of the South to the other, and almost every imaginable foodstuff seems to have its time in the limelight. Okra, chitlins, collards, peaches, peanuts, pecans, onions, sweet potatoes, hot peppers, oranges, strawberries—you name it, and chances are it's being celebrated somewhere in the South.

And in all the feasting and celebration thus far noted here, we've still hardly mentioned what many people consider the most outstanding Southern foods of all—fried chicken, grits, black-eyed peas, roasting ears, green beans, biscuits, cornbread, iced tea, and dozens of fabled sweets, from pecan and chess and Key lime pies to berry cobblers, strawberry shortcake, peach ice cream, boiled custard, coconut cake, and heaven knows how many other culinary delights.

◇

The South's gastronomical hall of fame is filled to overflowing with the finest in food and drink, the cumulative treasures of generations of superlative cooks. Far from being a "museum" cookery consigned to fading memory in the pantry of the past, Southern food is rooted in a vibrant heritage that has always risen to meet new challenges and necessities. No other aspect of Southern culture, not even its widely recognized speech patterns or its celebrated music, is more dynamic than its food.

In a book of Southern foodlore and folklore called *Cracklin Bread and Asfidity*, Alabama writers Jack and Olivia Solomon took note of that vitality. "The South is legend—legend begetting legend," they wrote. "As in all myth, truth holds fast at the center: We are hospitable, our women are beautiful, and our men are gallant and brave. And a whole lot of other things, all wildly improbable and richly contradictory. Whatever else the world has thought of the fabulous land below the Mason-Dixon line, it has granted us one supreme achievement— Southern cooking, which, like the South herself, is not one but many."

On the strength of that "one supreme achievement," succeeding generations of Southern cooks and eaters have built an enduring record of identity, satisfaction, and quality.

Breakfast

"In the morning they rose in a house pungent with breakfast cookery," wrote Thomas Wolfe sixty years ago in *Look Homeward Angel*, "and they sat at a smoking table loaded with brains and eggs, ham, hot biscuits, fried apples seething in their gummed syrups, honey, golden butter, fried steaks, scalding coffee. Or there were stacked buttercakes, rum-colored molasses, fragrant brown sausages, a bowl of wet cherries, plums, fat, juicy bacon, jam."

It was his own rising to the seductive aromas of breakfast in his mother's Asheville boarding house that Wolfe, the celebrated North Carolina novelist, remembered so vividly. He was not the first Southern writer to wax eloquent over a breakfast spread, nor has he been the last. Breakfast is a major meal in the region—some would say *the* major meal—and in almost every state from Virginia to Louisiana there remain many old and established traditions surrounding the morning repast.

One of the things I remember most vividly about my Kentucky grandfather is how much he enjoyed a good country breakfast. He loved it all—biscuits and bacon, fried tomatoes and fried apples, molasses and honey, strong coffee with cream and sugar, fresh fruit of every kind. He was a little man with a big appetite, and breakfast was his favorite meal. Seasonal specialties always pleased him—sausage and pork tenderloin at hog-killing time, rabbit or squirrel or game birds smothered with rich gravy in the fall, strawberries in May, blackberries in July, year-old country ham fried in a winter skillet.

And fresh fish. There was a little river near his house that generally yielded up to him a finny creature more or less on demand, and he loved to amble over there about daybreak and hook a couple of bass or bream or crappie. Within an hour, back home in the kitchen, he'd have those skillet-sized keepers scaled and cleaned, dusted with cornmeal, and eased into a pool of hot shortening. To the old man's pint-sized fishing and eating companion, a crisp crappie and a hot-off-the-stove hoecake with a bowl of grits and a pot of coffee made a singular feast. I wouldn't have believed finer fare existed anywhere on the globe.

Even now, nearly a half-century later, I find something especially appealing about the seasons of breakfast in the South. On a cool, shady patio in the spring, on a deck near the water in summer, on a mountain cabin porch in the fall, by an open fire in the winter—whatever the time or place, there is always food to suit the occasion, and the variety of it is not only surprising but eternally satisfying.

No, Thomas Wolfe was not the only breakfast-inspired Southerner to take pen in hand. Listen to this opening paragraph from the *Key West Cook Book*, a handwritten recipe collection still in print after forty years:

"It is morning—sunlight already brilliant on coral roadway and garden wall . . . . an emerald lizard stalks his prey on the grey bole of a palm, the yellow allamanda on the fence has called the bees to break their fast, and it is breakfast time for you, too. The patio is still shady, so put a green cloth on the old iron table, and let me bring you some chilled papaya, your morning coffee Havana style if you like, fresh Cuban bread with perhaps some carissa jelly for it, and a fluffy omelet with just a pinch of oregano in it. Work can wait . . . there is always mañana."

Accounts every bit as lyrical as this paean from the southern tip of Florida have been penned in honor of such diverse regional dishes as herring roe, red-eye gravy, lacy-edged griddle cakes and muscadine jam, just to name a few of the more uncommon breakfast delights.

Crack-of-dawn feasts go back a long way in the South. In the early colonial era, wide-eyed visitors to the region sometimes wrote rambling descriptions of gargantuan early-morning repasts that bordered on the incredible. Even in those days, people of means managed somehow to bring European opulence to their frontier tables. And, since hard-working people had to be fortified for long hours of heavy labor, it was considered altogether proper, if not essential, to get the morning off to a good start with a breakfast that included plenty of meat and potatoes and bread.

As the frontier receded, the fox-hunting Virginia gentry instituted a fabulous hunt breakfast for their upper-class guests, and elegant variations of that feast are still served on special occasions. Kentucky's version of that affair, the Derby breakfast, is a perennial favorite in the Bluegrass State on the first Saturday of every May. In the South Carolina low country around Charleston, morning feasts reminiscent of the colonial era are part of the local tradition, and in New Orleans, where Elizabeth Bégué revolutionized breakfast after the Civil War, restaurants such as Brennan's and Commander's Palace have gained national renown for their morning feasts. Spanish influences along the Gulf Coast from Tampa to Mobile still season and flavor the breakfast traditions of that slender crescent. Inland and upland across the Southern interior, in cafes and home kitchens alike, people of all classes still answer the call to country breakfasts that easily make up in quantity and quality anything they may lack in the way of elegance or formality.

As different as these delicious offerings are one from another, they are all closely bound to the culinary traditions of the South. In every corner of the region and in every season of the year, Southerners seem irresistibly drawn to the cookery that has for generations given special meaning and importance to their pre-luncheon gatherings.

One reason for the popularity of breakfast in the South has been the simple fact that it is the easiest to prepare and serve of all home-cooked meals. Breakfast lends itself to the talents of experienced and neophyte cooks alike, featuring as it often does a straightforward menu of no more than three or four dishes. A person who masters pancakes or biscuits or grits or omelets is already well along toward earning a sterling reputation as a breakfast cook.

Consider, for example, a traditional combination such as this: country sausage and sawmill gravy, fried eggs, biscuits, fried apples, and coffee. Nothing complicated there, not even the gravy, and yet such basic fare is almost certain to bring abiding pleasure to all who sit down to it, whether they be a table full of guests, a small circle of family and friends, or just the cook dining in peaceful solitude.

It's my contention that virtually no restaurant, be it a chain link, an old-time diner, a so-called upscale cafe, or a classier joint, can deliver a Southern breakfast as fine as the best you can prepare at home. To paraphrase the old song, anything they can do, you can do better. For example, almost no establishment is going to serve you real fresh-squeezed orange juice, or coffee made just the way you like it, or piping-hot homemade biscuits (read pancakes, griddle cakes, cinna-mon rolls, etc.) straight from the oven, or smoked and aged country sausage (ham, bacon), or real gravy made from scratch, or fresh fish like my grandfather prepared, or eggs cooked to order in any of a dozen ways, or stone-ground grits, or fresh fried tomatoes (apples, potatoes), or homemade jams and jellies, or real molasses and honey.

These are the basic elements of a traditional breakfast feast in the South. Now, as lifestyles change, the very survival of such elementary meals seems more and more in doubt. A breakfast revolution has taken place in this country since World War II ended less than fifty years ago. A majority of Americans now get their morning start-ups from a cereal box or a vending machine or the drive-up window of a fast-food outlet—if, indeed, they take the time to eat at all. The old menu is under attack, too; sometimes the very people who used to extol the virtues of a hearty breakfast (bacon, eggs, milk, coffee, cream, butter, hot breads) can be heard leading the assault on every one of those traditional foods—and doing so now, as before, in the name of good health.

By some accounts, breakfast as we have known it is gradually becoming a thing of the past. But before we say goodbye to this great institution, a few words of defense and reconsideration seem in order. At least on special occasions, and whenever time permits, the pleasure of lingering over a leisurely traditional breakfast may offer more in support of good mental health than it could ever take away from general well-being. To be sure, it might be unwise to eat large quantities of eggs, meat, dairy products and such every day, but to enjoy judicious servings of them once in a while seems a pleasure too innocent to abandon.

For my part, I intend to take my chances with measured rations of the foods that have made breakfast in the South a filling and fulfilling occasion, and I fully expect to fare better—in every sense of that word—than most of the contemporary advocates of no-food/fast-food/health-food approaches to forenoon nourishment.

Elsewhere in these pages, you will find descriptive passages touching on some of the major elements of breakfast dining—ham, eggs, grits, biscuits, fruit. Here, as a parting shot, is the formula for **camp coffee,** a hot beverage as old as the hills and as satisfying as any breakfast drink could ever be.

Scrub a large, old-fashioned enamel coffee pot and rinse it well with boiling water. Drop **8 tablespoons** (1/2 cup) **of freshly ground coffee** (coarse grind) into the pot. Break **an egg** over the grounds, crush the shell and toss it in too, add a **pinch of salt** and **1/2 cup of cold water,** and stir well. Set the pot over medium heat, pour in **6 full measuring cups of boiling water,** stuff the pot spout with a paper towel to trap the fragrant coffee aroma inside, and bring the coffee to a boil. As soon as it is boiling hard, reduce the heat to simmer and let the pot remain there for 3 minutes. Then set it off the heat for 3 to 5 minutes more to let the coffee steep and clarify. The egg, shell, and coffee grounds will settle to the bottom and coagulate into a lumpy mass, leaving 7 or 8 cups of the richest and most flavorful coffee

CAMP
COFFEE

you ever tasted, waiting to be poured and enjoyed. After you've poured a round, set the pot
in a pan of very hot water (not back on the stove)
to keep the coffee hot without letting it boil
again.

And with a cup of this eye-opening brew, drink a salute to
breakfast, one of the genuine pleasures of life in the South—or anywhere else.

POLITICS AND FOOD

A Tennessee politician of my acquaintance confided to me recently that only one major obstacle stood between him and a seat in
Congress. He identified that single vexing impediment as "the barbecue factor."

The incumbent, he explained, had mastered the art and science of
converting pit-cooked pork shoulder and ribs into votes. "He's got the
best cooks, the best sauce, the best guest list," my ambitious friend
lamented. "There's no way I can overcome that. I can't begin to
challenge him at the polls as long as he controls the pits."

If you think that's an apocryphal tale, you're entitled—but don't
bet the farm on it. Since time immemorial, serious Southern candidates
for practically every post from the town council to the White House
have used food as an integral part of their campaign strategy, and close
races have sometimes turned on a climactic oyster roast or pig picking
or catfish fry.

Politicians in these parts seldom get far without a food plank in
their campaign platform. You can have all the TV spots that money will
buy, but if you don't know how to put great barbecue or seafood or
some other specialty before the electorate, you're in deep trouble.

Even after they're in office, Southern politicians forget this recipe
for victory at their peril. The astute ones faithfully attend all the prayer
breakfasts, service club luncheons, garden club teas, cocktail parties,
pie suppers, and brotherhood dinners they can possibly work into their
schedules, confidently expecting to find there scores of votes ripe for
the picking. Whether to gain or retain office, a successful politician in
this region must go to the table and break bread with the people.

The 1988 presidential campaign held a certain gastronomical
interest for the hungry electorate as long as native Southerners Jesse
Jackson and Albert Gore, Jr., were in the race. Soul food and country
cooking were all the rage, and competing bands of supporters worked
feverishly to lay the finest spreads at one great banquet after another.
But then the two native sons fell by the wayside, and alas, gone were

the days of world-class dinners-on-the-ground in their behalf. George Bush and Michael Dukakis plodded on to the dreary climax, enduring unimaginative English peas and rubber chicken, gray roast beef and dehydrated potatoes, with only once in a while a little taste of Texas or Greece to relieve the monotony.

The real taste of grease will have to wait for Al and Jesse and a new wave of Southern aspirants to fire up the pits again in the future.

How did it come to be, this fast Southern bond between campaigning and eating? No one knows exactly when or where it started, but clearly the tradition is an old one. Almost from the beginning of the nation, our leaders from the Southern states have understood and exploited the unifying power of good food.

Thomas Jefferson, the second of fifteen Southern-born presidents of the United States, may have been the first politician to realize this. As governor of Virginia in the 1780s, Jefferson was a shrewd trader in the hog market, no doubt in part to keep a supply of country hams and barbecue meat on hand. His successes in this regard may have given rise to the practices now colorfully referred to as pork-barrel politics. In any case, scores of Southern politicians since Jefferson have used food as an essential tool of their trade.

There was, for example, Kentucky's Governor A. B. "Happy" Chandler. He and his wife invited a few political friends to the governor's mansion for a country ham breakfast before the running of the Kentucky Derby back in 1936. Now, more than half a century later, a crowd in excess of 10,000 swarms over the capitol grounds on the first Saturday morning in May to eat ham and eggs under a giant tent, and more elegant Derby breakfasts are served that same day throughout the Bluegrass region.

And Huey Long, the inimitable Louisiana Kingfish: After his elevation from the governor's office to the U. S. Senate, he delivered a famous filibuster oration that included such detailed and explicit instructions for frying oysters that a fellow senator complained of intense hunger pangs—proof, he said, that he and his colleagues were being "inhumanely treated" by the tantalizing descriptions of the Kingfish.

A. J. Liebling had Huey Long in mind when he wrote the opening sentences of *The Earl of Louisiana* , his classic 1961 biography of Governor Earl Long, Huey's younger brother.

"Southern political personalities, like sweet corn, travel badly," Liebling began. "They lose flavor with every hundred yards away from the patch. By the time they reach New York, they are like Golden Bantam that has been trucked up from Texas—stale and unprofitable."

Nobody could turn a phrase like Liebling. It was a striking simile, weakened only slightly by its inaccuracy (Southern politicians have, in fact, traveled rather well—sometimes too well—since the days of George Washington), and it lingers in the mind like the pungent aroma of a sack of smoked sausage.

But if Southern politicians do have greater range and staying power than sweet corn, Liebling's deliberate coupling of political and gastronomical images was entirely appropriate. New Yorker though he was, he was a heavy hitter in the food and drink department, and he frequently used food references in his political stories. (Besides politics, his favorite spectator sports were war and boxing; all in all, Liebling would have made an outstanding Southerner.)

When the South, shaken by its black citizenry, finally began to awaken from its segregationist slumber in the 1950s, the kitchen and dinner table were among the few arenas where some mutual interest and common knowledge between the races already existed. Politicians white and black were quick to see that, and they subsequently drew upon their shared food history to speed the process of social reconciliation.

Throughout the South today, food fairs and festivals and community banquets are so popular that no self-respecting local politician would dare ignore the ones within his or her jurisdiction. In every state, dozens of these events are staged annually, grand affairs such as the World Catfish Festival at Belzoni, Mississippi; the Chitlin Strut at Salley, South Carolina; the Blessing of the Shrimp Fleet at Bayou la Batre, Alabama; and the Collard Green Festival at Ayden, North Carolina. These high-spirited affairs draw thousands of spectators and eaters, and the politicians turn out in force to sup with the masses. They may even volunteer as cooks or servers, the better to be seen and admired by the greatest number of hungry citizens.

The annual Coon Supper at Gillett, Arkansas, is another of these not-to-be-missed events. In 1987, Governor Bill Clinton and Senator Dale Bumpers narrowly escaped tragedy when the plane in which they were riding to Gillett for the supper crash-landed. Once safely on the ground, the two men wasted no time in philosophical reflection on their close scrape with death; noting the late hour, they rushed on to greet the assembled throng of coon eaters.

In addition to being guests, Southern politicians are also hosts at some splendid repasts. For example, the high sheriff of Nashville-Davidson County, Tennessee, Fate Thomas, presides over the annual game supper of the Sure Shot Rabbit Hunters Association, and more than five thousand people pay ten dollars apiece to be seen there.

Even more spectacular some years ago was the ranch breakfast that L. K. Edwards, a state senator from Marion County, Florida, laid out every spring for his legislative colleagues. Some of his invited guests maintained that Edwards kept his hired help busy candling eggs for days before the event, so that every diner could be served a double-yolk egg with his grits and bacon and biscuits.

Lyndon Baines Johnson was the acknowledged master of the meals-and-deals school throughout his political career, and his Texas ranch was the main arena for countless functions combining politics and fine cooking. "Come, let us reason together," Johnson was fond of saying—and he might have added, "over beans and slaw, barbecue, bourbon and beer." Lyndon and Lady Bird knew how to entertain.

Later, when Jimmy Carter became president, the South returned to national attention, with the scene shifting from Texas to Georgia. The barbecue also changed—from beef brisket to pork shoulder—but the venerable food-and politics tradition continued and expanded, drawing on its deep roots in Southern history.

Jimmy and Rosalynn Carter knew the formula as well as the Johnsons, and so did Jimmy's mother, Miss Lillian. On one spectacular 1976 evening in Plains, she served a $5,000-a-plate Southern country supper to hundreds of guests and raised well over a million dollars for her son's presidential campaign. Reporters in attendance counted more than fifty-five different dishes on the groaning tables, including six meats, a score of vegetables and salads, five kinds of hot breads, and at least fifteen desserts. It was truly a feast to remember.

In that same campaign season, another Georgian, Betty Talmadge, honored Rosalynn Carter and Joan Mondale and the women of the Democratic Party at a festive "pig pickin'" on the lawn of her Tara-like home in Lovejoy, Georgia. The menu was not as extensive as Miss Lillian's, but the barbecue was said to be every bit as good—and the evening's receipts were almost as astronomical.

In the wake of that double serving of prime pork and Southern cooking, Carter and the Democrats rolled on to victory, and "the barbecue factor" soared to new heights in the folklore and mythology of Southern politics.

Such triumphs bring to mind the observations of one John R. Watkins, a reporter for *The Strand* of London, who visited Georgia in 1898 and sent back to his magazine a lengthy account of an institution known as "a political barbecue." In his dispatch were these passages:

"'Cue' is what they call it in Georgia, where it has been famous for many, many years. . . . So famous is it, in fact, that it has become a social and political force, and as a political entertainment has been duplicated in many states of the Union. . . . It is no exaggeration to say that many a gubernatorial election in Georgia has been carried by means of votes gained at barbecues, and no campaign for Governor is complete without a series of such popular feasts."

Now, almost a century later, the political entertainment continues as spectacularly as ever. Some things never change.

GRAVEYARD CLEANING

For as far back as he can remember, Charles Lewis and his family have gathered around the little north Alabama town of Somerville on the Saturday nearest to Memorial Day.

They used to meet on the farm of Doc and Maggie McDaniel, Charles' grandparents, but their two-story log house is no longer there. Now the out-of-town family members stay with relatives who remain in the Somerville area, or in nearby Athens and Decatur.

Charles Lewis and his brothers and sisters and most of their children and grandchildren usually make the pilgrimage. Together with a number of nieces and nephews, aunts and uncles, cousins, neighbors and friends, they come together annually to clear and clean the oak-canopied graveyard where the elders are buried.

They come to reconnect, to talk and laugh, to reminisce, to water the roots of the family tree. And they come to eat.

"Doc and Maggie McDaniel were my mother's parents," says Charles Lewis, who is now in his fifties. "We lived around here close to them when I was growing up, and my mother was living here when she died in 1953.

"Even before that—clear back to the 1930s, I guess—we always had a crowd around Memorial Day. The morning was spent cleaning off the old graveyard in town. In the afternoon and on into the evening, we'd gather at the homeplace to eat—and man, did we ever more eat!"

Almost everything was right off the farm—ham from the smokehouse, vegetables and fruits canned the previous summer, milk and butter from the cows, fresh eggs from the laying hens, tender young fried chicken, bread made from stone-ground cornmeal.

The Lewises, with kin and friends, still head for Somerville in late May, but they're more scattered now, and some of the older members have passed on, and without the homeplace it's harder to plan a common meal.

In 1988, after they had finished their work at the cemetery, Charles Lewis and his sons ate a big dinner late in the afternoon with some of their kinfolk in Athens. May Emma Bass, Charles's sister, was there, and so was Mack Lewis, their brother, but another brother and sister, Damon Lewis and Margaret Daniels, were unable to make the trip from Chattanooga. Alice Marie Shoulders, Mrs. Bass's daughter, did most of the cooking.

It was a small gathering, but the food was reminiscent of the country spreads of old. Stewed chicken and boiled ham led the platters, followed by candied sweet potatoes, stewed corn, field peas, sliced tomatoes, and hot rolls. There was plenty of iced tea, and the dessert feature was a cool and tangy lemon icebox pie.

"Alice Marie cooks the old fashioned way," said Charles Lewis approvingly. The field peas were an impressive case in point. Simmered for hours with a chunk of seasoning pork, they were as tender and flavorful as any could be.

Long one of the South's most prolific and abundant staples, field peas belong to a large family of legumes that includes black-eyed peas or cowpeas (first brought to this country by Africans in the seventeenth century), stock peas, crowder peas, and purple-hull peas.

Whether cooked fresh or preserved by canning, drying, or freezing, these basic vegetables have held a primary place in Southern cookery for almost four centuries.

The seasoning meat is important to their flavor (some would say essential). By whatever name—salt pork, white bacon, side meat, fatback—it adds a meaty flavor that complements the peas most favorably, and creates as a bonus, in conjunction with boiling water, a delicious pan broth known and loved by generations of Southerners as pot likker.

Here are some tips on cooking field peas. First, remember that two cups of shelled peas equal about a pound, and a pound will make four large servings. Use a large pot with a cover. Dried peas should be soaked overnight in cold water.

Cover peas with fresh water, add seasoning meat and a pod of red pepper, and bring to a boil. Reduce heat and simmer for 20 minutes to 2 hours (shortest if frozen, longest if dried), aiming for tender but not mushy peas. Add more water if necessary; season to taste with salt and pepper. This is a dish best cooked according to the tongue, not the clock. Taste frequently—and when the right flavor and tenderness are attained, turn off the heat and leave the covered pot on the stove to wait for dinner.

Whenever Charles Lewis encounters field peas, he automatically thinks of Somerville, Alabama, and his extended family and the old homeplace, long gone but not forgotten.

He also remembers the shady grove where his grandparents are buried, and the wonderful feeling of anticipation he knew there as a youngster, working with his kin to make the cemetery attractive—and waiting for the great afternoon dinner soon to come.

FOOD AND FUNERALS

Walking through an old farmhouse in Virginia a few years ago, a friend and I fell into conversation about antebellum architecture. He asked me if I knew why parlor doors were often made much wider than other interior passages.

I had no idea, so my perceptive friend told me what should have been obvious: Parlors were the funeral homes of the past. Undertakers laid out the bodies of deceased residents there, and pallbearers carried the coffins out to graveyards nearby. Thus, he said, parlor doors had to be wide enough for the bearers to pass through with the coffin.

We went on to talk about the rest of that somber scene from the distant past. Everything was centered in the home. When people of great longevity or prominence died, family and friends came in great numbers, and often from great distances. There being no motels, they had to stay at the homeplace or elsewhere in the neighborhood.

And, of course, they had to eat. Surely it was this necessity that generated the old and continuing tradition of taking food offerings to the family of the deceased.

Though it is by no means exclusively a Southern practice, it's obvious that Southerners, particularly in rural communities and small towns, have extended this courtesy to their loved ones for a very long time. What's more, they continue to do so—and it's hard to imagine how anyone could be more generous.

I was reminded of that most forcefully last summer when I went back to my boyhood home in Kentucky for the funeral of a much-beloved local community leader. A steady procession of mourners paid their respects at the home, the funeral home, the church, and the cemetery. And, an astonishing number of them brought food.

I counted six loaves of baked bread, five chess pies, four pecan pies, four platters of fried chicken, three pots of green beans, three baskets of cornbread muffins, three cold salads, three gallons of iced tea and lemonade, and three packages of barbecue totaling at least six pounds.

One lady brought a pound of bacon, a dozen eggs, a pound of coffee, and a supply of biscuits—"so nobody will have to think about what to fix for breakfast," she said. Others brought baskets of fresh fruit, soft drinks, trays piled high with sandwiches, and even supplies of paper cups and plates.

Some of the offerings were substantial dishes hot from the oven—baked ham, pot roast, chicken and dressing, baked apples, broccoli casserole, and poke sallet, a wild-greens dish not commonly seen even in the country. Deviled eggs and potato salad and cole slaw were also there in abundance.

Among the many desserts, I saw egg custard, apple, fried peach, lemon icebox, and sweet potato pies; loaves of cinnamon-raisin bread and zucchini bread; several sweet puddings, including banana; and a spice cake that was simply spectacular.

Altogether, nearly 100 offerings were received. The undertaker, obviously accustomed to such expressions of sympathy, provided the family with a "food book" in which to record the gifts for later acknowledgment. There was even a sheet of numbered stickers to identify dishes, so they could be returned to the proper owners.

Where but in the South, I wondered, is such an honorable and enduring tradition still followed so faithfully? Who else says "I'm sorry" with a cake or a casserole? Some people do, no doubt, for such a fitting and practical tribute could hardly be confined to one region. Still, Southerners have a special knack for tea and sympathy.

When the funeral was over, the family invited relatives and out-of-town guests to join them at the house. There, on the porch and the lawn and in the kitchen, the food that so many caring people had brought was spread before the throng, and a sad occasion ended on a happy note of fellowship and remembrance.

The deceased, a cheerful and gregarious hail-fellow named George Bleidt, had always taken kindly to down-home gatherings of family and friends and neighbors, whether the occasion was a reunion, a homecoming, a holiday, a wedding, or a funeral. He had his own term for such an event—it was "a coming-together"—and one essential unifying feature that always made it turn out well was Southern food.

As the assembled crowd partook of the wondrous display of cookery that day, one relative was heard to remark: "This is just the kind of event that George used to love. I wish he was here to enjoy it."

To which another promptly replied, "I imagine he is, honey. He wouldn't miss a feast like this for the world."

SUNDAY DINNER

Tommie Lewis is a man of many talents—television cameraman, gospel music producer, church pillar, cook, and caterer. I first met him in a TV studio during a taping session on food, and we started right in talking about Southern cookery as if we had known each other for years.

One of the things I learned from that first conversation is that Lewis and members of his family have been having dinner together after church every Sunday for the past 15 years or more.

As soon as the benediction is spoken at Olivet Missionary Baptist Church in Nashville, upwards of two dozen kinfolk and friends begin to move toward Dorothy Westmoreland's house, a few blocks away. Mrs. Westmoreland—"Big Mama" to everyone in the family—is Tommie Lewis's mother-in-law. Three of her thirteen children—Lillie Myers, Marie Winters, and Emma Jean Lewis (Tommie's wife)—share cooking responsibilities with Tommie and Big Mama. They all give part of Saturday to the preparation.

"I'm the meat cook," says Tommie, who is called "Daddy Bud" by the others. "I fix ribs, chicken, turkey and dressing, or some other main dish. Big Mama does most of the vegetables, and Lillie fixes the salads and desserts. Em and Marie always play some part in it, and Bernice, who's married to Readus Westmoreland, another one of Big Mama's children, usually makes macaroni and cheese. It's an old-fashioned, down-home dinner."

When I showed more than passing interest in this regular repeat of an old Southern ritual, Tommie graciously invited me to come as a guest to church some Sunday and stick around for dinner. It was an offer I couldn't refuse; truth be told, I think he may have sensed that I was on the verge of inviting myself.

The church service was long and eventful, filled with great singing and preaching and praying (by, among others, Elder Tommie Lewis), and I was so caught up in it that I didn't notice until the end that it was 2:30 in the afternoon. Suddenly, I was salivating in anticipation of the big dinner soon to be served.

At Big Mama's house, the crowd was already arriving when I got there. In the small kitchen, Lillie supervised the serving (I counted twenty-one plates as they were passed from the kitchen to diners in other rooms). Mrs. Westmoreland sat serenely on the sofa, her work completed.

And what a job she had done—turnip greens, green beans, fried corn and sweet potatoes, all seasoned to perfection. Tommie had prepared turkey and dressing and gravy, and Lillie had made potato salad and deviled eggs and hot water corn bread, and there was a bottomless pitcher of iced tea. There was abundance, and it was all perfectly delicious, up to and including Lillie's chocolate cake at the end.

"You should be here when she bakes carrot or coconut or pineapple upside down cake," said Monica, one of Tommie and Emma Jean Lewis's daughters, "or banana pudding, or sweet potato pie. Lillie knows how to make desserts."

Monica and her sister Marie and others of their generation were part of the clean-up detail, and they made short work of the dishes.

Mrs. Westmoreland, who is in her mid-seventies, grew up on a farm in rural Giles County, Tennessee, and she recalls fondly that both her mother and father were good cooks. "I learned how from both of them," she said. "There was five of us children, and I was the baby, so I grew up in a house full of good cooks.

"We always had a big dinner every Sunday, just like this, and the preacher would come, and others besides family. You never knew how many there would be. But you could always count on good food—just plain old home cooking, the same as we're still eating now."

The words of greeting and parting were the same, too: "Come on in . . . help yourself . . . feel free . . . come back any time." Here and there in the South, I'm glad to say, the wonderful tradition of Sunday dinner is still alive and well.

OWENSBORO BARBECUE

As sure as it's summertime, the Catholics of western Kentucky are deep into the picnic season, barbecuing sheep over hickory fires and cooking burgoo in huge, steaming black cauldrons.

Sheep? Burgoo? This side of Texas, barbecue means pork to most people. And as for burgoo, few outside the Bluegrass State would recognize that spicy concoction—unless it was called Brunswick stew.

It would be difficult to identify a more fascinating or improbable phenomenon in Southern food history than these church picnic/fundraisers. Nobody knows exactly how the events got started, but there's no question that mutton barbecue is *the* meat of choice around Owensboro, Kentucky. Most of the Catholic churches in the thirty-two-county Diocese of Owensboro that stretches along the south bank of the Ohio River are sheep cookers, and they invite the public to share it with them at outdoor feasts each summer.

At Fancy Farm, a small community in far western Kentucky, the annual picnic at St. Jerome's Catholic Church on the first Saturday in August has continued for 109 years. A crowd of over 10,000 people consumes more than 15,000 pounds of barbecued mutton, pork, and chicken there on that day, and no Kentuckian interested in statewide political office would dare miss the occasion.

Owensboro, not to be outdone, stages the International Barbecue Festival on the banks of the Ohio on an early weekend in May each year, and the resulting pall of smoke that hangs over the city has caused more than one distant observer to fear that a fire was burning out of control.

The 150-year-old tradition that ties Catholics to barbecued mutton goes back to a time when sheep were commonly raised on farms in the region and country parishes were first drawn to the idea of summer homecoming picnics.

As the years have passed, Owensboro's commercial barbecue pits also have gone for mutton in a big way. Consider, for example, the Moonlite, a gargantuan pit parlor whose dining room seats 300-plus. At the peak of the summer season, the Moonlite barbecues about two tons of mutton a day.

But it's the Catholic picnics that have the longest history, and they're a delightful outing for parishoners and visitors alike. The grand finale of about fifteen picnics in Owensboro and surrounding Daviess County each summer is the mid-September smokeout at St. Joseph, a rural parish and retirement center for elderly nuns.

"This is the biggest of all the picnics in the county," says David Warren, a member of the parish and a local-government official, "because all the parishes go together on it as a fund-raiser for the retired sisters. It's always held on the second Sunday in September—and if it rains in the morning, it always clears in the afternoon."

Warren's chief contribution to the feast is the barbecue sauce, which he and others cook in two seventy-five-gallon vats. (His recipe: vinegar, catsup, hot sauce, Worcestershire sauce, lemon juice, salt and pepper, combined "to suit my taste" and cooked over hickory fires.)

The pits, strung out on a shady hillside under tin-roofed sheds, expose about 100 yards of metal grates to smoldering coals. On both sides of the long, narrow cooking surface, aproned tenders last year prepared 6,500 pounds of mutton, 1,800 chicken halves, and a lesser amount of pork for about 6,000 picnickers.

At waist-high wooden tables under the trees, about 350 people at a time stand and eat as much as they care to be served of the entire menu—sliced and chopped mutton, the other kinds of barbecue, burgoo, loaf bread, slaw, potato salad, pickles, onions, soft drinks, and ice cream. The cost is $6 per person—$3 for children—and it's a feast worth driving to Owensboro for.

A festival atmosphere prevails. All manner of trinkets, bric-a-brac and other food items (cakes, pies, preserved goods) are on sale at booths scattered over the site. And strangers are made to feel welcome—the more the merrier, all for the benefit of the nuns.

You can't stay a stranger long at one of these affairs—and, says David Warren, "It's just about impossible to go away hungry." Thanks to the Catholics and the sacrificial sheep, a venerable Southern cooking tradition continues to thrive.

RELIGIOUS MINORITIES

Baptists and Methodists have long been so numerous in the South that the "Bible Belt" tag applied to the region has generally been understood to suggest an overwhelming preponderance of mainstream Protestants.

The largest Protestant denominations do attract a big majority of the South's churchgoers. But in fact, there has been much religious diversity in the territory below the Ohio River since colonial times.

Along with that variety has come many of our most celebrated food traditions. For obvious reasons, a number of them are highlighted during religious holidays such as Christmas and Easter.

Catholicism in the South is strongest in certain Gulf and Atlantic coastal regions, reflecting the centuries-long impact of Spanish and French influences there.

As one direct consequence, we are blessed with Louisiana's Creole and Acadian (Cajun) cookery, two of the finest culinary styles to be found under the broad umbrella of Southern food. The very names of many Creole and Cajun dishes—grillades, boudin, jambalaya, beignets, and pain perdu, to name a few—are straight out of the French lexicon.

Traces of Catholic Spain can be found in the cookery of Mobile, Pensacola, Tampa, and St. Augustine, where the fare includes such perennial favorites as gazpacho, bolichi, paella, and flan.

Another ethnic flavoring in St. Augustine is Minorcan, named after the Mediterranean island of Minorca, a port of departure for immigrants more than 200 years ago. (Actually, it was an English Protestant who recruited Orthodox Greeks and Italian Catholics as well as Minorcans from that Spanish Catholic-dominated jurisdiction, but their Florida descendants prefer the Minorcan identity.)

In St. Augustine you will find such dishes as pilau (probably Middle Eastern in origin), Minorcan chowder, Minorcan fruit cake, and fromajardis crispes, an Easter pastry.

Pilaus are also popular in Savannah and Charleston, two more seaport cities long open to the international currents of commerce (including food) that have always flowed between Europe and the United States.

Protestant Huguenots from France and Jews from all over Europe were among Charleston's earliest settlers, and thus even now you can find in the city's cookbooks recipes for a variety of fricassees (smothered meat dishes) and ragouts (hearty stews), as well as Huguenot tortes, blintzes, bagels, and borscht.

The Moravians, a German Protestant sect, settled early in the vicinity of Salem, North Carolina, and their breads, cakes, and cookies have since won more converts than the church itself. Around Winston-Salem now, especially in the Christmas season, a strong Moravian heritage persists in the array of "love feast" offerings: ginger cakes, streusel, sugar crisps, and citron tarts.

Farther inland, early settlers included Quakers in North Carolina, Dunkards (another German Protestant group) in Virginia, Shakers in Kentucky, Amish and Mennonites in Tennessee and Kentucky. Traces of some of those groups and their food heritage can still be found.

The Mennonites of middle Tennessee are justly noted for the quality of their food products, including breads and cheeses and sorghum molasses. In central Kentucky, the Shakers left a legacy of sumptuous feasting that can still be experienced in the restored public dining room at Pleasant Hill.

Foremost among many distinctive and outstanding menu items there are the sweets, including sugar-cream and Shaker lemon pies, mulberry cobbler, country thumb cookies, and oatmeal cake.

No doubt there are still more foods in the Southern kitchen and pantry that can be traced to the minority religious and ethnic communities of the region. As much as it owes to its white and black majorities of mainstream Protestants, Southern food nonetheless has ties that bind it to churches and nationalities around the world.

NEW YEAR'S FEAST

Foodlore—that's folklore seasoned to taste—is a fascinating guide to social history, a sort of cultural map that helps to describe and define individuals and communities.

You can tell a lot about people by observing certain things about them—how they work and how they play, how they care for their young and their elders, what they build and buy and throw away. And, of course, what they eat.

There are anthropologists and sociologists who study these patterns and interpret the behavior they find. That's always seemed like interesting work to me, though I sometimes wonder how reliable the findings are—as, for example, when a scholar attempted some years ago to draw meaningful conclusions from what he found in Henry Kissinger's garbage.

My interest in Southern food often leads me into amateur inquiries of that sort. I seldom nail down any startling new explanations for the habits and customs of eaters in this region, but the pursuit itself is instructive, and the food is almost always rewarding.

Consider this phenomenon: For generations across the South—and in the Caribbean, Central America, the warmer regions of South America, and maybe even around the entire girth of the earth—the eating of beans and peas, rice, and tender greens has long had a certain ceremonial importance. These foods are widely considered to be invitations to good luck, particularly in celebrations marking the beginning of a new year.

In the low country of South Carolina, for example, the rice and black-eyed peas dish known as Hoppin' John is an essential item on the New Year's Day menu. Black-eyed peas are also served—though usually without rice—at holiday gatherings throughout the interior South.

Black beans and rice are the people's choice at year-beginning parties along the Florida coast, as they are in the Caribbean and in much of Latin America, while in Louisiana and Texas, you'll be much more likely to encounter red beans and rice.

As for greens, many Southerners associate them with rising good fortune (green, they remind us, is the color of money), and so you'll often find turnip greens or collards on the first-day dinner menu.

Such rituals tend to be more whimsical and humorous than serious, and that's as it should be. But in addition, they offer a wonderful chance to enjoy some of the South's primary side dishes at their very best.

At the home of Al and Mary Ann Clayton in Atlanta, dozens of people show up for an afternoon beans and greens dinner on New Year's Day, and over the decade or so that these folks have been gathering there, the menu has grown to cover just about all of the good-luck bases.

White beans, black beans, red beans, black-eyed peas, and Al's near-legendary mess of collard greens are all featured, along with cracklin' cornbread, cole slaw, potato salad, and Mary Ann's celebrated fruit cobblers.

Dish for dish, the Claytons' feast packs about as much potential good luck as you could ever hope to get at one meal. Just getting invited is the best luck of all.

At the insistence of his friends, Al has made a videotape of his collard cooking method, and I have viewed it and taken notes.

He begins by selecting a large bunch of collard greens (three or four stalks bound together) at the produce market. He cuts off and discards the base of the stems, then chops the upper stems and leaves coarsely and washes them several times. A big double handful of the chopped greens goes into the food processor to make a purée for enrichment of the pot.

Then, in a 10-gallon stock pot half filled with fresh water, he brings the greens to a rolling boil with several smoked ham hocks, a couple of chopped onions, a generous amount of chopped garlic or garlic powder, and infusions to taste of the following: red pepper, black pepper, white pepper, hot pepper sauce, vinegar, salt, and cane syrup.

"It's hard to specify amounts of these seasonings," Clayton says. "It depends on how big the mass of your mess of greens turns out to be, and on your taste buds. What you're after is a sweet and sour tension that finally resolves itself in a nice balance."

Reducing the heat to low, he simmers this exotic pot for hours. You can also turn it off and boil again later, or refrigerate and reheat the entire pot, or even freeze them. Collards are well-nigh indestructible, and when you get the taste right, it stays right.

Call it what you will—original, inspired, bizarre—these collard greens and their pot likker are absolutely the finest I ever put in my mouth. My own efforts to match the Clayton genius have fallen short of the mark, and you may discover too that the unorthodox method is hard to perfect.

But the attempt seems worth making. I don't remember ever tasting anything more Southern in all my life than Al's collards, and I hope someday to claim mastery of the technique.

"These greens have healing powers," says the modest Georgia cook, with the slightest trace of a smile showing in his eyes. "They'll lift you up and carry you forward." We should all have that kind of good luck—on New Year's and every other day.

Minorcans

One of the oldest and most vigorous ethnic minorities in any Southern city is the Minorcan community of St. Augustine, Florida. Descended from immigrants recruited on the island of Minorca in the Mediterranean Sea more than two centuries ago, the contemporary residents maintain close ties to their predominantly Hispanic and Catholic heritage.

Among their oldest customs, now observed more in the telling than in the doing, is a strolling serenade on the night before Easter, with the singers receiving gifts of food and drink from appreciative residents.

According to the story, small groups of carolers went about the villages of Minorca (and later St. Augustine) singing hymns and verses, including a familiar religious folk song called "Fromajardis." The first seven verses in praise of the Virgin Mary were customarily followed by two or three more requesting a cake or tart as a token of thanks.

As time went on, the serenaders took to carrying bags to hold their pastries, and the pastries themselves became customized into a few basic types, one with a filling of cheese and spices, another a simpler sugar-and-spice tart called Fromajardis crispes (pronounced "cro-spays").

It's those crispes that I want to focus on here, both for their favor among the Minorcans and for their similarity to some other sweet treats found elsewhere in the South.

This is an old St. Augustine recipe: Make a rich pastry (your favorite pie dough will suffice). Roll out very thin and cut in circles with a saucer. Turn up and crimp the edges. Beat 1 egg well, adding 3/4 cup of sugar and enough cinnamon to assure a distinctly spicy flavor and a brownish color when cooked. Bake the plain pastries for a minute or two to set the dough and then put a tablespoonful of the flavored egg mixture and a little pat of butter on each one. Finish baking until crisp. The pastries are best when eaten fresh and hot.

Crispes make a nice, simple dessert as well as a good story. And not just in St. Augustine, either. Susan Davis of Charleston, South Carolina, has a vivid recollection of a similar little treat her mother used to make called stickies—and indeed, in a 1940 volume called *America Cooks*, I found a South Carolina recipe for them ("Make a rich dough . . . roll out thin, spread well with butter . . . sprinkle with sugar and cinnamon . . .")

And from widely separated Tennessee towns, Pat Braden and Karen Davis recall a monument to delicious simplicity called butter rolls or butter dumpling rolls. This is Pat's mother's recipe: Roll out pie crust dough very thin and cut in rounds with a saucer. Sprinkle bits of butter, sugar and vanilla on each. Roll up or fold into a square pouch and bake in a pan.

"Mom serves them hot, moistened with sweet milk and sprinkled with a little cinnamon," says Pat. Karen recognizes the basic recipe, but remembers her mother making a sweet sauce to spoon over the hot pastry.

And finally, in the turn-of-the-century *Picayune Creole Cook Book* from New Orleans, the recipe for pie crust ends with these words: "If any pie crust is left, do not think of throwing it away. Take all the bits left from cutting around the edges of the pie pans; roll very thin into small squares; bake lightly, and save for tea or luncheon. Put a spoonful of . . . jelly on each square, and they will be found delicious."

What's at work here is a combination of frugality and creativity. A long history of want, not to say hunger, taught Southern cooks never to waste food. Creole cooks turned stale bread into classic puddings. Appalachian cooks found dozens of ways to use apples—even the peels—before they rotted. Farming families at hog-killing time found uses for "everything but the squeal."

And so it is, I think, with Fromajardis crispes, stickies, butter dumpling rolls, and no doubt other pastries of similar make and taste. It has always been a mark of pride among great Southern cooks that they could take little or nothing in the way of raw materials and transform them into something deliciously memorable. These flaky little wonders in all their individualized styles and colorful names certainly prove the point.

MALE COOKS

While she was campaigning as the Democratic candidate for vice-president in 1984, Geraldine Ferraro found herself discussing blueberries with the agriculture commissioner of Mississippi, Jim Buck Ross.

"I grow those," Ferraro remarked.

"Do you?" Ross replied. "Can you make a blueberry muffin?"

"Sure can. Can you?"

Ross drew back. "Down here," he said, "men don't cook."

The notion is still abroad in some quarters that cooking is not a suitable activity for men. Wherever strong images of masculinity are nurtured—and the South has been such a place—men and boys who don aprons and bake cakes and exchange recipes may be thought a bit odd.

Apparently it's okay for "the boys" to stay up all night cooking a pig over a pit of coals, but they ought not to make a habit of hanging around the kitchen—except when they're eating.

Men cook in restaurants, of course, and always have. But it's not unusual for those who play an active role in food preparation at home to encounter ridicule or disapproval from other males.

The denial of a cooking role for men not only reveals a blindness to history, but also to the reality of contemporary male-female relationships.

In the first place, men have always cooked "down here" in the South, and I assume they have in other parts of the country too. Their overall contributions are not as great as those of women, certainly, but men have clearly helped to give Southern food a widely-shared reputation as the best and most popular style of regional cookery in the nation.

Cookbooks provide some supporting evidence. Two Mississippi women, Linda Ross Aldy and Carol Taff, compiled a book of outstanding recipes from male cooks in their state, and used Commissioner Ross's "down here men don't cook" remark as a mocking title.

For well over a century, men have written some outstanding books of Southern cookery, beginning with Lafcadio Hearn's 1885 New Orleans classic, *La Cuisine Creole,* and running through the more modern works of Eugene Walter, Peter Feibleman, Nathaniel Burton and Rudy Lombard, James Villas, Craig Claiborne, Bill Neal, Paul Prudhomme, and others.

Cookbooks aren't the only male literary contribution to cookery. Southern historians such as Richard Collin, Joe Gray Taylor, and Thomas D. Clark have also written perceptively about the region's foodways.

Virtually all of the riverboat and Pullman dining-car cooking of the nineteenth century was done by black men from the South, and the same can be said of barbecue. Even now, wherever real barbecue can still be found, the master cooks are usually black—and almost always male.

The women's movement and other social changes of recent years have brought men more frequently into home kitchens—but ironically, they are arriving just as people of both sexes are eating out with greater regularity.

"This is an equal opportunity kitchen," reads one apron slogan— but the apron is apt to be hanging in the closet while its male and female wearers are dining in a restaurant or eating fast food in the car.

But I'm convinced that home cooking will make a comeback. Over-processed and over-priced dinners served in the name of health or style or novelty can push us only so far before the inevitable course correction takes place and we return to the kind of home food that used to give us comfort.

For me, it's really not a matter of returning; I never left. Home cooking has always been my preference, and for the past ten years or so I have been honing my own meager but expanding skills as a cook.

Now, as I drift ever closer to "senior" status—whatever that means— I advocate equality in the kitchen with all the zeal of a latter-day convert and true believer. No matter where others may turn for their daily sustenance, my choice is clear: I'm in cooking to stay.

It's not, as I once thought, an art reserved for experts; it's an endeavor that invites beginners to learn by doing, and anyone with interest and motivation can gain skill quickly. Cooking is an activity that people of all ages can share—or enjoy alone. I cook instead of hunting or playing golf or watching football, and I wouldn't think of trading places with the sportsmen and spectators.

Not long ago, I spent two Saturday-afternoon hours making a black bottom pie for company. Researching the recipe led me back into some favorite old books by Duncan Hines and Marjorie Kinnan Rawlings and James Beard. Assembling the delicate confection was as challenging as working a jigsaw puzzle. Admiring the finished product gave me a genuine feeling of accomplishment. And then, watching and listening as the guests devoured it, I was rewarded once again. Seldom does any investment of time or money or effort bring me such a bountiful return.

The women who taught me to cook—my wife, my mother, others—gave me a useful skill and a permanent source of satisfaction and pleasure. I delight in returning the favor through my own cooking. Men who haven't discovered that for themselves are missing one of life's main courses.

BLACK COOKS

The cookery of the South is far and away the most diverse and developed regional culinary style in the nation. It stands out for many reasons, but one of the first and most important is the African-American contribution to it.

The facts speak clearly for themselves: Barbecue, historically speaking, is a black art. The justly famed Creole cuisine of New Orleans evolved from diverse elements skillfully united by black cooks. Elegant nineteenth-century plantation cookery was almost exclusively done by blacks.

Practically everywhere in the Old South, from private homes to hotels to steamboats and Pullman diners, it was black men and women who carried the lion's share of cooking responsibilities. Only in places where no blacks lived, or in the least affluent white homes—and not always in them—were there never any black cooks.

This is not to say that white women couldn't cook, of course, but simply to say that many of them didn't. Virtually all black women cooked, and many black men did too, especially on trains and boats and in hotels. As for white men, it was exceedingly rare to find them in the kitchen at all.

Living as they did from 1619 to the middle of this century under the heavy yoke of white control, blacks had few opportunities for unfettered self-development. The hard labor of food preparation caused most whites who could to shun it, and when the task fell to blacks, many of them discovered in the kitchen that cookery, as laborious as it was, also was a creative art.

Necessity is indeed the mother of invention. Combining instinct with experience, black cooks evolved most of the sub-regional culinary styles that come together under a single name: Southern food.

If the overwhelming majority of black Americans had lived north of the Ohio River instead of south of it, I dare say you would now find all the good barbecue in the North, along with the best hot breads, fried fish and chicken, well-seasoned garden vegetables; even many drinks, snacks, and desserts of the South probably wouldn't be here.

As it is, these and other elements of the South's culinary traditions are generally acknowledged by people in and out of the region to constitute the finest in native American food.

For a very long time, the enormous contributions of black cooks to our diet were virtually ignored. As social conditions have changed over the past three decades or so, credit has finally begun to come their way. One sign of the new order can be found in the growing number of cookbooks by blacks.

Except for two guidebooks for servants and waiters written by black men, Robert Roberts and Tunis G. C. Campbell, in Boston early in the nineteenth century, no other such books show up in the public record prior to 1912.

In that year, S. Thomas Bivins authored *The Southern Cookbook* and Emma Allen (Mrs. W. T.) Hayes wrote the *Kentucky Cook Book*. Between then and the end of World War II, only one other volume by a black writer—*New Orleans Cook Book*, by Lena Richard (1939)—gained any visibility.

Next came *A Date With a Dish*, by Freda De Knight, in 1948—not a Southern book in the strictest sense, but at least reflective of the Southern black heritage.

Jesse Willis Lewis, with help from Edith Ballard Watts, compiled *Jesse's Book of Creole and Deep South Recipes* in 1954, followed by the *Unusual Cookbook* of Nashvillian Flossie Morris in 1967.

In the 1970s, a rush of creative cookbooks by black writers appeared, starting with Vertamae Grosvenor's *Vibration Cooking*, a highly original slant on traditional African-American cooking.

Others included *The African Heritage Cookbook*, by Helen Mendes; *The Integrated Cookbook*, by Mary Jackson and Lelia Wishart; and soul food cookbooks by such well-known figures as Pearl Bailey and Mahalia Jackson.

Three more outstanding works of the seventies were *The Taste of Country Cooking*, by Edna Lewis; *Creole Feast*, by Nathaniel Burton and

Rudy Lombard; and *Spoonbread and Strawberry Wine,* a charming blend of food and family history by two sisters, Norma Jean and Carole Darden.

This much-belated trend has continued through the 1980s. To the eternal benefit of whites and blacks alike, generations of black Southerners have enriched the region's cookery out of all proportion to their numbers. Now, at last, they are beginning to receive the credit they deserve.

STUART'S PUBLIC COOKS

If there could ever be said to be such a place as a good town to get sick in—or, for that matter, to go to jail in—then I cast my vote for Stuart, Virginia, a pretty little county-seat community on the eastern slope of the Blue Ridge Mountains.

Not that I've been hospitalized there, or incarcerated. My choice isn't based on the quality of health care or the state of the lockup; it's strictly a result of talking to the cooks and checking out the food.

Some friends of mine who live in Stuart told me about the women who are in charge of the kitchen at R. J. Reynolds-Patrick County Memorial Hospital: food service director Betty Lou Simmons, supervisor Burgie Penn, and cook Shirley Carter.

Each has worked there for more than twenty years. They're a team of skilled professionals. Not only do they offer the patients some of the best hospital food in the country; they also have a contract to deliver and serve daily meals to the inmates at the county jail, they cater certain functions of the Rotary and Lions clubs, and they prepare the meal for the monthly dinner meeting of the county medical association.

There are a good many people around Stuart who claim that day in and day out, the women in the hospital kitchen serve the best food in Patrick County, maybe even the best in Virginia or the entire South. (That may reflect a wee bit of exaggeration, but it's also a measure of local pride.)

This is a far cry from the standard complaints about institutional food that are routinely voiced in most places. Nobody calls this fare "gruel," or worse; in fact, when a jail inmate made the mistake of griping about his dinner, local authorities were outraged.

"Anybody who would lie about this food would lie about anything," one public servant declared, dismissing the complaint.

What is it about the hospital kitchen and its daily output that makes so many people speak of it in such favorable terms?

"I think it's the menus," says Betty Lou Simmons. "Just good, earthy food—pintos, cabbage, pork chops, meat loaf, yeast rolls and such. And it's home-style cooking. Shirley's been here twenty-six years, Burgie twenty, and they know how to cook and season food properly."

With allowances for modern diet needs and health-centered eating, the Stuart public cooks turn out an impressive array of foods. They have cut back on the traditional elements of Southern taste— sugar, salt, butter, eggs, cream, bacon grease—but they still serve modified versions of the dishes that made Southern cooking famous.

"We strive for quality in food selection," says Burgie Penn, who in addition to her kitchen skills is also a Church of God minister. "That means fresh vegetables when we can get them—potatoes, cabbage— and dried beans, and first-quality chicken and ham and fish."

The daily menu at the hospital offers numerous choices for the health-conscious. Broccoli and cauliflower come with or without cream sauce, there's more fish than in years past, other meatless alternatives are served, and even the desserts are lighter.

"We still bake pies and cakes," says Shirley Carter, "but we use less butter and sugar and eggs than before—and more vegetable oil shortening."

Employees as well as patients at the Patrick County Hospital praise the cooking. "Those yeast rolls are so good," laughed one dining-room patron, "they'll make you swallow your tongue."

Considering how common it is to hear complaints about hospital food, the words of praise from this Virginia community are remarkable.

One of the eternal mysteries of life seems tied up in the question, "Why does institutional cooking have to be so bad?" The answer—in Stuart, at least—is crystal clear: It doesn't have to be, if you've got a team of real pros in charge of the kitchen.

People, Places, Books

MARGARET MITCHELL

Browsing through some dusty old tomes in an Arkansas bookshop several months ago, I came across something that startled me: a thin and stylish, silver-blue, hardcover collection of recipes called *Things You Have Always Wanted to Know about Cooking*. The author's name, printed in a flowing script under the title, was Margaret Mitchell.

Could this be *the* Margaret Mitchell, author of *Gone With the Wind?* I pondered the thought, and concluded that it well might be. The book was published in 1932, four years before the Atlanta author was catapulted to fame by the publication of her novel of the Civil War. The prospect of discovering a forgotten volume by a later-to-be-famous writer was too tantalizing to ignore. It could be worth hundreds, even thousands of dollars as a collector's item. I bought the little book for a few bucks and took it home for an identity check.

Gone With the Wind is generally thought to be Margaret Mitchell's only book (she died after being hit by a car on an Atlanta street in 1949). But before she wrote what turned out to be one of the most famous novels of the twentieth century, she worked for several years as a feature writer for the Sunday magazine section of the *Atlanta Journal*.

Her tenure there overlapped that of Henrietta Stanley Dull, a food editor and cookbook writer whose 1928 volume, *Southern Cooking*, is a classic of its kind. Knowing about Mrs. Dull, and about Margaret Mitchell's newspapering career before she became a novelist, I began to imagine how the two women might have been united behind the cookbook.

Things You Have Always Wanted to Know about Cooking was published by the Aluminum Cooking Utensil Co., a Pennsylvania-based manufacturer of cookware. Maybe, I thought, the company asked Mrs. Dull to write the book, and she, being too busy at the time, passed the freelance project on to her younger colleague.

I checked the Margaret Mitchell script on the cover against a sample of the author's signature. There were differences, but also some striking similarities—enough to suggest that the same person might have penned both. And, near the front of the book, a photograph of an attractive brunette talking with another woman in a kitchen seemed to bear a close resemblance to later pictures of the author.

Inquiries in Atlanta and among book collectors in various cities brought a mixed response. Some experts, noting the look-alike qualities in the signature and the photograph, spoke excitedly of the possibility; others were highly skeptical that the *Gone With the Wind* author could have done a cookbook without that achievement finding its way into her biographies.

But if she had, they all agreed, the book would be worth thousands of dollars. That was certainly reason enough to make me hope the little volume was authentic. Deep in my bones, though, I harbored doubts.

It didn't have to be titled something obvious, like *Gone With the Corn;* all it needed was a few tell-tale Southern recipes and a tone, an accent, with a hint of the South in it. But there was no cornbread, no seasoning meat in the vegetables, no barbecue, no chess or pecan pie, no boiled custard or iced tea—almost nothing, in fact, to identify the book with any region.

I did find a recipe for fried chicken, and others for cloverleaf yeast rolls, lemon tarts, and coconut cream pie, but those Southern favorites were also beloved by the rest of the country. If Margaret Mitchell was really a closet cook who turned to fiction writing, she certainly kept her culinary skills—and her Southern recipes—hidden from public view.

But I showed the book around, and even had a few offers for it (nothing in the three-figure range, let alone four), and finally I decided to take the matter up with the publisher, whose Wear-Ever aluminum cooking utensils are among the pots and pans in our kitchen.

Before I could do that, though, a friend showed me an advertisement in an old magazine, the June 1948 issue of *Ladies' Home Journal.* It was a Wear-Ever ad for pressure cookers—the food processors of that postwar era—and it contained a ringing endorsement by Margaret Mitchell.

Her picture was there—a round-faced, curly-haired, bespectacled woman, decidedly *not* the author—and the title under her name settled once and for all the question of identity. This Margaret Mitchell was the director of the Wear-Ever kitchens.

Oh, I thought to myself, *that* Margaret Mitchell—the cook, not the writer, the one for whom Rhett might have said, "Frankly, my dear, I don't care for yams," and Scarlett might have promised to plant a garden. Tomorrow, after she'd thought about it.

DUNCAN HINES

He was a silver-haired traveling salesman living in Chicago in 1936. By train and automobile, he had logged nearly a million miles on the road since the turn of the century. At 56, he was approaching the age when most American working men and women give up their jobs and retire.

But Duncan Hines had other plans. After years of information-gathering and one trial run, he was about to publish a traveler's guide to 490 restaurants scattered across the United States. *Adventures in Good Eating*, a 96-page paperback with a bright red cover, went on the market for $1 a copy that fall.

On the surface, the times hardly seemed favorable for such a venture. The country was between wars and just beginning to recover from the Great Depression. The automobile industry was barely three decades old, and most roads were narrow, rough, and crooked. There were no Holiday Inns; the word *motel* hadn't entered the language. McDonald's Hamburgers and Kentucky Fried Chicken were not even gleams in the eyes of Ray Kroc and Harland Sanders. Except for about two dozen Howard Johnson's ice cream and sandwich shops in Massachusetts, franchises and chains were virtually unknown in the world of public accommodations. Precious few guest rooms and no cars at all featured the summertime blessings of air conditioning.

Hines, a transplanted country boy from Kentucky, had acquired a degree of urban sophistication during his career. Furthermore, he possessed the two essential qualifications of a food and travel writer: an eclectic but discriminating appetite and an incurable case of wanderlust.

Still, as unlikely a visionary as he must have seemed when he first began opening doors and turning on lights for travelers, Duncan Hines confidently foresaw our collective transformation from a people who usually ate and slept at home to a figurative horde of nomads roaming the country in search of good food and comfortable lodging.

With the benefit of hindsight, his timing seems exquisite. In that pre-chain era of greasy-spoon cafes and spartan tourist courts, he imagined proliferating millions of travelers in need of his expert services. Hines took special pride in noting the "many motor car pilgrims" who came to regard him as "a reliable servant who has gone ahead, as it were, and posted the places where pleasant and satisfying meals can be had."

Just when the pilgrims were beginning to seek directions to the Canterburys and Tabard Inns of the land, and to want lists of places to sup and sleep along the way, they found their scout in Duncan Hines.

Adventures in Good Eating sold 5,000 copies the first year, and Hines lost $1,500 on it. In 1937, sales more than tripled and he almost broke even. From then on, the little red book never again swam in red ink. The *Good Eating* series prospered through 26 years of annual and semi-annual revisions. It and five other Hines books on food and travel recorded combined sales of half a million or more copies a year through most of the post-war period between 1945 and the mid-1950s.

For thirteen years on his own and then in collaboration with entrepreneur Roy H. Park, Hines parlayed his far-sighted idea into a personal fortune. In the process, his name became a household word throughout the nation.

◇

It often comes as something of a shock to today's roving diners to learn that Duncan Hines is not just a fictitious name on a cake-mix box. Unlike such "invented" characters as Betty Crocker and Aunt Jemima, he was very much alive, an in-the-flesh drummer on the perilous road to the top—and during most of his career, he seemed to stay at least a car-length ahead of the pack.

To be sure, the Hines label did appear on cake mixes and other food products—and it still does—but that was after the success of his guidebooks had given commercial value to his name. As an experienced traveling salesman who enjoyed what he called "the refinements of good living," he had in a sense been preparing for his later-life venture since the first decade of the century, when as a young man he went west to work for Wells-Fargo.

In Cheyenne, Wyoming, he met Florence Chaffin, an adventurous traveler from the East Coast. They were married in 1905 and settled in Chicago, where Hines developed a specialty in writing, designing, and printing promotional brochures for business and industry.

The work took him frequently on the road, and his wife often went along. Over the years, they made a game of "collecting" good inns and dining rooms worth revisiting. In careful notes, Hines maintained an updated roster of these "harbors of refreshment" scattered over the country. As their Christmas greeting to friends in 1935, Duncan and Florence Hines mailed a blue folder listing 167 restaurants in 30 states and the District of Columbia.

Hines was already accustomed to driving over 50,000 miles a year, and his reputation as a restaurant finder was such that people often called him for advice. The Christmas folder, far from halting the calls, brought a flood of requests for extra copies and more data. From there, it took just one small step for the Chicago printing salesman to become a freelance restaurant critic and travel guide.

"I make my money as a printer," he wrote in the introduction to the first edition of *Good Eating*, "and this adventure into the field of serving my fellow pilgrims rolling along the open road is just a piece of good fun." In an amazingly short span of time, the good fun also yielded big bucks.

Sales of the guidebook climbed to 16,000 in the second year. In 1938, soon after Hines published a companion volume called *Lodging for a Night*, he was featured in a long and favorable article in *The Saturday Evening Post*, and his fame quickly spread. By the end of 1939, sales of his books had zoomed to 100,000 a year.

The format of the guidebooks was simple and straightforward. Places were listed alphabetically by state and locality, with addresses, phone numbers, prices, and brief bits of descriptive information added. The number of restaurants cited soon grew from fewer than 500 to more than 2,000. It would have been impossible for Hines to keep the directory current by himself, but he attracted scores of enthusiastic sleuths and critics who volunteered their services to him, and with their help he updated and reissued the books once or twice a year.

Hines took great pains to maintain a reputation for objectivity. He charged no fees for inclusion in the books, accepted no advertising, and refused all offers of free meals and lodging. After his name became well known, he made reservations under a variety of pseudonyms. He also controlled the ownership and distribution of display signs bearing his seal of approval ("Recommended by Duncan Hines").

To be included in the guidebooks soon became both a mark of honor and a promise of profit for which restaurants yearned; conversely, to be dropped from the directories and to have the display of Hines's favor removed from the premises was a fall from grace akin to being drummed out of the corps or erased from the social register.

With his business booming, Hines quit his Chicago job in 1938 and moved to Bowling Green, Kentucky, his birthplace. There followed a period of declining fortunes for him. Florence Hines died in 1939, and World War II brought leisurely travel and dining almost to a halt, and Hines, then past 60, struggled through a brief second marriage that ended in divorce.

But by the time the war was over and people were eager as never before to enjoy a taste of peace and prosperity, the reinvigorated traveling gourmet was ready and waiting. Not only did he rush new editions of *Adventures in Good Eating* and *Lodging for a Night* into print; he also issued a cookbook (*Adventures in Good Cooking*) and began planning a vacation travel guide.

With a new wife (Clara Nahm, a Bowling Green widow twenty-four years younger than he), Hines happily took to the road again, and he soon became more of a celebrity than ever before. He drove a two-door Cadillac and traded for a new model almost every year. A precise and exacting man, he planned each trip meticulously. He and his wife took turns driving one hour each, and they held to a schedule that brought them to a prearranged stop by 4 p.m. each day, leaving time for a shower and a nap before dinner.

Hines was not given to habitual overindulgence, but he clearly enjoyed a wide variety of foods, particularly regional specialties prepared from fresh ingredients, and when circumstances required it, he was capable of facing five or six meals a day. He also looked forward daily to his afternoon toddy. As the years passed, his "spare figure," as one writer described it in 1938, progressively became "well set-up," "of robust size," "leaning to rotund," and "inching towards corpulence."

A nephew, John Hines of Bowling Green, remembers Duncan Hines as "a man who liked to do things big, to live well. He was good company, smiling and cordial, but he could also be blunt and demanding."

Jane Morningstar, another Bowling Green resident and a niece of Hines, recalls that "he had a successful man's ego. He knew what he wanted and saw that he got it, or else he spoke his mind. I think he got that from his father, who wouldn't eat off a plate if it had a flower print on it, and from his grandmother, who was a wonderful cook but a very fastidious person."

Even so, simple and unpretentious dishes—a good steak, a decent cup of coffee, a traditional country breakfast—seemed to please him most. "He had a real weakness for ice cream," says John Hines. "It was his favorite food. I've even seen him put it on a bowl of cereal in the morning."

By the end of the 1940s, with his guidebooks and related enterprises thriving, Duncan Hines had become a genuine celebrity in the eyes of millions of Americans. The image he projected was that of a well-traveled uncle, a silver-haired personification of worldly wisdom, good humor, courtly demeanor, and impeccable taste. Shortly before he turned seventy, he was invited by Roy H. Park, an advertising and public relations specialist in Ithaca, New York, to exploit his well-recognized name in a campaign to sell food products.

Park represented a group of clients in agriculture who wanted to create a brand name under which they could market a line of high-quality foods. Someone on his staff suggested that Hines personified the image they wanted, and Park made an appointment to meet the famous traveler.

Park, now in his eighties, still lives in Ithaca, where he is chairman and chief executive officer of a large chain of newspapers and broadcasting stations. "We met at the Waldorf Astoria in Manhattan," he says, recalling his first encounter with Hines. "He was thirty years older than I, and he had a flair for showmanship, a presence. He lived well, and it showed. I was very impressed with him."

They entered into a partnership that eventually controlled the marketing of about 200 food products, from hand-packed olives and whole tomatoes in glass jars to bread, ice cream, orange juice, and the cake mixes that still are familiar to supermarket shoppers. In addition, Hines and Park kept publishing the guidebooks and other volumes on food and travel, and through the Duncan Hines Foundation they funded scholarships in hotel and restaurant management at Cornell and Michigan State universities.

"We traveled together a good bit between 1949 and 1956," Park recalls. "He was a wonderful companion—a great storyteller, a humorous and entertaining gentleman, a connoisseur of fine food and drink. He was very distinguished looking, an immaculate dresser, a perfectionist. And, his first-hand knowledge of the regional and local food cultures of this nation was simply tremendous."

In 1956, after seven highly successful years in partnership, Hines and Park sold their publishing company and their food label to Procter & Gamble in a multimillion-dollar deal the sum of which was never disclosed. Park stayed on with the company to edit the publications for six more years. Hines retired to his home in Bowling Green, where he died of lung cancer at the age of 78 in 1959.

Sales of the Duncan Hines books began to tail off in the late 1950s, and in time the slide became a sharp and continuous fall. Along the nation's highways, chain restaurants and fast-food eateries and motels were popping up like summer daisies. Motorists weary of searching for decent places to eat and sleep were beginning to find an abundance of choices open to them.

Finally, in 1962, Procter & Gamble concluded that *Adventures in Good Eating* and the other Hines guidebooks were no longer profitable, and publication was halted. So many high-quality restaurants had come on the scene, declared Roy Park in a wistful farewell to the books and to his late partner, that "good eating has ceased to be an adventure in America."

Now, looking back on more than a quarter-century of dining in the post-*Adventures* era, Park speculates on what his old friend's reaction would be: "If Duncan Hines had lived to see the fast-food revolution and the enormous changes in travel and lodging, I'm sure he'd have been shocked. As far as the food is concerned, I don't think he'd be all that pleased with what has happened. He truly appreciated the regional foods of this country, the native specialties. He would tell you there's no substitute for fresh, individually prepared local dishes."

The interstate highway system, air travel, credit cards, microwave ovens and food processors, computerization, technological changes in food preservation and packaging, and a host of other modern developments have made *Adventures in Good Eating* and *Lodging for a Night* and even Duncan Hines himself seem like quaint artifacts from a distant past. In that light, it is all the more remarkable to realize that a half-century ago, Hines was already drawing from decades of road experience to create the models on which this generation's dining, lodging, and vacation guidebooks are based.

As much as anyone in American travel history, Duncan Hines deserves to be remembered as the king of the road.

VERTAMAE GROSVENOR

The first time I saw Vertamae Smart Grosvenor, she was emerging in noon-hour traffic from a Washington taxi. Her appearance was striking. Standing six feet tall and wearing brightly colored traditional African attire, she looked for all the world like a diplomat or a member of royalty.

So impressive was her appearance that it took me a moment to notice two other distinctive things about her. One was her voice, her accent; lilting and mellifluous, it resonated unmistakably with the low-country rhythms of coastal South Carolina—where, as I later learned, she was born and raised.

The other thing was her baggage. Somehow, in baskets and boxes, she managed with effortless grace to carry what turned out to be a complete home-cooked dinner: ribs, greens, cornbread. We were both bound for the same television studio to tape a late-night talk show. The host, Charlie Rose, a native North Carolinian, was waiting for us, primed for a conversation about Southern food. All I had brought was a copy of the book I had written on the subject; Vertamae not only had her book, *Vibration Cooking*, but her movable feast as well.

She was the star of the show. Midway into the conversation, I helped myself to a plate of food while she and Charlie were talking. Then, when he turned to me, Vertamae fixed him a plate and one for herself. Soon we were all eating and talking at the same time, the way Southerners are prone to do. I've been a fan of Vertamae Grosvenor's ever since. Her book, subtitled *Travel Notes of a Geechee Girl*, was first published in 1970 and reissued in paperback in 1986. It and her commentaries on National Public Radio's "All Things Considered" reveal a personality that combines warmth, pride, spunk, and humor. What's more, the lady can flat-out *cook*.

Vibration Cooking is a personal, informal, autobiographical travelogue with food at every stop along the way, and much of the food is that familiar blend of Southern soul and country that has been the staple cookery of this region for generations.

"I was 16 years old before I knew that everyone didn't eat rice every day," she writes. "Us being Geechees [the name is taken from the Ogeechee River in the Georgia-Carolina low country], we had rice every day." They had all manner of fish and game, too, and also collard greens, cowpeas, sweet potatoes, gombo (okra), chicken and dumplings, hoecake, pecan pie.

Africa, the Caribbean, South America and Europe also figure in her travels and in her cooking. Her basic message is that food is an international language—"as much so as music"— and the African contribution to it is the part she is most interested in documenting and sharing with others.

"Afro-American cookery is like jazz," she writes, "a genuine art form that deserves serious scholarship and more than a little space on the bookshelves." Her own saucy, irreverent book of cooking "by vibration"—by look and smell and taste and sound and touch—is a pleasure to cook from and to read.

Two of her works in progress are also aimed at bringing more long-overdue attention to African-American cookery. One is what she calls "a food opera," a stage production based on street cries, folk rhymes, songs, and sayings of the African people who came to America in bondage, who were "brought here and made to cook, and in this strange place created the only true nouvelle cuisine this country has ever had."

The opera is called *Nyam!*, a low-country vernacular term meaning to eat (come nyam/come eat). It has been performed once in a small theater in New York, and Grosvenor hopes to refine it further in other places where she spends time, including Washington, Philadelphia, and her hometown of Fairfax in Allendale County, South Carolina. "I keep one foot firmly planted there," she says.

The second of her current projects is a book—two volumes, actually—of social-cultural history focused on African culinary contributions to the nations on four continents facing the Atlantic Ocean. "It's African-American-Latin-European-Atlantic cookery," she explains, "the culinary routes to and from Africa. It's all there, waiting to be rescued." The first volume, she says, is nearing completion.

Vertamae Grosvenor and her diverse body of work collectively represent yet another example of the kind of personal vitality and creativity that has given Southern food a national and international reputation for variety, character, and goodness.

ELLA BRENNAN

"Food in New Orleans is like sex," said Ella Brennan with a wry Irish smile. "Everybody's interested. This is a food-wise city. To stay on top in the restaurant business here, you've got to deliver quality and satisfaction—in the cuisine, the service, the atmosphere."

It was the mid-afternoon interlude between lunch and dinner at Commander's Palace, one of the great dining places of New Orleans, and the lady of the house was holding forth at a quiet table in the shady embrace of the 200-year-old live oak tree that dominates the restaurant's courtyard.

"The role of the restaurateur fascinates me," she went on, with what sounded like echoes of Dublin and Boston and Brooklyn as well as New Orleans in her accent. "It's sort of like coaching a team, or conducting a symphony orchestra. The task is to get people with different talents to work together for a harmonious outcome—in this case, to make a dining experience turn out to the complete satisfaction of your guests."

She looked and acted the part of coach, of conductor. Stately and self-assured, her blue eyes unblinking behind owlishly round-rimmed glasses, her wavy, straw-colored hair showing faint streaks of gray, Ella Brennan managed without any apparent effort to exude a commanding air. She was dressed casually in slacks and a blouse and wore little makeup or jewelry, but there was something quietly formal in her manner, something disciplined and businesslike, that clearly pegged her as the boss.

More than four decades of single-minded devotion to her family's restaurant business in this most food-conscious and food-rich of American cities have not exhausted Ella Brennan's interest in the subject or her desire to keep growing and improving; like any creative artist, her mind is sharply focused on her work, and she strives constantly for perfection. To her, the restaurant staff truly is like a team, an orchestra:

"You have to perform as a unit, from the front door to the dining room to the kitchen—and you have to have someone to pull the whole thing together. That's what Dick and I do. We spend a lot of time in the kitchen—we were born there, and we've never left. We're in the dining rooms, we're out front, we're teaching, training, developing, bringing people along. We've got 200 employees here with one objective: to give our guests pleasure, to make regular customers out of the strangers who come through our door."

Ella Brennan and her brother Dick, with backup help from brother John and sister Dottie and several Brennan sons and daughters, have made the name Commander's Palace synonymous with culinary excellence since they took over the century-old restaurant in the Garden District fifteen years ago. Before that, going back to 1946, the senior siblings and their elder brother Owen, since deceased, operated Brennan's Restaurant in the French Quarter. That first family venture brought Irish charm and new luster to the venerable New Orleans culinary reputation, mainly through the introduction and refinement of a prodigious forenoon feast called Breakfast at Brennan's. (It's still being served there, under the direction of Owen's sons.)

The Brennan name now enjoys international stature in the restaurant world, and it is principally Ella and Dick who have raised Commander's Palace to the top echelon of American restaurants. The reasons are not difficult to determine. All you need to do is eat there.

As part of my preparation for our conversation, I had driven into New Orleans the day before—a sunny Sunday in 1988—and gone straight to the restaurant in hopes of getting a table for Jazz Brunch. As luck would have it, my companion and I had only a few minutes to wait before being escorted through the kitchen, bar, and courtyard to the glass-walled Patio Room.

For the next two and a half hours, we dined on a wondrous succession of classic Creole inventions—historic Ramos gin fizzes, rounds of buttered and toasted French bread flavored with cheese and garlic, thick and meaty turtle soup, fresh shrimp in a pungent remoulade sauce, two masterpieces of culinary beauty and taste called Eggs Creole and Eggs Hussarde, aromatic and richly flavorful New Orleans coffee with chicory, and a spectacular bread pudding soufflé, its hot center cooled with a creamy custard-whiskey sauce.

The food was truly memorable, the atmosphere captivating, the service faultless. No one said, "Hi, my name is Terry and I'll be serving you today." Instead, a legion of waiters and captains and managers moved quietly in and out of the room, functioning like a superbly drilled team of professionals. Outside the window, a benevolent sun filtered through the verdant foliage, giving the courtyard a languid look of tropical beauty. I can't remember a more satisfying dining experience. When a trio of jazz musicians strolled past our table playing the old Louis Armstrong favorite, "What a Wonderful World," we could only nod in speechless affirmation.

Ella Brennan's role in fine-tuning the Commander's Palace staff to its present level of excellence underscores her own uncompromising standards adopted over forty-three years in the restaurant business. She is to the present generation of New Orleans food mavens what the renowned Madame Elizabeth Kettenring Dutrey Bégué was to French Quarter "second breakfast" lovers for four decades prior to her death in 1906. (Here, surely, was the origin of what we commonly call brunch.) By virtue of both longevity and reputation, "Miss Ella" is now the doyenne of restaurateurs, the first lady of fine food—not just in New Orleans, but in the nation.

"I've known her for over forty years," said Herman Kohlmeyer, a retired New Orleans banker, "and I can tell you she knows how to run a great restaurant. She's the boss, no question. She'll come and sit down at your table, but she wants her back to the wall so she can keep looking around to make sure everything's running smoothly. That's why Commander's Palace is the number one restaurant in New Orleans."

Recalling her own early start in the business, Ella said, "I was barely 20 years old when Owen got the idea to open a restaurant in the Quarter. That was in the mid-forties, right after the war. He got our father to join him as an investor, and brother John came in with them, and I followed a few months later. Mother stayed at home and cooked for the family, she and a black woman named Leona Nichols, who lived with us. They cooked Creole, New Orleans style, and the food was marvelous, but we took it for granted. It wasn't French haute cuisine, and I wasn't smart enough to realize how grand it truly was. I didn't give Mother and Leona credit for being great cooks until I was much older."

The Brennans lived comfortably in the Garden District (their father was superintendent of a shipyard on the Mississippi), and they could afford what might be called a continental approach to the restaurant profession. Instead of going to college, Ella went to France and elsewhere in Europe to observe the postwar revival of the restaurant art. In New York, she spent two months under the tutelage of Max Kriendler, one of the owners of the 21 Club. Combining her home experience with the lessons of Europe and New York and the new restaurant on Bourbon Street, she was an accomplished cook, manager, and hostess by the time she turned 25 in 1950.

Before the end of the fifties, both the senior and junior Owen Brennans had died, and Dick, five years Ella's junior, had joined her in the management of the restaurant, which itself was relocated to Royal Street. Then, early in the 1970s, the older generation of Brennans parted company with Owen's three sons, leaving them to operate the French Quarter enterprise while they took on a new challenge: the restoration and revival of Commander's Palace.

Built by Emile Commander in 1880, the rambling Victorian mansion had known colorful times as a residence, a restaurant, and a Prohibition-era bordello. Noting the walled cemetery directly across Washington Avenue from the front door, Dick Brennan cracked that the family was moving to "the dead center of the Garden District." He and Ella jarred the neighborhood awake by painting the mansion a bright shade of aquamarine with white trim. Inside, they uncovered the windows and changed the color scheme to a compatible blend of softer, lighter shades.

Actually, it was Dottie Brennan, the "kid sister," who at Ella's request took charge of the redecorating. "She has very educated taste buds," Dottie later said of her sister, "but when it comes to patterns and colors, she can't envision the finished product. So she left it to me, and while she anxiously followed the progress, she never tried to tell me how to do it. She's so much in control around here that people tend to think she can do anything, but she can't. What she *can* do exceedingly well is delegate responsibility."

Upstairs, the wall facing the courtyard was replaced with glass, and a new dining area, the Garden Room, was created. Later, the Brennans built the Patio Room adjacent to the courtyard downstairs. The patio itself was replanted, and now, when the weather permits, guests can enjoy cocktails and dining outside. The bar was relocated to an area between the patio and the kitchen—an excellent vantage point for watching through the glass walls both the creative skills of the cooks and the dining enjoyment of the patrons.

Altogether, the refurbished Commander's Palace attained a capacity of more than 400 seats in four main dining areas (two upstairs, two down), and the staff has grown with it. The ratio of one employee for every two guests accentuates the Brennans' determination to provide service that is in every way as fine as the atmosphere and the food.

In the restaurant's internal organizational scheme, each of the four dining areas operates with its own staff of cooks and service people—all, of course, under the leadership of the chef and the maître d'. The chef in 1988, 31-year-old Emeril Lagasse, had been at Commander's for five years. A Massachusetts native of Portuguese and French Canadian descent, he was only the second American—after Paul Prudhomme—to head the Brennans' kitchen. "He's been great for us," Ella said, "and we're delighted with his leadership and his professional skill."

(Prudhomme, the now-famous Cajun chef, arrived in 1974 as a virtual unknown and spent five years with the Brennans. "He is outstanding," said Ella, "a natural cook and a marvelous teacher. We were very sorry to see him go, and we're proud of his many achievements. But his main interests were more Cajun than Creole, and we didn't want to move in that direction, so we worked out a mutually agreeable and altogether friendly parting.")

The maître d', George Rico, a native of Honduras, had worked at Commander's Palace since the pre-Brennan days—beginning, said Ella, as "the lowest-level cleanup person. He has complete knowledge of everything that goes on here. He's the kind of person who gets customers for you, not someone you have to get past in order to get into the restaurant."

Behind these two are the platoons of aides and assistants—thirty-five cooks and specialists of various kinds, party planners, dining room managers, captains, waiters, "a training lady who trains the trainers," and a "head shopper" who sees that the freshest and finest ingredients and foodstuffs are there for the kitchen staff to use.

And always, whenever the restaurant is open, there is a "BOD"— a Brennan on duty. "We have a rule," said Ella, "that at least one of us should be here all the time—Dick or me, or John or Dottie. It's the same as if we were having guests in our home."

That sense of dining with the Brennans, rather than simply having dinner in a restaurant, is a feeling that many regular customers appreciate. "My wife and I may go there for dinner two or three times a month," said Ron Thompson, a New Orleans advertising executive, "and though we don't expect it, it never surprises me if the evening ends up as a party. Ella knows so many people from different worlds, and she loves to bring them together and entertain them and leave them feeling good. She creates those evenings spontaneously."

Two of John's children, Ralph and Cindy, are co-managers of Mr. B.'s Bistro, a popular French Quarter restaurant started by the family ten years ago, and there is also a Brennan's in Houston; Dick's son Dick Jr. and Ella's son Alex manage it. Altogether, all but a couple of the senior Brennans' fourteen children are pursuing careers in the food business.

"We live and breathe this profession," said Ella. "All of us who work here talk food all the time—and when we're not working, we're going out to eat. New Orleans is very much on the rise as a restaurant city. When we went into the business forty-odd years ago, there weren't more than a half-dozen fine restaurants here. Today, there are a lot more than that, really first-rate places where you can go and enjoy a splendid meal. How many great ones, places I love to go to? I'm sure I could sit here and name a couple dozen. Dick says there aren't that many, but he doesn't eat out as much as the rest of us."

In keeping with her role as the leading lady of New Orleans cuisine, Ella Brennan is a persuasive spokeswoman for all of the city's fine restaurants and the traditions of Creole cooking and Southern hospitality that surround them. Foremost in her mind and heart, of course, is her own flagship, the venerable and ever-improving Commander's Palace, and it is to it that she gives most of her creative energy and all of her loyal devotion.

"We have a lot of fun here," she said, "but we're very serious about the quality of this restaurant. We want it to be the best, and we work at that very hard, every day. Many restaurants, when they get a little fame, take on an attitude of smugness that allows the service or the atmosphere or the food itself to be less than it ought to be. At today's prices, we believe our guests deserve the very best of everything, and that's what we're determined to give them."

And, said Tom Fitzmorris, editor of *New Orleans Menu* magazine and the city's foremost restaurant critic, the best is exactly what they get at Commander's Palace. "It's the culinary trendsetter in New Orleans," he said simply, and the credit for its success belongs to the Brennans—Dick, Dottie, John, and especially Ella:

"She's a perfectionist. No matter how good something is, she wants to make it better. She's also an operational genius; imagine putting close to 2,000 people through there on a good Sunday, and having virtually all of them go away delighted with the experience. Ella isn't flashy—she keeps a low profile, and gives others credit for things. But she's very much in charge, and at the top of the restaurant world in New Orleans."

ASHEVILLE FARMERS MARKET

On a wall of his office at the Western North Carolina Farmers Market in Asheville, general manager Clayton Davis has a map of the United States with about a hundred colored pins showing produce market locations.

Well over half of the pins are in the Southeastern states. "That's where the production is," says Davis.

Other states are famous for certain agricultural products—Hawaii for pineapples, Idaho for potatoes, Washington for apples, and so on—but only California can rival the Southern states for sheer diversity of edible produce.

Diversity is the essential foundation of a great farmers market. Like a roadside or fieldside stand magnified to gigantic proportions, it has to deliver a full range of foods at their peak of freshness and quality, and at prices generally lower than the supermarkets.

By all those measures, the state-owned market in Asheville is one of the best in the country. Its clean, well-lighted sheds are open to the outdoors in warm weather and heated in winter, and you can shop there every day of the year except Christmas and Thanksgiving.

Farmers and traders from a radius of a hundred miles or more bring a mind-boggling abundance and variety of fresh and preserved foodstuffs there to sell, and customers from the region and from the nearby interstate highways come by the thousands daily to bargain with them.

They go away with all kinds of farm-ripened fruits and vegetables, from apples to zucchini. They buy jams and jellies, pickles and preserves, honey and molasses, peanuts and pecans, dried and fresh flowers, seeds and shrubs, milled corn products and farm-cured meats and mountain-made crafts.

They even buy such exotic items as pickled possum, collard kraut, and pickled ramps, the latter a strong-smelling cousin of wild onions.

"What we've got here is a thirty-six-acre roadside stand," says Clayton Davis. "We've got 138 spaces for farmers and dealers to rent, and about 1,600 different people a year rent those spaces on a daily first-come basis." There's also a home-style restaurant on the premises.

The Western North Carolina Farmers Market is a $35-million-a-year operation of the state's Department of Agriculture. It serves over a million customers annually.

Since it opened in 1977, replacing an outdated and overcrowded facility, it has served as a model for numerous others, both in and out of the South. One of the most impressive of these is a new multi-million-dollar facility in Montgomery, Alabama.

North Carolina also has state farmers markets in Charlotte and Raleigh. Elsewhere in the South, the most impressive such retail centers include one near the airport in Atlanta, another in Columbia,

South Carolina, and several in Florida, where winter crops are so abundant.

Florida pioneered in the produce market field in the 1930s, and still has about fifteen regional centers that serve primarily as shipping points for agricultural producers. (Only in the Sunshine State can you drive through a tiny town like Cottondale, near the Alabama border, and find a dozen large roadside markets lining the main street.)

The oldest still-operating produce market in the country is said to be in Lancaster, Pennsylvania (closely followed by the French Market in New Orleans), and the largest by far is the privately-owned central market in Los Angeles, where the business volume is a colossal $4-billion a year.

But the South has the greatest number of markets, including most of the newest ones. And it also has, in places like Asheville, an inviting atmosphere filled with the sights and sounds and smells of the Southern countryside at its best.

"You can't beat produce like this," says Clayton Davis, "or good country people like these folks. We've got real quality here."

DEKALB FARMERS MARKET

Shopping for food can be a satisfying experience in the South, especially when what you take home is fresh and in season. Roadside and dockside markets offer much to whet the appetite. Think of such delights as spring berries, summer vegetables, fall nuts, and winter citrus, or think of slow-cured meats and just-caught fish, and you'll have to agree.

But our supermarkets are pretty much like everybody else's. When it comes to processed foods, and even some fresh things, we're no better served than the rest of the country. In fact, I've seen enough of big groceries in the East, Midwest, and West to wonder if they aren't sometimes better stocked than ours.

In light of that, the DeKalb Farmers Market in the Atlanta suburb of Decatur can truly be called a singular phenomenon. In a world of garden-variety supermarkets, this cavernous warehouse is something to behold.

Atlanta has an excellent state-operated farmers market near the airport and a fine little municipal market near the city center, but the DeKalb enterprise is altogether different. It's a privately owned food store offering the freshest, most varied, most distinctive and unusual array of foods I've ever seen under one roof.

And a big roof it is, covering 100,000 square feet. The temperature is always 57 degrees, the humidity 85 percent. In this ideal environment, you'll find 400 varieties of vegetables, 2,200 different staples, 500 kinds of cheese. The meat, fish, and pastries are near the peak of freshness; so are the roasted coffee beans and the cut flowers.

The aisles are always crowded with shoppers, and they're a heady mix of domestic and foreign, rich and middle class and poor—an economic and cultural cross-section. Blue-collar workers in hard hats rub elbows with blue-haired matrons from Buckhead and other exclusive neighborhoods, and they all forage side by side with citizens of the world.

A babble of voices from many nations seems to rise like a mighty chorus, to the accompaniment of clashing grocery carts and beeping forklifts being maneuvered into position to restock the bins and shelves. "The Russians would go crazy in this place," I heard one shopper say to another. "All this food—and no lines." There are checkout lines, of course, but in the arena itself there seems to be no end to the abundance, and every shopper has easy access.

To get a grasp of this market's magnitude, imagine a cornucopia of produce from dozens of countries, with 500 employees running the place (a majority of them Asians) and an astonishing 2 million pounds of foodstuffs going out the door in grocery sacks each week.

Rhode Island native Robert Blazer opened the first DeKalb County Farmers Market in 1977, and its popularity eventually caused gridlock in the aisles. In 1986, Blazer and his brother Harry, a one-time drummer in the Doc Severinson band, built the present facility. Harry and a sister, Linda, have since split away to open another market in northeast Atlanta.

Like an international bazaar with a hint of a Southern flavor, the market in Decatur offers tantalizing flavors to suit every taste.

Such exotic items as tumeric, dikon, bok choy, plantains, yucca, jicama root, lemon grass, calabaza melons, and octopus share space with the best of Southern produce—okra and squash, black-eyed peas and crowders, onions from Georgia, tomatoes from Tennessee, watercress from Kentucky, mustard greens from Arkansas, muscadines from North Carolina.

Grits are another popular staple, not only with Southerners but now increasingly with Orientals, who find them pleasantly similar to rice. And speaking of rice, you can find it here in gunny sacks, enough to feed armies.

The first time I entered this wonderland of smells and flavors, I fell upon the stock with a frenzy, as if it were about to disappear. My cart soon mounded up with leg of lamb, red snapper, flounder, Danish cheese, Dutch cocoa, mangoes, yams, collards, asparagus, pasta, bagels, rice cakes, balsamic vinegar, sun-dried tomatoes, pistachio nuts, black beans, garbanzos, dried apricots, hearts of palm, chutney, salsa, baklava, macadamia nuts, vanilla beans, artichoke hearts, and much more.

But now I behave more reasonably, like a veteran shopper—prudent, selective, controlled. I savor the feast of the senses, concluding with a sack of hot coffee beans right out of the roaster, and the wonderful aroma fills my car all the way back to Tennessee.

OLD COOKBOOKS

Some people read cookbooks from front to back as if they were novels. They're not looking for instructions on how to broil a fish or bake a cake; they're simply looking for entertainment.

"I may not cook a thing out of this book," such a person might say, "but when I finish reading it, I'll be able to tell you if it's a good book or not, and give you some specific reasons why I think so."

They're tough critics, these cookbook readers. They know the field—the books, the writers, the history. They understand the difference between a random collection of recipes and a carefully constructed presentation of social and cultural gastronomy.

The South has produced an abundance of excellent food writers and cookbook authors. Practically every state in the region can boast of contemporary sons and daughters who are nationally prominent in the field of food writing.

Immediately, I think of such luminaries as Mississippi-born Craig Claiborne, James Villas of North Carolina, Edna Lewis of Virginia, Eugene Walter of Alabama, Nathalie Dupree of Georgia, Camille Glenn of Kentucky, Rima and Richard Collin of Louisiana.

And in earlier times, too, the Southern states generated scores of fine cookbooks, many of which are still popular. The University of South Carolina Press has reprinted several excellent Southern cookbooks of the eighteenth and nineteenth centuries, including *The Carolina Housewife* (1847), by Sarah Rutledge, and *The Virginia House-Wife* (1824), by Mary Randolph.

Florida novelist Marjorie Kinnan Rawlings is almost as beloved for her *Cross Creek Cookery* (1942) as for her fiction. Another favorite of the cookbook readers is *A Place Called Sweet Apple*, written twenty-odd years ago by *Atlanta Constitution* columnist Celestine Sibley.

Finding a long lost and forgotten old cookbook is an unforgettable thrill for faithful fans of the genre. It's like digging up a buried treasure.

"Buried treasure" is, in fact, a good description for an old book that was reissued in 1988 by the University of Tennessee Press. It's called *Dishes & Beverages of the Old South*, and it was written in 1913 by a Tennessee woman, Martha McCulloch-Williams.

Born and raised on a plantation near Clarksville in pre-Civil War times, this remarkable Southerner went on to modest success as a writer in New York. Then, when she was 65 years old and near the end of her career, she reconstructed from her vivid memory a detailed description of the food and cookery of her early life.

She wrote in a breezy, humorous, entertaining way, and yet she also filled the pages of her narrative with a wealth of specific and revealing information about people and the times as well as the food.

Because it is so well-written and so perfectly intertwined with the customs and culture of the period, *Dishes & Beverages* is still as fascinating to read now as it must have been when it first came out seventy-five years ago. It's much more than a collection of recipes; it's really an enlightening essay on Southern social history.

Up to now, Martha McCulloch-Williams has not been well-remembered for her writing. Though she authored a half-dozen volumes for New York publishers, her work has slipped from sight, and even in the public and university libraries of Clarksville and most other Tennessee cities there are no volumes bearing her name.

But the reissue of *Dishes & Beverages of the Old South* will no doubt introduce her anew to cookbook readers and others interested in social history. She certainly deserves to be "rediscovered." Her book of Southern cookery and history does too.

It's one of those rare buried treasures that cookbook readers are always searching for but rarely find. Now, fortunately, it's been resurrected for the enjoyment of a new audience.

NEW COOKBOOKS

If ever there were two more popular cookbook writers in the South than Henrietta Dull and Marion Brown, I can't imagine who they'd be.

Dull's *Southern Cooking* can still be found in bookstores, sixty years after it first appeared. So can Brown's *Southern Cook Book*, which was first published almost forty years ago.

A few national cookbooks have been more long-lived—there's the immortal Fanny Farmer, of course, and the encyclopedic *Joy of Cooking* —but no one with a strong Southern accent comes close to matching the records of Georgia's Mother Dull and Mrs. Brown of North Carolina.

In the style of the times, Henrietta Stanley Dull used her husband's name as her byline; she was "Mrs. S. R. Dull." *Southern Cooking*, though, was strictly her production, a 400-page compendium of 1,300 recipes straight from the heart and soul of Dixie.

Twenty years as editor of the *Atlanta Journal's* home economics page gave her the experience and confidence to write her classic recipe book in 1928. She was a master cook and a no-nonsense taskmaster who didn't waste time with small talk, and the book reflects that businesslike character.

Marion Brown was a tad less serious and thus more entertaining, but every bit as skillful and authoritative. Her *Southern Cook Book* is even larger than Mrs. Dull's—more like 500 pages and 1,800 recipes—and it has the added virtue of giving credit to scores of contributing cooks.

Southern cooking has changed tremendously since the salad days of Dull and Brown, but irrefutable proof that it remains a viable and vigorous cookery is no farther away than your nearest bookstore.

In the 1980s alone, dozens of outstanding new cookbooks have emanated from far-flung corners of the South. Each one is distinctively different from the rest, but all qualify as worthy inheritors of the Dull-Brown legacy. I've picked up three at random to prove the point.

For openers, there is *The Heritage of Southern Cooking*, by Camille Glenn (Workman Publishing, 1986). Her mother and father were innkeepers in Dawson Springs, Kentucky, and Camille Glenn, now in her late seventies, speaks with the assurance of one who has spent her life around fine food.

No greasy-spoon eatery, theirs was a great old Southern hotel dining room in the lofty tradition of Alabama's Purefoy and Tennessee's Sedberry. This wide-ranging book, brimming with culinary history and creativity and timeless quality, is a delight to cook from as well as to read. Camille Glenn has directed a cooking school, been a caterer, and written a popular food column for the Louisville *Courier-Journal*. Her *Heritage of Southern Cooking* is the crowning achievement of a woman whose entire life has been devoted to the pursuit of excellence in regional cookery.

The South's regional and sub-regional diversity is often overlooked or taken for granted, even by natives who ought to know better. In light of that, a book like *Tropic Cooking*, by Joyce LaFray Young (Ten Speed Press, 1987), comes as both a surprise and a reassurance. Billed as "the new cuisine from Florida and the Caribbean," this soft-cover collection might seem at first glance to be too modern and too "offshore" to qualify in any sense as truly Southern.

But look again. Joyce Young has a deep appreciation for social history, for the foods of Crackers and Conchs (terms denoting certain native-born Floridians, among others), and for the Indian/African/Spanish/British/French/Dutch fusions from which have come the cookery and culture of south Florida and the Caribbean.

Many of the most Southern of foods, from barbecue to beans and rice to seafood and sweet potatoes, are so much a part of Caribbean cookery that the styles can only be understood as extensions from the same roots. Joyce Young's *Tropic Cooking* makes the necessary connections for us.

New Southern Cooking (Alfred A. Knopf, 1986), Nathalie Dupree's major attempt at uniting the traditional and contemporary schools of regional cookery, is to my way of thinking a major success—even if some of her inventions (turnip green pasta, grits with yogurt and herbs) seem a bit outlandish to my admittedly less imaginative palate.

Several things about Dupree and her book are particularly impressive to me. First, she's daring—unafraid of new ideas, new combinations, new foods. Second, she's also very forthright about her food heritage and her appreciation of old Southern cookery at its best.

And third, she's very good at what she does. As the founder of Rich's Cooking School in Atlanta, as a cook and writer, and as a network television chef ("New Southern Cooking with Nathalie Dupree"), she demonstrates time and time again her sure-handed mastery of the region's old and new cuisines.

In all three of these books, as different as they are, there is an unmistakable mark of professional quality. Henrietta Dull and Marion Brown surely would be pleased with them. No wonder Southern cooking remains the richest and most vital of America's regional cuisines.

COOKBOOK PUBLISHERS

The written record of Southern cookery is almost as old as the South itself. Under lock and key in libraries and other repositories in the region are some handwritten recipe collections going back to the seventeenth century.

In 1742, a printer in Williamsburg, Virginia, brought out the first cookbook ever published in this country. Eight decades later, in 1824, Mary Randolph wrote *The Virginia House-Wife;* most food historians now agree that it was the most influential American cookbook of the nineteenth century.

From those early times to the present, both the quantity and quality of Southern cookbooks have been at least as high as any other region's. With the possible exception of France, no country in the world has had as high a level of interest and involvement in books about food as the American South.

Cookbooks are almost as plentiful as Bibles in the South, and the more there are, the more people seem to want. Even with home cooking on the wane, people still buy cookbooks to read for entertainment, if not to guide them in the kitchen.

Since the end of World War II, Junior League chapters all over the country have raised a major portion of their budgets by publishing and selling cookbooks—a practice begun in Montgomery, Alabama, and Charlotte, North Carolina, and Dallas, Texas, before the war. Southern chapters of the service organization still publish more recipe collections and sell more copies than those in other states.

Given this long history of fascination with cookbooks, it's no wonder that the South is still spawning new publishing enterprises that specialize in recipe collections. Among them are a number of small-town, home-based cottage industries using modern tools such as computer technology to make themselves competitive with the bigger houses. Here are a couple:

Quail Ridge Press got its start in Brandon, Mississippi, in 1978 when Gwen and Barney McKee put together a book on the twelve days of Christmas and sold 4,000 copies in about three weeks.

"We weren't total neophytes," Gwen explains. "Barney had worked for the university presses of Louisiana and Mississippi, and had directed the Old Miss press. But free enterprise is a lot riskier. That first success gave us the confidence to keep going."

They published another book the next year, and another the year after that. Gradually, they have built a catalog of 23 titles, including 14 food books. A friend, Barbara Moseley, joined them in the venture, and so in time did three of the McKees' children.

Centerpiece of the Quail Ridge collection is the "Best of the Best" series: cookbooks from Southern states featuring selected recipes from the most popular cookbooks in those states. Volumes on Mississippi, Louisiana, Florida, Kentucky, Tennessee, Texas, Georgia, and Alabama have been produced so far; the latter two were among six new titles on the 1989 list. *Best of the Best from Louisiana* has been the company's sales leader. It's been reprinted four times, and there are 50,000 copies in print.

Quail Ridge has operated out of the McKees' home in Brandon, a suburb of Jackson, since the beginning. "We're moving to outside quarters in 1990," says Gwen McKee. "With six employees and three computers, we have to have more space. We're doing our own typesetting now—in fact, doing everything in-house except the actual printing. If you had told me ten years ago that all of this would happen to us, I'd have laughed out loud."

McClanahan Publishing House in Kuttawa, Kentucky, a country town about thirty minutes' drive from Paducah, is an even smaller enterprise—but in its own way, it's just as impressive.

Paula Cunningham started the company in 1983 after she and her husband, Bill, a lawyer, had published a local history manuscript of his in league with a Bowling Green, Kentucky, printer.

"Bill wanted to do another book, on the Night Riders and the tobacco wars in western Kentucky back at the turn of the century," says Paula, "and we decided to do that one ourselves."

On Bended Knees: The Night Rider Story is now out of print, but nine McClanahan titles, seven of them food books, are not. They include two by Paducah restaurateur Curtis Grace; three on historic restaurants (in Ohio, Kentucky, and Tennessee) by Marty Godbey; and *The*

American Sampler Cookbook, a collection of favorite recipes of political families nationwide.

Dining in Historic Kentucky, the leading seller on the list, has 20,000 copies in print. Now, after five years in the Cunninghams' home with the couple and their five young sons, McClanahan (named for a cousin of Bill's) has moved to new quarters in his law office and hired its first employee.

"Book publishing is unpredictable," Paula says, "but it's very exciting. I've decided to make cookbooks our specialty because people in this part of the country never seem to tire of them—and fortunately, neither do I."

COOKBOOK BOOKSTORES

Like collectors in general, people who accumulate cookbooks seem always to be looking for a few more elusive items to complete a set. Sifting through the miscellany at flea markets and garage sales, they harbor an eternal hope that the next volume they turn over will be the very one they've sought for so long.

Used-book stores and antiquarian bookshops often prove to be valuable searching grounds for collectors, and so do libraries and other institutions that hold periodic sales of surplus volumes.

And now, in the age of specialization, another source is emerging: bookstores that handle nothing but cookbooks. Following inevitably in the pattern established by specialty bookstores in other fields (religion, travel, mystery, science fiction, metaphysics, computer technology), cookbook specialty shops are popping up like soufflés in all parts of the country.

Within the past five or six years, book dealers in New York, Boston, Baltimore, Chicago, Denver, San Francisco, Portland, and Seattle have entered the cookbook field. A few shops, such as Jan Longone's Wine and Food Library in Ann Arbor, Michigan, and Jean Bullock's Gourmet Guides of San Francisco, have been in business for well over a decade.

Nach Waxman, a former book editor, opened Kitchen Arts & Letters on Lexington Avenue in New York City in 1983, and his store has inspired others—even served as a training ground for like-minded entrepreneurs.

One of Waxman's first employees was a South Carolinian, John Taylor, whose experience as a food writer and editor led him to an interest in cookbooks and then in bookselling.

"I apprenticed with Nach," says Taylor, "and then, in November 1986, I came home to Charleston and opened my own shop." Hoppin' John's, Taylor's enterprise, is located on Pinckney Street in the Battery, the old coastal city's historic district.

The following summer, another Southerner, Stephen J. Lee of Louisville, opened a shop called the Cookbook Cottage on Bardstown Road in Kentucky's largest city. The Charleston and Louisville stores are the first—and, as far as I know, the only—cookbook specialty shops in the South.

Lee, a professionally trained cook, caught "book fever" in the mid-1970s while building his personal collection of cookbooks. "I burned out pretty fast on cooking in restaurants," he says, "but not on food, and certainly not on cookbooks."

The Cookbook Cottage keeps about 3,500 titles in stock—60 percent of them old books, the rest new, Lee estimates—and the shop also sells gourmet foods and kitchen accessories. Cooking classes are another feature in Lee's array of services. All in all, books make up slightly less than half of his business—but it's the most visible half and, to Lee, the most important.

"There's an ongoing interest in cookbooks," he says. "A major part of my trade is through the mail—people looking for rare, out-of-print titles, old favorites. I really enjoy finding those books for them."

John Taylor also sells things besides books in his Charleston shop— hand-made knives, food-related art and greeting cards are three of his other specialties—and he is continuing his involvement in writing and editing too.

"I inherited 1,200 cookbooks from my mother," he says. "I've been interested in food since I was a kid, so this seems like a natural business for me to be in. With about 4,000 titles and an active search business, I stay immersed in cookbooks."

As an extension of his book business, Taylor is also active as a speaker and consultant on food. He enjoys cooking, too, and eating, and he is investing a major portion of his time now in writing. *Hoppin' John's Foods of the Lowcountry,* his book on South Carolina cookery and history, will be published in 1991.

The success of Hoppin' John's and the Cookbook Cottage will no doubt encourage others in the South to open trade in this long-favored commodity. Though the trend didn't originate in this part of the country, it seems bound to prosper here, where cookbooks have been so common and so prominent for more than a century.

Encyclopedia of Southern Culture

Food and history seem to fit together in the South about as easily as biscuits and gravy or beans and cornbread. I wouldn't go so far as to say that our food lovers are all history buffs, or that our historians all enjoy talking about and cooking and eating Southern food, but there is an affinity.

More precisely, it's the history of food I'm talking about. Whenever you find people enjoying a festive traditional Southern meal together, you'll likely hear plenty of talk about yesterday's garden and pantry, and memorable meals of the past, and great cooks since departed.

Southern food history is especially rich in folklore and anecdote, as well as rich in taste and quality. Many a good cookbook from the region has preserved those stories for us, and they add immeasurably to the storehouse of treasures that gives Southern cookery such strength and appeal.

Now comes a new book—not a cookbook at all, but an encyclopedia— that puts the region's foodways in a larger context. *The Encyclopedia of Southern Culture* is a 1,650-page volume crammed with just about anything and everything imaginable having to do with the South.

Compiled and edited by staff members of the Center for the Study of Southern Culture at the University of Mississippi and published by the University of North Carolina Press, the massive resource book was ten years in the making, and more than 800 writers contributed to it. The price is a little hefty—$49.95—but it figures out to only about $6 a pound. That makes it similar in weight and cost to good barbecue pork shoulder or ribs—and like the 'cue, it's worth every nickel.

In a quick perusal of the contents, I found about thirty separate articles on Southern food, and there are others that deal indirectly with the subject. In a major section on agriculture there are pieces on gardening, poultry, corn, fruit, peanuts, pecans, rice, dairy products, meat products, and sugar. Elsewhere in the book, these topics are covered:

Barbecue, beverages, bourbon, Cajuns and Creoles, catfish, chitterlings, Coca-Cola, collard greens, cookbooks, country ham, Craig Claiborne, fried chicken, Goo Goo Clusters, grits, gumbo, Jack Daniel's Whiskey, mint juleps, Moon Pies, moonshine, okra, soul food, and watermelon.

The list is by no means comprehensive; missing, for example, are such quintessentially Southern foods as shrimp and oysters, yams and sweet potatoes, beans and peas, cornbread and biscuits, hush puppies, cakes and pies and cobblers, iced tea. Restaurants don't get much attention, either, and neither do the many contributions of blacks and other ethnic groups to our cookery and foodways. But regardless of these oversights, the inclusions are well-researched, interesting, and informative.

The short biographical sketch of Craig Claiborne, long-time food editor of *The New York Times*, describes his Mississippi boyhood and other background and experiences from which grew his reputation as one of the nation's most respected and influential food writers.

The article on soul food (a term that came into vogue in the 1960s) describes the cookery thereby identified as "a distinctive, traditional southern style of cooking . . . that is the native fare of both black and white southerners of all economic and social strata." History certainly supports that inclusive definition.

Okra and collard greens are also properly chronicled. Among other things, we learn that the world's record for eating collards was claimed at a North Carolina festival in 1984 by one C. Mort Hurst, who "ate 7-1/2 pounds in 30 minutes, and kept them down just long enough to claim his prize."

The Moon Pie entry records the sweet snack's "humble beginnings" at a bakery in Chattanooga seventy years ago, and the Goo Goo Cluster, a candy bar created in Nashville in 1912, is described as a staple whose "ingredients (caramel, marshmallow, peanuts, and milk chocolate), cooking methods, and essential southern identity have remained the same."

The Encyclopedia of Southern Culture seems likely to become another distinctive feature of the region, like Goo Goos and collards and hickory pit barbecue. It's a book for food lovers—and for all others fascinated by the Southern mystique.

Cafe Society

GREEK CAFES

George Metropol had no money and spoke no English when he arrived in the tiny village of Manning, South Carolina, in 1900. Driven in desperation from his native Greece by a severe economic depression, he joined thousands of other Europeans in the quest for a new life of prosperity in America.

But unlike the vast majority of immigrants, Metropol chose not to live with his fellow countrymen in the ethnic enclaves of New York, Boston, and other Northern cities.

About a quarter of a million Greeks entered the United States in the half-century between 1865 and 1915, but only one in ten moved into the South, and most of them dispersed to settle in scattered communities where no Greeks had lived before. George Metropol belonged to that minority within a minority. Rather than attempting with others to transplant and perpetuate the Greek cultural heritage, he was one of a relative few who set out alone to find a new home in an unfamiliar society.

The door he entered in Manning led to the kitchen, simply because there was work to be had there, and the language barrier was not a serious handicap for dishwashers and cooks. By 1909, Metropol had gained enough of a foothold to open a restaurant of his own on Manning's main street. A decade later, that place—the Central Coffee Shop—was the most popular cafe in the rural midlands of South Carolina.

In 1989, the Central Coffee Shop proudly celebrated its 80th birthday. It's still owned and operated by the descendants of George "Papa Jack" Metropol. The restaurant's appealing combination of Greek and Southern cookery has brought it a loyal and devoted clientele down through the years.

When Papa Jack died a few years back, the legislature of South Carolina passed a memorial resolution in his honor, taking special note of the fine food and hospitality he had bestowed upon his customers.

The phenomenon of turn-of-the-century Greek immigrants entering the restaurant business in the South is an obscure but fascinating slice of regional culinary history. Even more interesting is the fact that many of them developed their enterprises into family-run institutions that are still thriving—and still in the family. Here's a random list of some of them:

♦ The great seafood emporium of the Louis Pappas family in Tarpon Springs, Florida.

♦ The Elite Cafe in Montgomery, Alabama, a long-time venture of the Xides family.

♦ John's, a popular downtown restaurant in Birmingham that has been passed down through the family to its present owner, Phil Hontzas.

♦ The Bright Star in Bessemer, Alabama, owned and operated by the Koikos brothers, who inherited it from their uncle.

♦ The Mount Vernon, latest in a long line of restaurants owned by Gus Tombras and his descendants in Chattanooga, Tennessee.

♦ The Peerless, a steak house in Johnson City, Tennessee, that John Kalogeros and his children have made into an all-time local favorite.

♦ The Mayflower, a downtown cafe in Jackson, Mississippi, that has become a standard by which local neighborhood restaurants are measured.

There are numerous others scattered about the South, from Yorktown, Virginia, to St. Augustine to New Orleans to the Arkansas Ozarks. In all of them you will find traces of the Greek food heritage compatibly blended with generous dimensions of Southern cookery.

Unlike the Italians, Germans, Chinese, French, Mexicans, and others who have clung tenaciously to the cuisines of their homelands, the Greeks have seemed more interested in combining the old with the new.

With the Greeks, you get seafood and country cooking. Souvlaki and Southern fried. Pilaf and purloo. Baklava and buttermilk pie. Jimmy Metropol, Papa Jack's son, calls the happy union "Greek and Southern, white and black, the best of both worlds."

In cafes and confectionaries and fine restaurants scattered across the Southern landscape, a century of Greek immigration has added a richness of flavor—cultural as well as culinary—to the American character.

GROCERY-CAFES

Since the end of World War II, supermarkets and fast-food chains and auto service centers have become common fixtures on the American scene, as common as churches—and more frequently used. These new institutions are the modern equivalents of the neighborhood groceries, cafes, and filling stations that were so numerous and familiar in earlier times.

The South certainly had its share of those pre-war institutions, though by no means a monopoly on them. Now they are fast disappearing. Even in small towns and rural areas, family-owned commercial enterprises of the so-called "mom and pop" variety are becoming a rare species.

But here and there in the rural South, I keep running into a modern response to the giant chains, something you might call consolidated mom and pop: country stores with gas pumps out front, groceries inside, and a cafe in what used to be the living quarters or the stockroom.

If you happen to be driving around the back roads of north Mississippi, you can stop at Ruth and Jimmie's in Abbeville for a loaf of bread, a can of motor oil, a fishing license—or a plate lunch at the 12-stool counter in the rear.

In Taylor, another small Mississippi town, the Taylor Grocery is no longer simply a country store with gas pumps; it now has a far-reaching reputation as one of the best catfish cafes in a state where catfish (not cotton) is now king.

Tennessee also has some prime country store-cafes. There's the James Grocery & Cafe, for example, in the village of Brushy, between Centerville and Hohenwald. It was a grocery first, and it still dispenses a variety of staples and sundries, as well as fresh meats and rental videos. You can pump yourself a tank of gas, too.

And best of all, you can sit at one of a half-dozen or so oilcloth-covered tables back beyond the shelves and enjoy a short-order meal or a homemade country dinner of meat, vegetables, hot bread, cold tea, and dessert.

"I just cook the old-fashioned way, just plain old Southern," says Betty James, who with her husband Bobby owns and operates the enterprise, including an adjacent chainsaw repair shop.

From 6 a.m. to 6 p.m., six days a week, Mrs. James and three helpers cook and serve meals and keep store. They make biscuits every day, and meat-and-vegetable plates, and some kind of dessert—pie, cake, or cobbler. There's usually soup, too, and cornbread.

"One of our most popular dinners is chicken and dumplings," Mrs. James says. "We try to fix what people seem to like best. We even tell our regular customers to call us up ahead of time and let us know when they're coming and what they want—and if we can, we'll cook it for them."

If that sounds like your mama talking, you'll understand why those regulars look to the James Grocery & Cafe for all the comforts of home.

Farther west across the Tennessee River, another country store with food service is Guy's Grocery & Cafe near Trenton, in Gibson County. The store is open every day, but on Thursdays, Fridays, and Saturdays from 4 to 8 p.m., customers come in droves to enjoy catfish and chicken dinners in an atmosphere as traditional as the food itself.

Owner Hollis Guy bought the grocery when he got out of the service in 1951. One Friday about twenty years later, he "fired up a big black kettle and cooked a mess of Tennessee River channel cats" for some fishermen friends of his, and that was the start of a cafe that some faithful customers say now has the best fish and chicken dinners in west Tennessee.

Guy and his wife Beatrice, with major help from Mary Lynn Utley and Syble Baker and a crew of cooks and waitresses, have a buffet line and most of their tables in what used to be an apartment attached to the grocery. There are also a few tables and chairs in the main room of the store.

"The grocery business is slow," says Hollis Guy, a large, flinty-eyed man with an easy-going manner and a deadpan sense of humor. "I'm about half-way trying to retire. I used to pump gas here too, until about four years ago. The same thing is killing gas and groceries: chains. It's about over with for these little stores. The big-volume boys have undercut us."

But food, says Hollis Guy, is a whole 'nother thing. The superstore dealers can beat him selling the same items—aspirin, say, or motor oil—but the fast-food chains "can't serve you a dinner as good as ours, and that's why our customers keep coming back week after week."

What they get, for a few bucks a person, is a fresh and plentiful array of fried chicken and catfish, french fries, hush puppies, white beans, cole slaw, sweet onions, pickled beets, and assorted other servings. The Mississippi pond-raised fish are deep-fried in hot peanut oil that is changed often.

"The life of any business," says Guy, "is to keep the customer satisfied. And the way to do that in the fish business is to change your cooking oil very frequently."

Good cooking may be harder and harder to find, but wherever it exists, it's always in demand. That's why places like the James and Guy grocery-cafes may keep on being cafes long after the groceries are gone.

ALLEN'S HISTORICAL CAFE

In all his 71 years, Carl Allen has seldom ventured far from the central Florida back-country land of his birth. "I never left it," he says with a rueful smile, "but it's just about left me."

Urban sprawl has almost overtaken him. If you go looking for Allen at his restaurant outside Auburndale, you won't see enough undeveloped land in the fifty-mile drive from Tampa to convince you that Florida still has much back country remaining—and in truth, it hasn't.

Which makes Carl Allen, a self-described pack rat, all the more valuable to his state, and to the preservation of its history. The son and grandson of range-riding cow hunters, he has collected and saved everything he could get his hands on from Florida's frontier era, and the artifacts cover every square inch of his sprawling, five-room cafe.

"The early cowboys down here rode what they called cracker ponies, tough little horses that had got loose from the Spaniards and lived wild," he explains. "The riders carried whips that they cracked when they rounded up the bony longhorn scrub cows that roamed through the brush. That's why they—and eventually, any native resident of the state—came to be called Florida crackers."

Slim, bald, and bespectacled, the cowboy-clad Allen looks like he just rode in from the range. In fact, though, it's more likely that he's been working on his weekly newspaper column, or painting a Florida frontier scene, or adding to his collection of memorabilia, or dealing with some of the musicians who play for him three nights a week (bluegrass on Thursdays, gospel on Fridays, country on Saturdays).

Or cooking (though he leaves most of that to others now). His place is, after all, a restaurant first and foremost, and Allen likes to serve as much "frontier food" as he possibly can. Much of it he remembers from his own childhood experience.

"My mother taught me to cook on a woodstove," he says. "I was a teenager during the Great Depression, and in those days, she and my grandmother could make a nice dish out of practically nothing. That always impressed me."

The menu at Allen's Cafe features plenty of seafood, fresh-water fish, chicken and beef, along with slaw, white beans, grits, hush puppies, and cornbread. But there's also a sampling of the fare of bygone days: rattlesnake, armadillo, alligator tail, rabbit, turtle, frog legs, deer, wild turkey, quail, poke sallet, swamp cabbage (hearts of palm—tender shoots of the sabal palm tree), guavas, and a fiery hot sauce made from "bird-eye" (datil) peppers.

"My ancestors and the others who came in here after the Civil War learned survival from the Indians, as the Spaniards had done centuries ago," says Carl Allen. "They never knew nothing but hard times, making do, living off the land. But there was something romantic about all that, to me. I've always wanted to hold on to time, cling to the past. This place is about all there is left of it."

Surrounded by his menagerie of artifacts and antiques, Allen lives for the frenzied weekend evenings when the musicians come to play and sing their own nostalgic tributes to the past, and upwards of 300 customers jam the place to listen, eat, and socialize.

They may get a bit of alligator tail or rattlesnake meat to go with their stock orders of fried chicken or catfish or shrimp, and they may eat the homemade biscuits and gravy, or the grits and greens, or the cornbread and beans. If there is homemade pie or berry cobbler, they'll certainly go for that in a big way.

But mainly, I suspect, the customers come to look and listen and wonder, to sample Carl Allen's smorgasbord of history, to get a literal and figurative taste of the Florida that used to be.

It may not be the very best restaurant fare you ever put in your mouth, but it's mighty tasty all the same, and the experience will hold your attention like a cow hunter's whip-crack.

HOME-STYLE CAFES

At first glance, the assignment seemed quite simple: to single out twelve Southern home-style restaurants—one in each of a dozen states—and present them as sterling examples of a class or type of eatery beloved by Southerners everywhere.

You know the sort of place I'm talking about. It has a certain homey atmosphere, a comfortable familiarity, and the food looks, smells, and tastes very much like the fare your mama served at the family table when you were younger—simple, unpretentious, filling, quite delicious Southern food.

But things are seldom as simple as they seem. The problem here is that terms—"Southern," "home-style," "country," "soul" and such—mean different things to different people. Sometimes the descriptions connote diversity and variety; sometimes they hide a multitude of sins. And, there are countless little differences that mark the food, the cooks and servers, the customers, the dining rooms, the history—subtle nuances of style and quality and character that show up from state to state, town to town, even kitchen to kitchen. It would be a mistake to rank or label such places (good, better, best); the only fair way to characterize them is to say they're among the cafes you remember fondly when you think of traditional Southern cooking.

Now as always, the best home-style food is more likely to be found in somebody's home than in a restaurant—home, after all, is where the definitive dishes originated. And, it is certainly true that many—

probably most—of the really great Southern cafes of a generation ago have since disappeared, and the surviving remnant is endangered by competition and changing lifestyles. But it's certainly not impossible to get a wonderful old-fashioned meal in a public dining place; in fact, deciding which one to name in each Southern state is a problem in itself, there being more than a few.

So my Delicious Dozen are an arbitrarily chosen set. They're quite different one from another—and that's intentional, to underscore the variety that exists. They're not necessarily the best of their class by anybody's measure, though you might well consider some of them so. They are, though, broadly representative of the South's most venerable and valuable food traditions. More to the point, they all have a nice, homelike feeling about them, and they tend to be long-established and consistent places—dependably, predictably good—and most of them boast a presiding elder who reminds you of someone you used to know and like.

These are not the best, then, and certainly not the only—but they're good enough to make me want to go back whenever I can. I offer no addresses, phone numbers, prices, or hours of operation—not even any assurance they'll be open at all. There's too much built-in eccentricity here for such formality to be effective—and besides, half the fun is in the search.

ALABAMA: The Waysider Restaurant, Tuscaloosa. Elizabeth Snow Farr bought this cafe in the late 1950s, and Archie Farr, her son, eventually inherited the keys to the kitchen. Breakfast and lunch are the daily meals, and the menu of hot breads, main dishes, side dishes, and sweets will remind you of your own mother's table.

ARKANSAS: Jones Cafe, Noble Lake. This tiny community, ten miles southeast of Pine Bluff on U. S. 65, has become a mecca of sorts, thanks to the small gem of a cafe operated by Ruby Jones and her son, W. R. A restaurant cook for more than forty years, Mrs. Jones is such an accomplished pie maker that folks drive from Little Rock, sixty miles away, just for a taste.

FLORIDA: Flora & Ella's Restaurant, LaBelle. Ella Burchard—with her sisters and their parents before them—has kept alive a record of more than half a century of fine cooking at a picturesque street-corner cafe in this little village west of Lake Okeechobee. There's still a feeling of the 1940s here, and the food is as fresh and tasty as you'd expect to find in any good Southern cook's home kitchen.

GEORGIA: Mrs. Wilkes' Boarding House, Savannah. Sema Wilkes, another forty-year veteran of the food business, has gained considerable fame for the tables she sets in the small basement dining room of her old house in Savannah's historic district. There's no sign out front, no ad in the tourist guides, not even a number in the phone book, but the crowds are always there waiting patiently when Mrs. Wilkes opens for midday dinner.

KENTUCKY: Bailey's Restaurant, Hazard. "Fresh" and "home-made" are the bywords at James and Pauline Bailey's 1950s-style establishment, which is perched on a sharp curve and lacks parking space but still draws a steady stream of regular patrons. Whoever said location means everything to a restaurant obviously has never been to Bailey's. The biscuits here are as good as any home-baked hot ones you ever tasted.

LOUISIANA: Lasyone's Meat Pie Kitchen & Restaurant, Natchitoches. James Lasyone, a butcher, remembered vendors who sold meat pies on the streets of Natchitoches when he was a boy. Seeking to recreate the flavor, he came up with a spicy beef and pork hash that he deep-fried in a half-moon pastry. Now it's the house specialty at this family restaurant owned and operated by Lasyone and his wife, Jo Ann (whose own signature dish is Cane River Cream Pie). Besides the specialties, there are plenty more basic dishes.

MISSISSIPPI: Revolving Tables Restaurant, Mendenhall Hotel, Mendenhall. Successive generations of the same family (including the current owners, Fred and Natalie Morgan) have operated this small hotel since it first opened in 1915. The dining room features enormous round tables with lazy-Susan centerpieces on which dinner is served in a score or more of bowls and platters. Here you can sit and quite literally watch Southern culinary history pass before your eyes.

NORTH CAROLINA: Nu-Wray Inn, Burnsville. The Wray family has owned this mountain inn since 1870, and it is justly famed for the breakfasts and dinners its guests have enjoyed at the long, linen-covered dining room tables. The late Rush Wray, once the patriarch of the clan, was famous for his salt-cured, hickory-smoked country hams, and ham is still the breakfast specialty, along with biscuits, grits, red-eye gravy, eggs, and fried apples.

SOUTH CAROLINA: Mrs. Frances Kitchen at Prince's Place, Myrtle Beach. Frances Iwilla Gainey Bowens built a thirty-five-year reputation for quality in her soul-food restaurant before she died in 1983. Her son, Prince Bowens, and his wife, Queen, have kept the family flag aloft with faithful renditions of the dishes Mrs. Bowens was praised for, among them chicken bog, shad roe, and barbecued coon. The field peas, collard greens, and cobblers are equally as impressive.

TENNESSEE: Miss Mary Bobo's Boarding House, Lynchburg. Until she died at the age of 102 in 1983, Miss Mary was known far and wide as the proprietor and hostess of a superlative country-home lunch place in this citadel of the Jack Daniel family of whiskey-makers. Miss Mary almost never touched the hard stuff; her passion was for eggs, butter, cream, sugar, pork, fresh vegetables, cornbread and such, and she served some of the very best Southern food to be found anywhere. The tradition continues with Lynne Tolley as the hostess. Six days a week at the stroke of one o'clock, sixty fortunate guests who have called ahead for reservations sit down to feast. Here is your classic Southern grandmother's table, laden as of old.

TEXAS: Threadgill's, Austin. The late Kenneth Threadgill put his stamp on this Austin landmark (as did a star-crossed singer named Janice Joplin), and present owner Eddie Wilson has sustained the eatery's reputation with great fresh vegetables, chicken-fried steak, biscuits and cornbread, homemade pies, and Shiner Beer in long-neck bottles.

VIRGINIA: The Chesterfield Tea Room, Richmond. "Old Virginia Cooking Since 1903," says the menu, and that's what brings the regulars back—that, and the comfortable quaintness of this inner-city lunchroom on the main floor of an apartment building. The Chesterfield is where your grandmother might go for a little light refreshment if she weren't home cooking for you.

There are other home-style restaurants still operating in the South, of course, and they span the scales of style and quality. All are threatened, to one degree or another, by fast-food competition, changing diets, the rising cost and declining quality of fresh foodstuffs, and numerous other modern developments. That should be reason enough for you to do your patriotic duty by supporting your local home-style cafe, if you have a good one nearby. Places such as these are treasures worth preserving for future generations.

CRACKER BARREL RESTAURANTS

Danny Evins was still in his thirties when he looked around and realized that two of the things he loved most about country living in the South were fast disappearing.

One was the old general stores that used to thrive at dusty rural crossroads throughout the region. The other was home cooking of the kind and caliber that has elevated legions of grandmothers to sainthood.

Like it or not, Evins concluded, Americans were turning from the backroads to the interstate highways and leaving grandma's kitchen for the fast-food chains. They might miss those simple pleasures of earlier times, but they weren't going to roll back the clock and return to them.

So Evins had a bright idea. He decided to take the old country store and the homey little cafe that looked and smelled like grandma's kitchen, and plunk them down beside the interstate.

The first of these he opened on Interstate 40 near his hometown of Lebanon, Tennessee, in 1979. In addition to the gift shop-country store and the restaurant, it also had gas pumps.

The pumps are gone now, but otherwise, not much has changed—not much, that is, except the number of Danny Evins' store-cafes.

He and his partners and stockholders—collectively, the Cracker Barrel Old Country Store Corporation—now have about eighty almost identical outlets in a dozen states. A few of the restaurants are outside the South (in Indiana, Ohio and West Virginia); the others reach into most of the Southern states. Eventually, they may be all over the country.

By affecting a down-home country air without sliding into hillbilly caricature, the Cracker Barrel outlets have rapidly gained popularity as places for the traveler to stop, relax, and refresh—sit in a front-porch rocker, browse through an old-fashioned store, and enjoy a home-style meal.

Interstate traffic accounts for about 75 percent of the company's trade, but in many places the restaurants have taken the place of local cafes that once served Southern cooking to small numbers of regular customers.

"This is the only place I know of around here to get a good country breakfast," said a man on the Cracker Barrel porch in Valdosta, Georgia.

"I don't know what's around here," the man in the rocker next to him, a tourist from Minneapolis, responded, "but to me it's the best breakfast I ever ate anywhere."

"Well, I wouldn't go that far," the first man replied, "but then I had two Georgia grandmas and a mother that could cook mighty well."

With about 160 seats, a Cracker Barrel restaurant may serve 1,500 or more customers a day in the busiest season. No restaurant with that kind of turnover can operate literally like a home kitchen, or even a small cafe. Time-consuming preparations made from scratch with only fresh ingredients are luxuries that seldom can be indulged.

But the menu is full of familiar main dishes—ham, barbecue, catfish, pork chops, chicken and dumplings, meat loaf—and the vegetables are also traditional (buttered corn, country green beans, pintos, fried okra, turnip greens, fried apples), and the biscuits and corn muffins are made in-house, and the fruit cobblers are impressively reminiscent of homemade.

The task for Danny Evins and his cooks at Cracker Barrel has been to make mostly processed foods look and taste as much like home-grown, all-fresh, individually prepared dishes as possible. With well-chosen recipes, proper seasonings, and practice-makes-perfect repetition, they seem to be handling the job with ever-increasing confidence and success.

As home cooking continues to fade out of the American experience and more of our meals are eaten in restaurants—and as country stores linger only in museums and memories—the Cracker Barrels and other enterprises similar to them seem certain to grow in number and importance.

They may not be as diverse, as distinctive, as authentic, or as excellent as we like to think things were back in grandma's glory days, but they're not bad, not bad at all—and considering the fast-food alternatives, I'll happily take them without complaint.

CEDAR KEY

Cedar Key basks in a quiet byway of Florida hype and history like a sleeping pelican on an abandoned pier. Once a lumbering center and a busy port, the little village now appeals mainly to fishermen, artists, and a modest number of late-winter tourists eager for spring.

Though it has qualities reminiscent of Key West, it is not one of the Florida Keys but rather a narrow spit of land far to the northwest in the Gulf of Mexico, near the great bend that defines the Florida Panhandle. In its relative isolation from the state's main attractions, Cedar Key retains the placid charm of an earlier time that is now all but forgotten.

There is, for example, the Island Hotel, a ten-room, Jamaican-style inn built in 1849 and now a creaky, quirky oasis for lodgers and diners grown weary of hectic journeys in the fast lane. There's a pot-bellied stove in the lobby, and a shady wooden veranda on the second floor. Segovia guitar music wafts softly through the dining room.

Marcia Rogers, a native New Englander, bought the hotel in 1980 and managed to get it listed on the National Register of Historic Places, not by modernizing it with contemporary comforts but by restoring and preserving as much of its nineteenth-century character as possible.

The hotel's dinner menu is probably the most modern aspect of the inn, featuring as it does a number of vegetarian/gourmet/natural-food specialties created by Ms. Rogers. But seafood still predominates, as it has throughout Cedar Key's history, and in that sense the Island Hotel dining room remains true to its heritage.

A somewhat faster pace is kept in the restaurants down by the dock—places with names like the Brown Pelican, the Captain's Table, Frog's Landing—and one inevitable consequence is that they all seem to be more or less indistinguishable from the other seafood eateries that predominate in coastal communities everywhere.

But back on the somnolent main street, where the Island Hotel is, a pervasive calm gives the storefronts a movie-set quality, and it's easy to hear seagulls crying and the breeze rustling through the palms and the namesake cedars.

At the Heron, a restaurant just down the street from the hotel, owner and chef Janice Coupe serves guests in a Victorian setting such as might have existed there a century ago. The atmosphere is inviting, but not sufficient by itself to make lunch or dinner there something to remember. It takes good food to do that—and good food is precisely what came to our lunch table in two simple but outstanding and alto-gether Southern dishes: crab bisque and Cedar Key lime pie.

The bisque—thick, creamy, and loaded with lumps of blue crab meat—was rich almost to a fault and so delicious that I easily could have tossed caution to the winds and eaten a second bowl.

"I threw this together in a hurry one night when I ran out of clam chowder," Ms. Coupe explained, "and it went over so well that I've been making it ever since."

The other memorable offering was one of those lighter-than-air desserts that seem elementary—until you try to make one yourself. The chef gave it that same off-handed dismissal as "just the traditional Key lime filling, frozen in a Graham cracker crust and topped with whipped cream."

I tried it when I got home, combining 3 well-beaten egg yolks, a 14-ounce can of sweetened condensed milk, and a half-cup of fresh lime juice. The first time, I poured just this mixture into the crumb crust, froze it, and served it with whipped cream.

Then, for a variation, I dissolved a teaspoon of plain gelatine in the lime juice and folded the well-beaten egg whites into the custard. This second version held together better when served, but tasted about the same as the first—very good, even worth doing again, but not truly outstanding.

Not memorable, like Janice Coupe's. It's going to take more practice, more trial and error. A tough job, as the saying goes, but somebody's gotta do it. With the Heron's example as my inspiration, I hereby volunteer.

DINING OUT IN NEW ORLEANS

When it comes to traveling and eating out, there's one destination that always pops into my mind first: New Orleans, the Crescent City, the Big Easy. I'm no French Quarter fanatic, no Mardi Gras maniac, but the restaurants are another matter. I can easily lose everything there—my diet, my budget, my good sense—when the city's fabled Creole chefs are doing their stuff.

Arguments can be made for New York or San Francisco as our greatest restaurant cities. Internationally, Tokyo and Paris win high praise. But you can have Manhattan and the others with my blessing, as long as you call me in time for dinner with NOLA—that's New Orleans, Louisiana.

This has to be the premier food city in the world. Whatever else it lacks—and most critics will tell you the list is long—New Orleans remains a place where residents and visitors alike seem obsessed with fine food, not just in its numerous classy and expensive restaurants but in countless small and unpretentious cafes as well.

In the groceries and open-air markets and on the docks, in the kitchens and dining rooms of restaurants and private homes, in little shops and old bookstores and even out on the street, interest and attention and conversation seem to revolve around cooking, serving and eating, whether the focus is on great dinners past, meals at hand, or feasts yet to come.

Part of the explanation for New Orleans food madness is traceable to nature, to geography, and climate. The semi-tropical setting and the surrounding network of fresh-water and salt-water wetlands and rich soils bring an incredible abundance and variety of fresh foods to the city daily.

History adds another dimension. Beginning with the Natchez and Choctaw Indians before 1700, the area has thrived on the contributions of many diverse people—French, Hispanic, African, English, Italian, German, Greek, Asian. As a port city, it has always attracted world travelers.

But the strongest and most reinforcing element in the New Orleans reputation for greatness as a food city is tradition. Its image as a genial and hospitable Southern dinner-table host to diners from around the world was already beginning to spread when the nineteenth century opened. Now, nearly 200 years later, that identity is more firmly established than ever.

Its ties to France in the colonial period certainly helped, but New Orleans has added its own distinctive touches. The old cookbooks are full of French names, from bouillabaisse (fish stew) to vol au vent (puff pastry), but local cooks have given distinctive character to the dishes by adding their own ingredients and seasonings.

The New Orleans reputation is built upon homemade gumbos and jambalayas, on shrimp and oysters, grillades and grits, beans and rice, poor-boy sandwiches, coffee with chicory, beignets, pralines and dozens of other specialties that have become timeless and universal.

Its fame is also built on continuity. There is Antoine's, for example—first opened in 1840, and now presided over by a great-great-grandson of the founder. And Galatoire's, another restaurant of nineteenth-century origin, guided by four generations of the same family.

And then there is the Brennan clan, Irish purveyors of the finest in French cuisine. Not only Brennan's in the French Quarter but Commander's Palace in the Garden District and Mr. B.'s Bistro in the Quarter are showcase establishments of this one creative family.

The list could go on—Arnaud's, Dooky Chase, Masson's, LeRuth's, Broussard's. And still, as outstanding as all these famous restaurants are, the most impressive fact about New Orleans dining may be the number and variety of Crescent City eateries that are less well known but excellent in their own right.

New Orleans restaurant critic Tom Fitzmorris, drawing on "almost 20 years of dining out a minimum of 12 times a week," publishes annually a descriptive list of his 100 favorite eating places in the city. Even 100, he says, is not enough to include "all the restaurants I think are good."

On almost anybody's list of the South's top ten restaurants, New Orleans would probably fill at least half the slots. If the list were the top 25 or the top 100 or the top 500, the city would still be dominant.

The South has earned its reputation for producing the finest regional foods in America. New Orleans is the heart and soul of that well-deserved reputation, the once and future kingdom of cookery.

THE FUTURE OF SOUTHERN COOKING

Over pot likker and cornbread at Mary Mac's one day recently, my table companions and I fell to talking about the state of Southern cooking.

"Look at this place," one of them said, waving a hand around the crowded dining room. "This is one of the busiest restaurants in Atlanta, day in and day out. If you're looking for proof that Southern food is alive and well, here it is. We're bullish on pork and greens."

From across the table came a dissenting voice: "You're dreaming, Ace. The main reason this place packs 'em in is that so many of the other plate lunch palaces have gone belly up. This food is living on borrowed time. Fast-food joints and microwaves on the left, health nuts and food reformers on the right—the squeeze is on, and this comfort food of our childhood is about to get mashed, wasted, iced. Better enjoy your meal, friends. This kind of cooking won't be around much longer."

They both looked to me for confirmation. "Well," I said, putting on my best gloom and doom expression, "it probably *is* just about over. When you think of the limited availability and rising cost of fresh foodstuffs, and the low pay that makes good cooks and servers turn to other kinds of work, and the time it takes to prepare real Southern food from scratch, and the cheaper imitations being mass-produced by the chains, it's hard to see how even a big-time restaurant like Mary Mac's can stay on top."

Our server arrived with the main course: meat-and-threes for each of us, and a platter of hot rolls. Fried chicken, meat loaf, pork chops. Green beans glistening with bacon grease, mashed potatoes and brown gravy, candied yams, fried okra, stewed tomatoes, cole slaw, black-eyed peas, butterbeans, boiled cabbage. Our iced tea glasses were refilled, and we were left to our knives and forks—and to our thoughts. After a few bites, I started to speak again. But somehow, the Pollyanna gremlin had crept into my head, and I felt the fog of pessimism lifting.

"But on the other hand," I began, wiping chicken grease from my lips, "Mary Mac's is not the only real home-style eatery left in the South . . ."

"Probably not even the best, good as it truly is," one of my friends interjected.

" . . . and even though some great ones have closed, I can still think of several outstanding places in every Southern state. There's also the other dimension to this issue: private cooking. I know, I know—everybody's deserting the home kitchen. But I can name you plenty of cooks, men and women, who are just as good as their mamas were, and almost as faithful to the traditional style. They may not do it every day, but they do it often enough to stay good at it. They'll keep this cookery alive."

Our desserts showed up—pecan pie with ice cream, banana pudding, blackberry cobbler. An air of contentment enveloped our table. "Never mind the future," somebody said, and between bites we began to reminisce about Creole and Cajun cafes in Louisiana, and political barbecues in Kentucky, and oyster roasts on the Carolina coast.

◊

It's easy to get schizophrenic about this subject. Southern food is a hot culinary item . . . Southern food is dying. It takes forever to fix . . . It's worth every minute. Eggs/butter/cream/sugar/salt/bacon grease will kill you . . . What a way to die. Nobody does it the right way anymore . . . This is the best gumbo (burgoo, hot Brown, hoppin' John, chicken mull, Brunswick stew, pain perdu) I ever tasted.

Fortunately, Southerners come by their schizophrenia naturally, and they never let it get in the way of a good contradiction. This *is* the best regional food in the country, it's always been great and always will be—and, it's also suffering from modern technology, mass production, accelerated living, family disintegration, cultural homogenization, yuppie grazers, tofu eaters, scientifically raised hogs, shellfish depletion, and instant grits. We believe the good stuff will last forever, and at the same time we recognize it as an endangered species with slim prospects for long-term survival.

The South has been losing its identifying characteristics, good and bad, since the end of World War II. We've gone from one-crop domination in an agricultural economy to the point where not just the crop (cotton) but agriculture itself is under siege. Our colorful ways of speaking are being sifted down and rounded off to a bland national standard of television newspeak. Racism and sexism, though still visible, no longer dominate and govern our society. Southern fundamentalist religion has spread via the airwaves into the national arena. Our politics now resembles everybody else's politics, so much so that the Solid South regularly joins the nation in sending Republicans to the White House and Democrats to Congress. Even our music—blues, jazz, gospel, country, rock 'n' roll—has been appropriated by the rest of America and the world, and has been changed in the process from its primitive characteristics to something more sophisticated but not necessarily finer.

Compared to all that, the evolution of Southern food seems relatively uneventful. In spite of the critical stereotypes (all fried, overcooked, too fat, too greasy, too sweet, too salty), and in spite of the plethora of bad joints that prove the stereotypes, there remains a network of eateries and a body of professional and private cooks who assure our cuisine of diversity, quality, and fidelity to its traditions and its history.

Though it originated in a culture of racism and sexism, Southern food has excelled and prevailed and finally transcended its origins. Blacks and women, once its slaves and vassals, are now its primary guardians, its insurance and assurance. Our cookery offers a striking parallel to jazz and the blues: Born out of misery, tempered and flavored by hard times, the food and the music have soared to immortality. We properly condemn and despise the root causes of the misery, but we praise the food and the music for their excellence, and we celebrate the women and men who historically gave so much to them and got so little in return.

If African-American history had been centered in the Midwest instead of the South, I'm convinced that the best barbecue and roasting ears would be there, where the pigs and corn are. Not all good cooks are black and not all blacks are good cooks, of course—but blacks have given quality to Southern cooking out of all proportion to their numbers, and that one fact above all else has made our regional food superior to any others.

We have other unique strengths as well: the long growing season; the cornucopia of vegetables, fruits, nuts, berries, and other edible things that grow; the everlasting sea with all its harvest. We also have Louisiana, which means Creole and Cajun cookery, which means more good eating in one state than you can find in thirty or forty others combined. And, we've got pond-raised catfish, Mississippi's replacement for King Cotton. They're better than the old channel cats we used to get out of our rivers, primarily because pollution is killing the rivers. Pond-raised catfish are an impressive sign that Southerners *can* change and adapt and improve on the past.

There's more. We've got the foods of Appalachia and the Ozarks—trout, goat, lamb, wild game, wild greens, and specialty dishes such as stack cake, persimmon pudding, leather britches (dried green beans), big hominy, and sausage gravy. We've got colonial cookery in Virginia, Spanish cookery in Florida, Greek-American restaurants scattered over the landscape, and soul food cafes in every state.

All this—and I've barely mentioned barbecue, hot breads, and the multitude of desserts for which the South is justly famed.

So is it Pollyanna or Dr. Doom? If you're pressing me to take a position here, I might as well go ahead and bite the bullet. As much as I lament the undeniable decline in quality and quantity of authentic Southern food being served to the public, and the decline of home cooking in general, I'm not so pessimistic as to believe that the distinctive cookery of our foremothers and fathers is in imminent danger of extinction.

Food has been too important throughout Southern history to be summarily relegated now to a lowly position of minor significance. It has been our livelihood, our preoccupation, and at times our very salvation. In the eras of the Civil War and the Great Depression, Southerners of every rank and station learned as few Americans ever have what it means to go hungry. I wonder sometimes if the modern "all you can eat" invitation of so many Southern restaurants isn't a subconscious response to those historical traumas. The message is, "Get plenty while it's here; no telling what's coming tomorrow."

In the not too distant past, we responded to history by building our lives around food—growing it, preserving it, cooking it, serving it, cleaning up, and starting over. Now, as a consequence of many social changes, we have bought into modernism with a vengeance. No other Americans are more addicted to fast food than Southerners (indeed, many of the chains originated here). And it's not just carry-out hots in styrofoam and plastic that have won us over—it's also frozen TV dinners, microwave ovens, canned biscuits, home-delivered pizzas, shake-and-bake chicken, and even pre-cooked Thanksgiving dinners from the supermarket deli.

But it's all part of the schizophrenic contradiction (or so I choose to believe). We meekly fall in step with all the fads and trends and movements—but we still produce more cookbooks and generate more cookbook sales than other Americans, and we still express reverence for our wise elders who cook the old-fashioned way, and we still associate traditional Southern foods with all the momentous occasions in our lives, from holidays and birthdays to weddings, anniversaries, and funerals.

And one more thing: Even though the vast majority of Southerners have already abandoned the lifestyle that brought family members to the table together for breakfast and supper every day, a substantial number of people at least remember how to prepare breakfast and supper, and they do it occasionally, and the experience is generally positive and satisfying. I hear lots of people say cooking is too time-consuming, or too much work, or too hard, but I seldom hear anyone say the food doesn't taste good or isn't well received by those who eat it.

What this tells me is that traditional Southern food, though it is no longer the foundation of our principal daily diet, is still very much a part of our culture, and will remain so for a long time to come. It's our forever food. Country ham, pork barbecue, skillet-fried chicken, cat-fish, grits, corn, green beans, okra, squash, black-eyed peas, turnip greens, collards, sweet potatoes, biscuits, cornbread, yeast rolls, iced tea, boiled custard, coconut cake, pecan pie, blackberry cobbler, straw-berry shortcake, peach ice cream and all the rest, the best of soul and country, of Creole and Cajun, of coastal plains and mountain hol-lows—these crown jewels of the Southern kitchen are indestructible, and I don't expect to see the day when they have disappeared from table and memory, never to rise again.

As long as there is corn, there will be roasting ears and cornbread and sour mash whiskey. As long as there are pigs and fire, there will be barbecue. As long as there is remembrance, there will be Southern-ers cooking and eating the immortal foods of their history.

RECIPE INDEX

(See "Subject Index" for recipes organized by category)

SUBJECT INDEX

A

B

C

G

garlic, 5-6; breath, antidotes for, 6
Garlic for Health, 5
gaspacha-Spanish: recipe, 55
Gatorade, 18
gazpacho: about, 54-56
gazpacho: recipe, 55
Glenn, Camille, 40, 176, 178
Godbey, Marty, 180
Gold Medal, 38
Goo Goo Cluster, 183
Good Hearts, 126
Grace, Curtis, 180
grapefruit, broiled: recipe, 76
greens: about, 80-82
greens, collard, 80
**greens, collard, Al Clayton's New
    Year's: recipe, 150-51**
greens, turnip, 80
greens, turnip: recipe, 81
Griffin, John Howard, 47
grits, 29-30; about, 90-92
grits, Mabry Mill: recipe, 30
grits, Nassau: recipe, 92
Grosvenor, Vertamae Smart, 166-67
Grover, Geneva, 98
**gumbo, duck and sausage: recipe, 59-
    60**
Guy, Hollis, 188

H

Hach, Phila, 123
ham, country: about 69-70
ham, country: recipe, 72
Hardy, Jean, 3
Hearn, Lafcadio, 128
herb butter: recipe, 4
herbs, in Southern food, 3-4
Heritage of Southern Cooking, The,
    40, 178-79
Hill, Madalene, 3
Hilltop Herb Farm, 3
Hines, Duncan, 100-02, 161-65
Hines, Florence Chaffin, 162-63
hoecake 30
hoecake, Beck's: recipe, 35
Holland, David, 47
Hoppin' John's, 109, 179, 180
Hoppin' John's Foods of the Lowcountry,
    182
Housekeeping in Old Virginia, 99
Huguenot torte, 109
Hurst, C. Mort, 184
Hutcherson, Ben, 80-81

I

Irwin S. Cobb's Own Recipe Book, 21
It's Grits, 90

J

James, Betty, 187
Jaubert, Gus, 57
Jefferson, Thomas, 109, 127, 139
johnnycake, 30
Johnson, Lady Bird, 141
Johnson, Lyndon Baines, 140

K

Kane, Hartnett T., 25
Kentucky Hospitality, 98
Kentucky whiskey. *See* Bourbon
Key West Cook Book, 135
Kirkum, Harlee, 61-62
Kirkum, Henry, 61-62
Knight, Harold, 66
Kohlmeyer, Herman, 169
Koonce, Gladys, 48-49

L

La Cuisine Creole, 128, 154
Lagasse, Emeril, 171
lagniappe syrup: recipe, 8
Lane, Emma Rylander, 40
Lau, Dr. Benjamin, 5
Lee, Stephen J., 182
lemon curd: recipe,100
lemon pie, about, 99-100
Lewis, Charles, 142-43
Lewis, Edna, 176
Lewis, Tommie, 145
Liebling, A. J., 139
Little Rock Junior League cookbook, 11
Lodging for a Night, 163, 165, 163
Long, Huey, 29, 139
Looney, J. T., 57

M

maple syrup, mock, 7
Martha White, 38
Mary Mac's, 198-99
McClanahan Publishing House, 180
McCulloch-Williams, Martha, 108, 176
McDaniel, Doc and Maggie, 142
McKee, Barney, 180
McKee, Gwen, 180
McLaurin, Mel, 61-62
Minorcans in St. Augustine, 152
mint julep, 20-21
Miss Lillian and Friends, 9

About the Author

John Egerton has been a freelance journalist and author in his native South for the past two decades. His weekly newspaper column on Southern food appears in *The Atlanta Journal-Constitution* and other papers, and his food essays have been published in *Food & Wine, Travel & Leisure, Southern* Magazine, *Atlanta* Magazine, *Southern Living,* and other periodicals. His previous books, in addition to SOUTHERN FOOD, include GENERATIONS and THE AMERICANIZATION OF DIXIE. He lives in Nashville, Tennessee.